UNDERSTANDING
FLANNERY O'CONNOR

Understanding Contemporary American Literature
Matthew J. Bruccoli, General Editor

Volumes on

Edward Albee • John Barth • Donald Barthelme • The Beats
The Black Mountain Poets • Robert Bly • Raymond Carver
Chicano Literature • Contemporary American Drama
Contemporary American Science Fiction
James Dickey • E. L. Doctorow • John Gardner
George Garrett • John Hawkes • Joseph Heller
John Irving • Randall Jarrell • William Kennedy
Ursula K. Le Guin • Denise Levertov • Bernard Malamud
Carson McCullers • Vladimir Nabokov • Joyce Carol Oates
Tim O'Brien • Flannery O'Connor • Cynthia Ozick
Walker Percy • Katherine Anne Porter • Thomas Pynchon
Theodore Roethke • Philip Roth • Mary Lee Settle
Isaac Bashevis Singer • Gary Snyder • William Stafford
Anne Tyler • Kurt Vonnegut • Tennessee Williams

UNDERSTANDING
Flannery
O'CONNOR

Margaret Earley Whitt

UNIVERSITY OF SOUTH CAROLINA PRESS

For
Vuron Thomas Earley
(1905–1991)

And his grandchildren after him:
Todd, Steve, Barber, Jean, and Will
Charley and Wintry

Published in Columbia, South Carolina by the
University of South Carolina Press

Manufactured in the United States of America

Library of Congress Cataloging-in-Publication Data

Whitt, Margaret Earley, 1946–
   Understanding Flannery O'Connor / Margaret Earley Whitt.
     p.   cm. — (Understanding contemporary American literature)
   Includes bibliographical references and index.
   ISBN 1–57003–036–7
   1. O'Connor, Flannery—Criticism and interpretation. 2. Women
and literature—Southern States—History—20th century. I. Title
II. Series.
PS3565.C57Z94 1995
813'.54—dc20   94–18748

CONTENTS

EDITOR'S PREFACE

The volumes of *Understanding Contemporary American Literature* have been planned as guides or companions for students as well as good nonacademic readers. The editor and publisher perceive a need for these volumes because much of the influential contemporary literature makes special demands. Uninitiated readers encounter difficulty in approaching works that depart from the traditional forms and techniques of prose and poetry. Literature relies on conventions, but the conventions keep evolving; new writers form their own conventions—which in time may become familiar. Put simply, *UCAL* provides instruction in how to read certain contemporary writers—identifying and explicating their material, themes, use of language, point of view, structures, symbolism, and responses to experience.

The word *understanding* in the titles was deliberately chosen. Many willing readers lack an adequate understanding of how contemporary literature works; that is, what the author is attempting to express and the means by which it is conveyed. Although the criticism and analysis in the series have been aimed at a level of general accessibility, these introductory volumes are meant to be applied in conjunction with the works they cover. They do not provide a substitute for the works and authors they introduce, but rather prepare the reader for more profitable literary experiences.

M. J. B.

ACKNOWLEDGMENTS

I acknowledge the following people for help with this book. First, Peggy Keeran and the supportive staff of Penrose Library at the University of Denver saved me untold hours by their willingness to pursue the answers to my dozens of questions. Carol Taylor and Jennifer Moore-Evans in the Faculty Computing Lab at the University of Denver were always helpful. Jane Smith read and commented on the manuscript. Through the years, my ongoing talks with Sarah Gordon have provided me with a deepened insight to O'Connor's work and life in Milledgeville, Georgia.

My parents, Ruth and Tom Earley, made the decision to live in the South and let me experience first hand, with my sister Jackie, the world that O'Connor created in her fiction.

Conversations with colleagues and friends helped my own understandings of O'Connor become more clear: Marilyn Heim, Karen Gaddy, Anne Daniel, Judy Goldberg, Sally Kurtzman, Kathleen Barr, Gail Brown, Dodi Vaughn, Carol Samson, Joyce Kinkead, Jeanette Harris, M. E. Warlick, Abbey Kapelovitz, Burton Feldman, Hyman Datz, Gerald Chapman, Diana Wilson, Douglas Wilson, Sudarshan Kapur, and members of the Loose Canon.

Further, I am indebted to the 1990 Interterm class that traveled with me to middle Georgia and helped me see anew this part of the South. Finally, I am grateful to students and friends who have shared in the discussion of Flannery O'Connor for the past seventeen years.

UNDERSTANDING
FLANNERY O'CONNOR

CHAPTER ONE

Understanding Flannery O'Connor

Career

When Flannery O'Connor's first novel, *Wise Blood,* was published in 1952, Sylvia Stallings of the *New York Herald Tribune Book Review* wondered "where, after an opening performance like this one, she has left herself to go."[1] These words suggested and predicted the puzzling and disturbing effect that O'Connor's writing had and would come to have on her readers. She was a devout Roman Catholic, with a Southern upbringing. Her keen eye for observation and sensitive ear for the dialogue that comes naturally to a story-telling people assisted her in capturing the language and obsessions of a people congenitally "Christ-haunted," as she once explained. Hazel Motes, the fanatical frustrated preacher protagonist of this first novel, becomes a symbolic prototype of the most repeated question in O'Connor's fiction: "What about this Christ? What are we supposed to do with Him?" She readily admitted the importance of Christ's resurrection to her way of seeing the universe.

This Christian orthodoxy was reiterated in her first collection of short stories. Each of the ten stories of *A Good Man Is Hard to Find* (1955), with the exception of "Good Country People," had been previously published in *Sewanee Review, Kenyon Review, Shenandoah,* and *Harper's Bazaar.* By the time of the collection's publication, O'Connor had been included in the 1953 O. Henry Prize anthology for "The Life You Save May Be Your Own," the story of a one-armed tramp who seduces a babbling idiot and her desperate mother in order to get a car that can take him away. The following year, "A Circle in the Fire" won second place in the O. Henry Awards; in this story, three young boys set on fire a farm woman's property for the devilment of it. Contemporary reviewers vacillated on what to do with her writing. The reviewer for *Time* saw her stories as "witheringly sarcastic"; here was a writer who used "a brutal irony, a slam-bang humor and a style of writing as balefully direct as a death sentence."[2] Something was going on in these stories, but most critics were not sure exactly what to call it, and a representation of orthodox Christianity did not cross their collective minds. "There is brutality in these stories, but since the brutes are as mindless as their victims, all we have, in the end, is a series of tales about creatures who collide and drown, or survive to float passively in the isolated sea of the author's compassion, which accepts them without reflecting anything," suggested a review in the *New Yorker*.[3]

Her stories continued to appear in journals and magazines. In 1960 she published her second novel, *The Violent Bear It Away*. The novel's title comes from Matthew 11:12 of the Rheims-Douay Version of the Bible: "From the days of John the Baptist until now, the kingdom of heaven suffereth violence, and the violent bear it away." The protagonist is fourteen-year-old Francis Marion Tarwater, designated a prophet by his late great-uncle, old Mason Tarwater. Like *Wise Blood*'s Hazel, Tarwater must do everything in his power to run in the opposite direction before finally accepting the call to "GO WARN THE CHILDREN OF GOD OF THE TERRIBLE SPEED OF MERCY."[4]

CAREER

Contemporary reviewers were beginning to understand that something significantly deep—Southern and Catholic—was happening in her work. Although early critics had placed her in the "Southern sunlight Gothic" school, the term was being recast, expanded. Her work was violent, grotesque, and horribly funny, but with a twist. Granville Hicks, after reading *The Violent Bear It Away,* for example, asserted: "From now on there can be no doubt that Miss O'Connor is one of the important American writers."[5]

To affirm her literary reputation, *Esquire*'s fiction editor Rust Hills placed her squarely into "red hot" status in his "The Structure of the American Literary Establishment"'s chart in July 1963. O'Connor was assigned to "the hot red blob in the middle," which represented "the critics, agents, universities, book publishers, and magazines that habitually work together to establish a literary reputation."[6] By this time, she had won first place in the 1957 O. Henry Prize Collection for "Greenleaf," the story of a farm woman who is gored to death by a scrub bull. She won first place in the contest again in 1963 for "Everything That Rises Must Converge," the story of a young man's response to his mother's eccentricities and her subsequent stroke on a dark street outside her weight-reduction class. And she garnered a third first-place O. Henry Award for "Revelation" in 1965, the story many critics consider her finest.

By August 1964, Flannery O'Connor was dead. But her literary career did not end with her death. The posthumous collection of nine short stories, published as *Everything That Rises Must Converge* (1965) and edited by Robert Fitzgerald, firmly established her reputation as a significant contributor to American literature. In an important biographical essay included in this volume, Fitzgerald illuminates O'Connor's darkness, bringing to light the essentially positive view that Christianity makes possible. The collected stories explore an essential theme of the Catholic theologian Pierre Teilhard de Chardin, whom O'Connor had begun to read in the late 1950s. His concept of the Omega Point, that particular nexus where all vital indicators come to a convergence in God, O'Connor interpreted through a character in each story who would have a moment where he or she would see or come to know the world in a way that possessed a touch of ultimate insight.

A collection of essays and occasional writings edited by Sally and Robert Fitzgerald was published as *Mystery and Manners* (1969). In a review in the *New York Times Book Review,* Keith Mano's reaction to the work is one of "gratitude," for he had never read "more sensible and significant reflections on the business of writing."[7] His response was often repeated; reviewers regarded this work with sincerity in their appreciation for both who she was and what they could know of her and her writing. Through the decade of the 1970s, this collection of essays, more than any other piece of O'Connor criticism, became the chief lens for O'Connor interpretation. From beyond the grave, O'Connor herself became the chief influence on O'Connor criticism.

Farrar, Straus and Giroux published O'Connor's *The Complete Stories* (1971), making available in one edition thirty-one short pieces of fiction that included the nineteen stories from the previously published two collections, her thesis stories from her graduate work at the State University of Iowa, previously published early drafts of short stories that became chapters in her novels, other stories not included in the collections, and a fragment of what could have been her third novel. This edition enabled critics to reassess O'Connor's development as a writer.

OVERVIEW

In 1979, Sally Fitzgerald edited for Farrar, Straus and Giroux a collection of O'Connor's letters, *The Habit of Being.* Paralleling her writing life from her days at Yaddo in 1948, the writer's colony in Saratoga Springs, New York, until her death in 1964, these letters brim with candid comments about her writing, her awards, her critics, her disease, and her friends. They portray, more than any other contribution to the knowledge of O'Connor, a person and writer who are inextricably entwined. In the 1980s, the letters did for O'Connor criticism what the essays did the decade before. The two most persuasive and pervasive commentaries on O'Connor come from her own hand.

Overview

To see more deeply into O'Connor's work is to understand the two essential components, in all their multiplicity and merging, that drive her fiction: O'Connor was both Southern—ripe with its manners—and Roman Catholic—replete with its mystery. The blend of these two provided her a rich milieu out of which her worldview develops. And a blend of these components provided her a way to accept lupus erythematosus, the disease that cut short her life at age thirty-nine. On first encounter with an O'Connor story, the reader is likely to find the work disturbing because the violence is most notably present on the surface. O'Connor can be dismissed by a simple rejection of the crazily distorted characters that stretch credibility, or she can haunt by that important observation that Elizabeth Hardwick made at the time of O'Connor's death: "You'd have to call 'A Good Man Is Hard to Find' a 'funny' story even though six people are killed in it."[8] Either way, one is not likely to forget an O'Connor story precisely because it is so strikingly, stridently different.

UNDERSTANDING FLANNERY O'CONNOR

Born in Savannah, Georgia, on 25 March 1925, she was the only child of Edward Francis and Regina Cline O'Connor. She spent her formative years in a narrow three-story row house nestled between larger, more resplendent residences of relatives. Across from this Charlton Street home is one of many park squares, and perpendicular to the home is the Cathedral of St. John the Baptist, a magnificent edifice. Her first years of schooling, coinciding with the Depression, took place in this cathedral, and it was here also that she participated in mass. Her father encountered business difficulties, but O'Connor's vision of the world was being formed by hours spent sitting inside St. John the Baptist. The young Mary Flannery, with an imagination bursting from reading and visualizing, was deeply impressed with a sense of disparateness: on one side of the street was the house, plainly appointed and often full of her mother's relatives—O'Connor's aunts and uncles—telling stories, some of them about her father's increasing economic misfortune; on the other side of the street was the dazzling cathedral, lavishly appointed, each detail of the stations of the cross illuminated in rich and vibrant color, with mass delivered in Latin in these pre-Vatican II days. Mystery and manners were beginning to merge in her mind and in her heart.

By 1938, she moved with her family to Milledgeville, her mother's birthplace, and the place she lived for the rest of her life, with the exception of about five years. In the spring of 1945, she graduated from the local Georgia State College for Women, now Georgia College, with a major in social science. She received her M.F.A. from Iowa in the spring of 1947, but remained another year (fall 1945 to spring 1948), followed by several stints at Yaddo (summer 1948 to spring 1949). She moved briefly to an apartment in New York and within the year boarded with the

OVERVIEW

Robert Fitzgeralds in Ridgefield, Connecticut (spring 1949 to Christmas 1950). Early in 1951, she was diagnosed with lupus erythematosus, the disease that had taken her father's life in 1941. This disease brought her back permanently to the South, with an anguished comfort. In a letter to Maryat Lee, she recounts the "Return": "This is a Return I have faced and when I faced it I was roped and tied and resigned the way it is necessary to be resigned to death, and largely because I thought it would be the end of any creation, any writing, any WORK from me. And as I told you by the fence, it was only the beginning."[9]

For the rest of her life, the next thirteen years, O'Connor lived with her mother at Andalusia, their farm home, a few miles outside Milledgeville on the road to Eatonton. She wrote each morning for three hours; the rest of the day, she read, visited with friends, wrote letters, and took trips with her mother into town for lunch, usually at the Sanford House. A place similar to Andalusia figures prominently in many of her stories. "The Life You Save May Be Your Own," "A Circle in the Fire," and "Good Country People" all feature a single mother with a single daughter who has either a physical or attitudinal affliction that makes it necessary to depend on the mother who does not understand her. But each story in turn has its reversal; just as the dependent daughter is asserting herself to separate or be separated from her mother, the mother prevails in a way distinctively sympathetic.

The larger portion of *Wise Blood* was written and rewritten during those years she was away from the South, but daily letters to and from her parent kept her constantly aware of local happenings in and around Milledgeville: about the black hired help that lived within what Alice Walker termed "calling distance from the back door,"[10] about her mother's day-to-day activities of living in middle Georgia, where the likes of Hazel Motes, Sabbath Lily Hawks, and Enoch Emery actually exist in the flesh. In "The Nature and Aim of Fiction," O'Connor says, "The novelist makes his statements by selection, and if he is any good, he selects every word for a reason, every detail for a reason, every incident for a reason, and arranges them in a certain time-sequence for a reason."[11] Those reasons for the selections became clear to her once she returned home where she was able to finish this novel: the South was her community, and if she was to write "anything enduring," she needed to be at the "crossroads where time and place and eternity somehow meet."[12] To write about "place" was to live in it and observe it, but to do so with a bemused attachment.

For readers not familiar with the South that exists beyond the interstate,[13] as Reynolds Price once termed it, her characters are grotesque. They wear strange clothes: uniforms "clotted" with stains (50), pink nightgowns that "would better have fit a smaller figure" (17), shiny blue suits, black cotton stockings, pea green ties, yellow socks that get sucked down into shoes, gorilla suits. They hold unusually fierce attachments to family members: disrespectful and abrasive adult children do not leave home, but parents do their duty nevertheless, as though they are used to being told, as Mrs. May is in "Greenleaf," "I wouldn't milk a cow to save your soul from hell" (510). Unwelcome grandparents stay with their adult children, and grandchildren think nothing of insulting them to their faces, as John Wesley and June Star attempt to banish their grandmother from the automobile trip in "A Good Man Is Hard to Find." These children also physically abuse their grandparents, as Mary Fortune Pitts demonstrates in "A View of the Woods." They have physical, mental, and attitude afflictions: loss of limbs, muteness, deafness, a club foot, heart disease, undulant fever, obesity, insanity, bad disposition, and severe acne, to name a few. They have a collective inability to hold normal conversations with each other: "Mrs. Hitchcock told the woman about her sister's husband who was with the City Water Works in Toolafalls, Alabama, and the lady told about a cousin who had cancer of the throat" (6). O'Connor explains that her characters have "an inner coherence, if not always a coherence to their social framework. Their fictional qualities lean away from typical social patterns, toward mystery and the unexpected."[14]

Placing her characters in socially unlikely circumstances is precisely the crossroads "of time and place and eternity" that O'Connor was determined to capture. She delivers a blend of manners—a way of living and doing that is distinctly Southern—and mystery—a religious vision that defies rational explication. The more she became aware that the South was "not alienated enough" from the rest of the country, the more necessary she found it to "observe our fierce but fading manners in the light of an ultimate concern."[15] O'Connor's most interesting characters listen to something inside themselves, and for many of them it is a Catholic vision that prevails.

From 1956 until her death in 1964, O'Connor reviewed a wide range of books for local Catholic diocesan papers, the *Georgia Bulletin* and the *Southern Cross*. In a 1961 review of Raymond of Capua's *The Life of St. Catherine of Siena,* O'Connor writes of Catherine's family, who must have been full of "consternation" to find themselves "with a visionary in the house, a daughter who scourged herself three times a day until the blood ran, ate nothing but herbs, and occasionally fell in the fire during her ecstasies." For O'Connor, however, St. Catherine's behavior is responsive to an inner coherence. She concludes the brief review with a line that is helpful in understanding O'Connor's fiction: "Altogether this is not a book to give anyone faith, but one which only faith can make understandable."[16]

In every story, O'Connor suggests that if the Christian faith is in place for the reader, the work will be understandable. She knows, though, that this is not the case. Assuming a hostile audience, one that does not understand the world her way, she draws "large and startling figures."[17] She wants to make sure that the distortions are seen and understood as distortions to "an audience which is used to seeing them as natural."[18] So the grotesque images alert the reader to both sides of the spectrum: those characters who are Christ haunted, whose lives do not follow "typical social patterns," but rather have an inner coherence, such as Motes, Tarwater, the Misfit, Rufus Johnson of "The Lame Shall Enter First," young Harry/Bevel Ashfield of "The River," Mrs. Greenleaf, and those characters who are in denial, who see the world separate and apart from a meaning vested in Christ's redemption, but ultimately understand that some mystery lurks, that there is more in this world than meets the eye, such as Joy/Hulga Hopewell of "Good Country People," the grandmother in "A Good Man Is Hard to Find," Mrs. Turpin in "Revelation," and Mr. Head in "Artificial Nigger."

O'Connor does not create characters who take religion moderately, halfway. Her theological and artistic vision merges in an all-or-nothing religious perspective on life. If the message is accepted, then it is accepted *en toto,* and if it is rejected, then it is rejected with a fury because the premise would be too ridiculous to countenance. The characters in this latter group will come to new understandings within or beyond their respective stories, and it is at this point that mystery enters the story. Clearly, one of the reasons that readers turn repeatedly to an O'Connor story is to see exactly how, as Ralph Wood phrased it, these characters are "laid low by the whammy of grace."[19]

Borrowing from the violence of Christ's death on the cross, O'Connor once said in a letter to a friend: "What people don't realize is how much religion costs. They think faith is a big electric blanket, when of course it is the cross. It is much harder to believe than not to believe."[20] O'Connor's use of violence was her way of "returning [her] characters to reality and preparing them to accept their moment of grace."[21] By bringing characters to the point of death, the best example of ultimate violence, the character reveals the essence of the best possible self, the truest self, the self most clearly in touch with inner coherence, the self most ready for eternity. Violence is never gratuitous in O'Connor's stories; it is essential as a device to move the reader toward something else, something that could be seen as the embodiment of the story's mystery.

To understand O'Connor's fiction is to accept the intricate blending, the complex weaving of manners and mystery. The economically poor, Southern rural Bible Belt fundamentalists who people her fiction are uncomfortably funny. They say the unexpected; they do not answer questions directly. Most readers will be repulsed by these characters. They elicit a visceral response that emanates from a reader's sense of superiority, which, at some transcendent moment in the story, becomes false. These characters are seeking some answers to unstated yet fundamental questions about life. They are in the world, consumed by their fanaticism, not cloistered safely away in a convent or monastery. Every day they go forth to grapple with what matters to them uniquely. To attempt, then, to pull the South away from the mysterious concerns of the characters' lives or to wrench those ultimate queries from the place in which the characters live is fruitless; the relationship of mystery and manners is symbiotic. Both are essential to a more nearly complete understanding of O'Connor's fiction.

Notes

1. Sylvia Stallings, "Young Writer with a Bizarre Tale to Tell," *New York Herald Tribune Book Review* 18 May 1952: 3.

2. "Such Nice People," *Time* 6 June 1955: 114.

3. "Briefly Noted," *New Yorker* 18 June 1955: 105.

4. Flannery O'Connor, *Flannery O'Connor: Collected Works,* ed. Sally Fitzgerald (New York: Library of America, 1988), 478. All parenthetical citations are from this edition.

5. Granville Hicks, "Southern Gothic with a Vengeance," *Saturday Review* 27 Feb. 1960: 18.

6. Rust Hills, "The Structure of the American Literary Establishment," *Esquire* July 1963: 41–43.

7. D. Keith Mano, "Mystery and Manners," *New York Times Book Review* 25 May 1969: 6.

8. Elizabeth Hardwick, "Flannery O'Connor, 1925–1964," *New York Review of Books* 8 Oct. 1964: 21.

9. Flannery O'Connor, *The Habit of Being,* ed. Sally Fitzgerald (New York: Farrar, Straus and Giroux, 1979) 224.

10. Alice Walker, "Beyond the Peacock: The Reconstruction of Flannery O'Connor," *In Search of Our Mothers' Gardens* (New York: Harcourt Brace Jovanovich, 1983) 57.

11. Flannery O'Connor, *Mystery and Manners,* ed. Sally and Robert Fitzgerald (New York: Farrar, Straus and Giroux, 1969) 75.

NOTES

12. O'Connor, *Mystery* 59.

13. Reynolds Price, "The South, Beyond the Interstate," *U.S. News and World Report* 13 June 1988: 62.

14. O'Connor, *Mystery* 40.

15. O'Connor, *Mystery* 28–29.

16. O'Connor, *The Presence of Grace and Other Book Reviews,* comp. Leo J. Zuber, ed. Carter Martin (Athens: U of Georgia P, 1983) 111–12.

17. O'Connor, *Mystery* 34.

18. O'Connor, *Mystery* 33.

19. Ralph Wood, *The Comedy of Redemption: Christian Faith and Comic Vision in Four American Novelists* (Notre Dame: U of Notre Dame P, 1988) 91.

20. O'Connor, *Habit* 354.

21. O'Connor, *Mystery* 112.

CHAPTER TWO

Wise Blood

When the slim first novel *Wise Blood* appeared on 15 May 1952, it represented an effort on O'Connor's part that, according to Sally Fitzgerald, had begun in December 1946 at the Writers' Workshop in Iowa City.[1] Four of its fourteen chapters had already been published in various stages of similarity to the final version: "The Train" in *Sewanee Review* (spring 1948); "The Heart of the Park" in *Partisan Review* (February 1949); "The Peeler" in *Partisan Review* (December 1949); and "Enoch and the Gorilla" in *New World Writing* (April 1952). O'Connor's struggle to put this novel on track is evidenced by some 2,000 pages of typescript housed in the Flannery O'Connor Collection at Georgia College in Milledgeville, files 22 through 151, half the entire manuscript collection.[2] Because O'Connor had won the Rinehart-Iowa Fiction Award, Rinehart had first option to publish the finished novel. The response from one of Rinehart's editors was disappointing. In 1949, replying to her agent Elizabeth McKee, O'Connor shows her fully developed integrity: "The criticism is vague and really tells me nothing except that [Rinehart's people] don't like it. I feel the objections they raise are connected with its virtues, and the thought of working with them specifically to correct these lacks they mention is repulsive to me. The letter is addressed to a slightly dim-witted Camp Fire Girl, and I cannot look with composure on getting a lifetime of others like them."[3] Three years later, after many rewrites, Harcourt Brace, not Rinehart, published the novel.

WISE BLOOD

Hazel Motes, the Jesus-denying preacher protagonist, bursts on the scene snarling, "I reckon you think you been redeemed" (6) into the faces of people he does not know. Motes, just released from World War II, takes a train to Taulkinham to do some things he has "never done before" (5). And it is here that he meets the sordid characters that comprise this modern world: among them, Asa Hawks, a phony blind street preacher and Sabbath Lily, his homely daughter; Leora Watts, a too-large prostitute; Enoch Emery, a hangdog guard at the gate of the zoo; Slade, a sour used-car salesman and Slade, Jr., his Christ-cussing son; Solace Layfield, a wheezing fake prophet; Hoover Shoats, a sleazy radio preacher; and Mrs. Flood, an aging and prying landlady.

Contemporary reviewers were quick to notice that the characters in *Wise Blood* were beyond strange: in the *New York Times Book Review,* William Goyen said that "they seem not to belong to the human race at all,"[4] and from Oliver LaFarge in the *Saturday Review,* "the individual is so repulsive that one cannot become interested in him."[5] Other reviewers suggested the novel's "oddness,"[6] its "strange, predatory people,"[7] and "its insane world, peopled by monsters and submen."[8] The book was seen as angry, not comic, and classified as "an important addition to the grotesque literature of Southern decadence."[9] At the time, no critic saw the novel as a unique contribution to American literature. A more appreciative critical understanding was to come after O'Connor added a short note to the 1962 second edition of *Wise Blood.*

When she received word in the fall of 1961 from Robert Giroux, her editor, that *Wise Blood* was going to be reissued, she could not bring herself to reread the book in order to write an introduction. Reluctantly, she submitted a terse paragraph, to "prevent some of the far-out interpretations."[10] In this 226-word note, she calls Motes a "Christian *malgré lui,*" whose integrity lies in his efforts to try to get rid of Jesus, "the ragged figure who moves from tree to tree in the back of his mind." She further states that, for her, his integrity rests in his being unable to do so (1265).

Throughout the novel, Enoch Emery has the "wise blood," which sets him on a series of activities beyond his understanding. His wise blood hounds him, controls him. It is Enoch, however, who points out to the reader that Hazel acts as though he has "wiser blood" (33). O'Connor's note directs the reader to pay closer attention to the deeper symbolic significance of the title; Enoch possesses the comic version of wise blood, but Haze is racked by it. He is an insistent, flat, geometrically poised young man, whom O'Connor has designed as the medium through which she delivers her message: the Christian religion is serious business and must be accepted *en toto* or rejected similarly.

On this level, then, the novel is the story of Haze's rejection of the Christ who died on the cross, and his eventual return to this Christian belief. Haze moves through the story as though he has a rubber band attached to his back, and when he moves far enough away from this inescapable truth, when the rubber band is pulled taut to the point of near breaking, he snaps back to the position he cannot shake. He will blind himself with lime, sleep with barbed wire wrapped around his chest, walk with broken glass in his shoes. He is not "clean," and he must pay. As Paul on the road to Damascus or Jonah sailing away from Nineveh felt the power of reversing their directions both literally and figuratively, and as the saints in the early days of the church demonstrated with their hairshirts, Haze's ultimate acceptance is fiercely resigned and complete, yet his longing is not stated, his understanding is not articulated. His acceptance does not make life easier; on the

WISE BLOOD

contrary, shortly thereafter he is clubbed to death by a fat young policeman with a new billy. O'Connor uses the literal Mrs. Flood to acknowledge Motes's return to her boardinghouse: "I see you've come home" (131). The word *home* doubles its meaning; Haze Motes, at novel's end, has also found his spiritual home. His integrity is intact; he has served his purpose.

Haze's name, "Weaver," "Wickers," and "Moats" in earlier drafts, becomes the finalized "Motes," suggested by the Rheims-Douay Version of Matthew 7:3–5: "And why seest thou the mote that is in thy brother's eye, but seest not the beam that is in thy own eye? Or how sayest thou to thy brother: Let me cast the mote out of thy eye; and behold a beam is in thy own eye? Thou hypocrite, cast out first the beam out of thy own eye; and then shalt thou see to cast out the mote out of thy brother's eye." In this name selection, O'Connor calls attention to the eyes, specifically to Hazel's eyes, which are mentioned repeatedly in the text: "But his eyes were what held her attention longest. Their settings were so deep that they seemed, to her, almost like passages leading somewhere" (4). Motes ultimately turns inward; the focus, after his self-blinding, is to rid his own eye of the beam that is there.

"Hazel" is a reminder of the biblical Hazael; both tried to expunge God from their lives by using violence to destroy God's people. The biblical Hazael (which means "God has seen"), king of Syria, oppressed the Israelites, the chosen people of God (2 Kings 8–13). Hazael sought power and the fictional Hazel, ultimately and ironically, sought God's empowerment. Throughout the book, "Hazel" is most often referred to as "Haze." The shortened name is a reference to a glazed, impaired way of seeing.

O'Connor chooses all her characters' names with care. Enoch Emery, described as a "friendly hound dog with light mange" (23), shares a name with the biblical Enoch, one of two people from the Old Testament who was taken up into heaven without dying. The biblical Enoch had exemplary faith. O'Connor's Enoch is eighteen years old, has been in impersonal Taulkinham two months, and has a job at the zoo, in the heart of the city. When Enoch's wise blood tells him to step up and shake the hand of Gonga, he receives the first welcome he has had in this unfriendly city. Interrupting the personal narrative that pours from Enoch's mouth, Gonga growls at him: "You go to hell" (102). The name choice is a reminder that the faithful, trusting biblical Enoch never did go to hell; but this Enoch, who sells out to the modern materialistic world, will do just that. As an emery board is a rough surface for smoothing fingernails, Emery's personality irritates and grates on others.

For the street preacher-beggar-blasphemer, who poses as a blind man, O'Connor selects the name "Asa Hawks." In earlier drafts he is called "Moats," and later "Shrike," and is in some stages husband to a fifteen-year-old Sabbath; and, in the final version, is her father. Asa is the name of a king of Judah who goes to Syria for help in war instead of to the Lord. He is chastised by the prophets for demonstrating this display of unbelief (2 Chronicles 16). O'Connor's character announces to the world that he will blind himself "to justify his belief that Christ Jesus had redeemed him" (64), but then in a moment of seeing Jesus in front of him, "he had fled out of the tent into the alley and disappeared" (65). The name "Hawks" reminds the reader of the bird with the keenest eyesight, calling attention literally to Hawks's supposed blindness and figuratively to an important theme of the novel—how all these characters view the world and their places in it. Also, "to hawk" something is to sell it on the street, exactly what Asa Hawks is doing, delivering the word of Jesus through tracts that shout: "Jesus Calls You" (21).

WISE BLOOD

The explanation for Sabbath Lily's name is part of the story: "My mother named me [Sabbath] just after I was born because I was born on the Sabbath and then she turned over in her bed and died and I never seen her" (66). Lilies are most closely associated with Easter Sunday. Their whiteness suggests purity, but Sabbath Lily, who dresses in black, is mainly interested in going "the whole hog" since she is an illegitimate child, and a "bastard shall not enter the kingdom of heaven!" (67). She also appears as a perverse Virgin Mary when she accepts the shrunken mummy from Enoch, who has delivered what he thinks is the "new jesus" to Haze. Carrying the new jesus into Haze's room, she announces to him this new role for herself: "Call me Momma now" (106).

In the choice of the name "Onnie Jay Holy" for the former radio preacher, O'Connor employs a form of pig latin, suggesting Holy John, the one who would come before and announce the Messiah. One of his functions in the novel is to introduce the "True Prophet" after Haze rejects Holy's scheme for money. O'Connor extends the pig from the pig latin when Holy tells Hazel Motes that his real name is "Hoover Shoats." A shoat is a just-weaned small pig, and Hoover is not only a dam, a president, and a former director of the FBI, but more relevant to the text, a popular vacuum cleaner at the time O'Connor was writing the novel, one that enabled the operator to "Hoover" through dirt and make everything clean. The choice of "Hoover" highlights the emergence of machinery in a modern world that substitutes desire for gadgets for matters of eternal consequence.

Solace Layfield, the "True Prophet" whom Holy introduces and whom Haze runs over with his high rat-colored Essex, has a name with literal application. He ultimately will find his solace "laying in a field" after Haze has forced a confession from him and flattened him with the tires of his car. Other supporting characters in the book have names that reflect their personalities: Slade, a cold, hard man, who has nothing but cuss words for his son; Slade, Jr., a chip off the old block, with nothing but cuss words for Christ; Leora Watts, a speckled green-toothed prostitute with low mental wattage; Mrs. Flood, the eager-to-marry-Motes landlady with a flood of compassion for his money and a lost-in-the-deluge understanding of his internal quest for home.

One by one, Motes goes through these characters, for each of them represents something that he must reject if he is to reach his spiritual home. Enoch Emery represents an obsessive, compulsive attachment to meaningless ritual acts. Every day when his stint at the zoo gate has ended, he goes to the swimming pool, hides in the bushes or sits on the bank, and looks at the women. The second station is the Frosty Bottle, where he makes "suggestive remarks" (46) to the waitress. At station three he insults the animals. After these three stops, his wise blood directs him to the center of the park where he gazes at the shrunken mummy and is filled with "a terrible knowledge without any words to it" (45). When he attempts to take Haze to see the mummy, Enoch cannot go directly there; he must go through his usual ritual, the stations of his own cross. When Motes flings the rock at Enoch, he is literally rejecting the ridiculous stupidity of the limp zoo guard who does not remember where the Hawkses live, but he is figuratively rejecting the kind of religion that includes meaningless acts of ritual.

Asa Hawks represents the lie, the man who says he believes, who purports to be blind for that belief, but neither believes nor is blind. Motes, strongly attracted to Hawks, needs to follow him everywhere, knocks on his door throughout the day, and "couldn't understand why the preacher didn't welcome him and act like a preacher should when he sees . . . a lost soul" (82). When Motes finally breaks into his room, lights a match in Hawks's face, and discovers the sham, the moment is so startling for Motes that he temporarily ceases to be human. Hawks throws a punch in the direction of the intruder's face, but "it moved back, expressionless under the white hat, and was gone in a second" (92). The movement from a third-person masculine pronoun to a third-person neuter happens several times in the novel and it is always deliberate. Motes, then, figuratively rejects the approach to religion that would use it to obtain money and speak about Christ without believing the ideas behind the words.

Motes rejects Sabbath Lily before he knows of her father's deceit, when she tells him she is a bastard, because "him and her wasn't married" (66). Motes interrupts Sabbath's babbling more than half-a-dozen times to tell her she could not possibly be a bastard since Hawks had blinded himself for Christ. His spurning her is the result of his indecisiveness about her bastard status in his new Church Without Christ. He knows she "wouldn't be any different from anybody else," but "something in his mind was already contradicting him" (69). His attempt to leave her in the woods fails because the rejection in his mind is not yet clear. The night after his discovery of her father's false claims, he finds Sabbath in his bed. The white hat Haze wears symbolically represents his innocence in the scene where he discovers Hawks's fraud, and when Sabbath removes the hat from his head and sails it across the room, O'Connor suggests that Haze's innocence has taken wing. Sabbath tells him that, like her, he is "pure filthy right down to the guts," only she likes being that way and he does not (95). He recognizes, without acknowledging, the truth in her words, "as if he were waiting to remember one more thing" (96).

He worries that he is filthy, and he knows all too well that he does not enjoy being filthy. After he blinds himself, much to her horror because "she hadn't counted on no honest-to-Jesus blind man" (121), she leaves and then returns, but Motes is indifferent to her presence, wanting her to leave, willing to "pay her to stay away" (121). It is Mrs. Flood who calls the authorities to have her removed. Motes, who never acts as a willing participant in their sexual encounters, such as they are slightly alluded to, rejects Sabbath in perhaps the cruelest way of all. Literally he ignores her, and figuratively he rejects the nonreligious heathen filth of her ways. Sabbath is comfortable as a bastard who will not enter the kingdom of heaven, and because of her already doomed afterlife she seeks out lusty earthly benefits.

Motes violently rejects the "new jesus" that Enoch Emery has stolen for him. Snatching the mummy from Sabbath's arms, he throws it against the wall, pops off its head, and lets the dust inside spray out. When he sees the shrunken man through his mother's glasses, he realizes that his own literal words preached on the street are an exact description of his call for a "new jesus": "One that's all man, without blood to waste, . . . that don't look like any other man" (80). Motes understands that what he has called for is not what his church needs, and not what he needs or believes. He must reject literally the "baby" that Sabbath clutches to her breast and his own "fatherhood" in this fraudulent momentary drama. Figuratively, he rejects the religion behind the words he has spoken on the street, a first step on his path to salvation. When he throws his mother's glasses out the door behind the mummy, he repudiates her brand of religion. He has only used her glasses when he reads the Bible he has brought from home. He banishes her view, discerning that he must come to his religious perspective through his own vision, unadorned with her spectacles.

Physical violence is also the manner through which Motes destroys both Hoover Shoats and Solace Layfield. Shoats recognizes a potential monetary windfall from Motes's Church Without Christ, immediately moving in on Motes's preaching turf and renaming his church the "Holy Church of Christ Without Christ" (86). As he speaks Motes's message in order to collect money from the listeners, he sees the "new jesus" idea as full of possibilities, only in need of "a little promotion" (90). Motes slams Shoats's thumb in the car door, sending him howling into the night streets, and literally rejecting his intrusion. Figuratively, Motes denies the kind of religion-turned-flash that would earn money for something that its spokesperson sees only as an end in itself, a way to financial gain. Solace Layfield, Shoats's replacement for Motes as the "True Prophet," represents Motes's double. "Him and you twins?" (94), he is asked on the street. When Motes hears Layfield, he recognizes his own echo and knows he must "hunt it down and kill it" (95). Although the literal death of Layfield by Motes's running over him with his Essex is barbarous, the figurative meaning is the turning point on Motes's road to salvation. He realizes that Layfield is preaching against what he truly believes: "What do you get up on top of a car and say you don't believe in what you do believe in for?" (114), and he sees that he, too, is also guilty. When he kills Layfield, he symbolically kills his own Church Without Christ.

The last thing to stand in the way of Motes's return to that "wild ragged figure" of Jesus (11) is his prized possession, the high rat-colored Essex, as much a character in the novel as any human because of the important roles it assumes as woman, with its "bulging headlights" and "thin wheels" (38) and Slade's invitation to "get under and look up it" (40); as home, with Haze's ready admission to Slade, "I wanted this car mostly to be a house for me . . . I ain't got any place to be" (41); and as his identity— "nobody with a good car needs to be justified" (64). When Haze becomes a preacher, the car is his means to reach the arbitrary church site, his place to preach from, and his way to depart. Here, too, is Haze's double. The car is as good as Haze is. When Haze finds out from one mechanic that the car cannot be put in "the best order" (65), he drives to another who promises what Haze wants to hear—about himself and his car: that it was a "good car to begin with . . . with good materials in it" (65). Since Haze denies original sin at this point, he advocates innate goodness. Haze listens to what he wants to hear, not truth. O'Connor, in writing about symbols, calls the Essex a "kind of death-in-life symbol" suggesting that its roles include as Haze interprets them: "pulpit . . . coffin" and mistakenly a "means of escape."[11] When Haze asks young Slade the cost of the car, his response is symbolically important: "Jesus on the cross . . . Christ nailed" (38). He is letting Haze in on the secret mystery—his sacrifice for the car as symbol of spiritual home and identity must be complete; it will cost everything Haze has. Only Haze does not see young Slade's point. He believes in his car because "nobody with a good car needs to be justified" (64); however, when the policeman pushes his car over the embankment, Haze instantly needs justification. The literal need and the figurative point come together. In this new understanding, found in Haze's gaze across the clearing, he now sees fully that he is not clean, so he blinds himself for Jesus, succeeding where Hawks has failed, acknowledging through further persecution of the flesh that he must pay.

WISE BLOOD

After his self-blinding, the direction of the action changes; Motes has nothing else to discover from the world around him or the people in it. Now it is his landlady, Mrs. Flood, who becomes obsessed with what it is that Motes knows. She feels as though she has been cheated somehow. When she discovers that he walks on rocks and wraps barbed wire around his chest, she is entirely baffled, likening his actions to something she might have read in an Edgar Allan Poe story. In an exchange in which the literal Mrs. Flood talks with the figurative Motes, O'Connor demonstrates how the same words move in opposite directions: Motes explains that he does these things because he is "not clean." Mrs. Flood responds, "I know it . . . you got blood on that night shirt and on the bed" (127). When Motes explains that he means another kind of clean, she tells him there is "only one kind of clean" (127).

When the policemen return the dead Motes to Mrs. Flood, she spews forth her confessional apology to the corpse with a face "stern and tranquil" (131). Still attracted to his scarred blind eyes, she is now completely perplexed as she attempts to see into his eyes with her eyes shut. She has not solved the mystery that she finds somewhere in Haze; she is "blocked at the entrance of something" (131). O'Connor suggests with this powerful and mysterious conclusion that death has some answers that life simply cannot give, but those who are willing to make the sacrifice, who are willing to center their lives in Christ, go into that life after life with a perspective denied the Mrs. Floods of the world.

O'Connor's 1962 note assists the reader in interpreting the novel through Christian dogma. She does not mince words about her own belief: "I see from the standpoint of Christian orthodoxy. This means that for me the meaning of life is centered in our

UNDERSTANDING FLANNERY O'CONNOR

Redemption by Christ and what I see in the world I see in its relation to that."[12] But she was also a product of the South and knew well the voices and idiosyncrasies of her neighbors, their nuances and incongruities. Louis Rubin leads the school of thought that speaks for her as a "Southern writer rather than as a theologian."[13]

One of the ways O'Connor delivers her serious message through a comic novel is by exploiting what is most well known about Southern manners. One example is through the dress and hairstyles of women. She plays on the Southern stereotype of afternoon tea with ladies in lace and voile, describing their dress with various details that undercut at once any notion of Southern charm. Sabbath Lily, in her black dress and black knitted cap, replaces the proper purse with "a white gunny sack hung over her shoulder" (22). Leora Watts, a prostitute who gets at least some business from the men's toilet at the train station where her name has been written on the wall, dons the clothes of her trade, "a pink nightgown that would better have fit a smaller figure" (17). Mrs. Wally Bee Hitchcock is dressed appropriately for her train ride with "pink collars and cuffs" (3), and later as she prepares for her berth, she will grace the narrow train corridor in a pink wrapper. On the other hand, Maude, who drinks "whisky all day from a fruit jar under the counter" (51), wears a "once-white uniform clotted with brown stains" (50) to serve her customers at the Frosty Bottle. The reputed Southern hospitality and down-home cooking are served up by a woman who wipes her nose with her hand and greets Haze by asking, "What you come in here with a son of a bitch like that for?" (51). O'Connor's minor female characters are often either no-nonsense women, such as Maude or the unnamed women Haze has lunch with on the train, one of whom repeatedly blows cigarette smoke directly in his face while ignoring him, or ladies who appear ridiculous in spite of themselves. In this mastery of detail about the limited people she depicts, she shows how clearly she has observed them from a distance; her audience, as she well knows, is far more likely to be sophisticated enough not to see themselves as the people she describes.

In the South, a code of manners determines not only how women and ladies should dress, but also how men should treat the "fairer sex." Popularized by *Gone with the Wind,* Southern myth abounds in the images of the gentleman caller and his belle dressed in her finery under the shade of a magnolia tree. Men listen to "ladies" out of respect and in order to reflect positively on their mothers who have labored unceasingly in teaching them proper manners. When Haze joins Mrs. Hitchcock on the train seat, his attitude toward her mocks Southern gentility: "He didn't answer her or move his eyes from whatever he was looking at" (3). When she speaks to him, he ignores her on three separate occasions. Although he accepts the food and company of Mrs. Flood after he blinds himself, he also slights her. After she has asked him to marry her and tells him she "has a place for [him] in [her] heart, . . . he passe[s] her, expressionless, out the door and into the hall" (129). When he does speak to women, he does not generally respond to their questions, but utters out loud whatever occupies his thoughts. For example, when he is told by Leora Watts to make himself at home, he responds, "What I mean to have you know is: I'm no goddam preacher" (18). Hawks verbally abuses his daughter, reminding her that Haze "don't even know [she] exist[s]" (62). Enoch insults whatever women cross his path—Maude at the Frosty Bottle to whom he owes fifteen cents for his milkshake: "You're worth more than that, baby girl" (51), and Sabbath Lily when he delivers the "new jesus" and sees Motes in the bed: "I see why he has to put theter washrag over his eyes" (103). He hides in the bushes to spy on a woman in a public forum, but he will openly visit a prostitute. There are no gentleman callers here and no Southern belles. Each character is depicted as having some sense of appropriate Southern behavior, but then O'Connor directs them otherwise in order to highlight both the expected mode and the deliberate flagrant twist.

Protestant church buildings are so present throughout the South that O'Connor finds it "safe to say that while the South is hardly Christ-centered, it is most certainly Christ-haunted."[14] O'Connor's creation of Motes, whose grandfather was a shouting, backwoods fundamentalist, Bible-declaring, evangelist preacher, and arrives every fourth Saturday "just in time to save them all from Hell" (10), makes sense within her orthodox views as well as within the milieu of her region. For the supporting cast in *Wise Blood,* O'Connor employs a secular use of religion to call attention to its abundant visibility and often surface meaning in the lives of Southern people. So powerful is the code of Southern manners that it often dwarfs religion, dominating the nature of its potential capacity for ultimate good. The references to "Jesus" or "Christ" and the Christian Trinity represented by the number three proliferate throughout the novel. At times, the words are clearly used as a way of cussing; other times, the words appear to be a prayer of supplication. When Haze is trapped in his berth on the train, he receives no help for his stifled cries of "Jesus, . . . Jesus" (14); ambiguity exists in the utterance. The words are a curse of frustration and/or a prayer of desperation. When the porter finally speaks, his comment could answer the prayer or the curse: "Jesus been a long time gone" (14). The porter means either that the world has lost Jesus, who is not around to answer the call for help, or that Haze's swearing has removed "Jesus," as the one signified, from the word itself, the signifier.

O'Connor uses the words *Jesus* or *Christ* 133 times in this novel, and references to Jesus by pronoun or inference abound. The use of the word in a pejorative manner dominates the text. When Motes becomes a preacher to "the church of truth without Jesus Christ Crucified" (31), a name he later shortens to "Church Without Christ" (59), his message on the streets is one of denying Christ: "Nothing matters but that Jesus was a liar" (59). However, once Motes creates his church and becomes its preacher, he does not use the word *Jesus* as a cuss word again. Before his decision to preach, he is partial to "My Jesus" (27), which he mutters in such a tone that Sabbath Lily notes: "Listen at him cursing" (27).

The obsessive play on the word *Jesus* calls attention to its paradoxical tension. The word is recognized as profane, but because of the repetition and the content of the story, the word takes on multiple meanings. The potato peeler seller, whose message is interrupted by the Hawkses' distributing tracts, unleashes "damn Jesus fanatics" and "goddam Communist foreigners" (21) at them, which establishes "Jesus," by proximity of word, as a displaced person. While the peeler seller's message denigrates Jesus, the gathered crowd does not have any response. Maude admonishes Haze for being with Enoch: "Jesus. . . . There ain't anything sweeter than a clean boy. God for my witness. And I know a clean one when I see him and I know a son a bitch when I see him and there's a heap of difference and that pus-marked bastard zlurping through that straw is a goddamned son a bitch and you a clean boy had better mind how you keep him company" (51). The woman who would use "Jesus" as a cuss word, call on "God" as her "witness" to identify a "pus-marked bastard . . . , a god-damned son a bitch" has had her thinking affected by the whisky she drinks from the fruit jar. The language of "God" and "Jesus" have become so routine to her that the words mean no more than just "a way to say something" (90), an expression Haze uses to explain the "new jesus" concept to Hoover Shoats.

This attitude is evident in Mrs. Flood's greeting to Haze when she considers renting a room to him in her boardinghouse. When he tells her he is a preacher, she wants to know the church: "Church Without Christ," to which she asks "Protestant? . . . or something foreign?" Of the two, Haze chooses "Protestant" (60). Mrs. Flood obviously knows the words, but she pays no attention to their meaning. "Protestant" has respectable associations. She does not see "Christ," neither the word nor the idea, as relevant or necessary to a definition of Protestant. The fear of the unknown, the foreign, is what worries her. Haze assumes her stand and answers, for a Southerner, correctly; he is successful in obtaining a room to rent.

For O'Connor, the entwining of mystery and manners was inevitable. A discussion of manners in isolation is possible as long as religion can be kept at bay. In this novel, there is no escaping it. Her references to specific numbers with Christian associations are most apparent with "three," representing the Trinity—the Father, Son, and Holy Ghost. This number emerges as the most often chosen after Haze has declared his preaching vocation. In chapter 6, the first chapter in which he begins to preach from his car, he pays three dollars for his room, reads Hawks's clipping three times, preaches to three "portly" women, three boys in "red satin lumberjackets" (58), and he repeats the message three times and moves on to three other picture shows before returning to Leora Watts for the last time. The symbolic suggestion through repetition is clear in this chapter. In other uses of "three," a car will be driven around the block three times before its occupants park and challenge Motes's message. The "True Prophet" earns three dollars for his first night's work. After his blinding, Haze wraps "three strands of barbed wire" around his chest (126). While each of these uses points toward a possible reminder of the Trinity, each time the number is used in Enoch's antics, the obverse is insinuated. Enoch, in responding to the call of his blood, washes three items: the bed, the chair, and the washstand that was "built in three parts" (74). He has three pictures on his wall, and he goes to three movies, which as Frederick Asals points out, are the "cosmology of his universe as heaven, hell, and earth."[15] Of all characters in the novel, besides Haze, Enoch deserves attention.

Critics have often noted the doubling that parallels Haze's and Enoch's roles in the novel. In many ways, Enoch serves as a foil to Haze's spiritual quest. Haze works insistently to determine what kind of religion will ultimately center his life. Enoch, on the other hand, works toward a literal center where he finds symbols of the modern world that are as tawdry and inconsequential as they are trivial and momentary. Enoch guards the gate at a park that is "the heart of the city" (45), and his fascination with what he will come to identify as the "new jesus" Haze alludes to rests in a glass case in "the center of the park" (45). After Haze knocks him out with the rock, Enoch hears his blood beating "in the center of the city" (57). When his blood tells him to clean his room, he wants to go straight to the center, but he is crippled by his unswerving attention to an incomprehensible order, one that includes beginning with the least important item and working "toward the center where the meaning was" (75), saving the washstand for last because "this piece had always been the center of the room and the one that most connected him with what he didn't know" (74–75). What he does not know is symbolized by an empty space within the washstand, suitable for storing something of value, a kind of lost ark of the covenant. Enoch raids the glass case in the center of the park and stores the shrunken mummy in this gilt-painted shrine. The mummy, soon to be dashed to dusty pieces by Haze, is empty of substantial meaning for Enoch, and after he gives the "new jesus" away, the storage vault remains empty, symbolically duplicating Enoch's core belief system. What is telling is the mirror that sits on top of the washstand, with its wooden carved "hunched eagle wings" (74) protruding on each side, framing the face of anyone who would gaze in the mirror. This serves as a prediction for "THE young man of the future" (108) that Enoch hopes to become. In actuality he will be more animal than human and incapable of seeing himself as others see him.

With his blood still heated and unconversant with himself, Enoch goes to Walgreen's in the "center of the business district." Scratching his back against the window as he inches his way inside, he must pass the displayed chaos, representing an accumulation of stuff that has some essential sway in modern life: "alarm clocks, toilet waters, candies, sanitary pads, fountain pens, and pocket flashlights" (77). O'Connor has selected items that appeal to the senses; they can be heard, smelled, tasted, felt, and seen. Grouped as they are, however, she has a plan for the chaos. Candies, which can be tasted, next to sanitary pads, which can be filled and felt, create a grotesque impression, helpful in marring the city's image. The pocket flashlight assists its owner in seeing better in the dark, for O'Connor has already highlighted the indifference the Taulkinham folks demonstrate to the night sky's beauty and magnificence: "The black sky was underpinned with long silver streaks that looked like scaffolding and depth on depth behind it were thousands of stars that all seemed to be moving very slowly as if they were about some vast construction work that involved the whole order of the universe and would take all time to complete. No one was paying any attention to the sky" (19). Haze, however, does not look in the store windows.

Once inside the store, Enoch heads toward the "center of a small alcove" (77) to a "belching" popcorn machine. The city, brimming with superfluous gadgetry, is the place most likely to swarm with evil. Enoch's encounter with the "pasty boy" who was "there to serve the machine" (77) highlights the ugliness of modern city ways, where humans yield to technology. The machine attendant feels around in "its vitals" and fills a bag, delivering the perversely acquired popcorn to Enoch, who pays with coins from his purse that, to the "pasty boy," looks like "a hawg bladder" (77). The biblical reference to Jesus' removing the demonic spirit from the people to the herd of swine, which then "ran violently down a steep place into the sea" (Mark 5:13) where they drowned, is a reminder of Enoch's possession of the purse of pig. O'Connor appears to be suggesting that without Christ, Enoch is a prime target for the devil's territory.

In fact, still haunted and controlled by his blood, Enoch goes to the movies. "Down a long red foyer," that color most associated with the devil, Enoch, "like Jonah," finds his seat in the belly of this movie whale (79). The message of each of the movies foreshadows Enoch's coming gorilla transformation. *The Eye* suggests that he is about to lose something he "couldn't do without" (79), literally, his physical presence. The unnamed second picture is about life at "Devil's Island Penitentiary," where Enoch appears destined to roam when his gorilla hospitality days are done on earth. The third and final picture, *Lonnie Comes Home Again,* is about a baboon "who rescue[s] attractive children from a burning orphanage" and eventually receives "a medal" (79); Enoch's own desire to reach out to people is apparent in the Gonga costume. Upon watching this movie, however, Enoch is repulsed by what he sees and is in a great hurry to leave the maw of this theater. After the three movies are over, he falls down "the two higher tunnels" and races out "the red foyer and into the street" (79). Unlike Jonah, Enoch does not appear to have changed his mind, heart, or direction; he remains other-directed, blood-guided. And the street he returns to is still in the city.

Finally, armed with his "denuded" umbrella stick, he makes his way toward the "Victory," where he anticipates having his own kind of superior finish. Echoing the message in the forgotten *The Eye,* he tells a waitress, "You may not see me again . . . the way I am" (110). Once Enoch disposes of the Gonga impersonator, he buries his own clothes. Although the dense Enoch believes this is "not a symbol to him of burying his former self," it is certainly a symbol to the reader. As Enoch eases into the Gonga costume, he erases his personhood. O'Connor shifts the pronoun from "he" to "it" (111), acclaims supreme happiness for this gorilla, and reduces God to a "god," who "had finally rewarded it" (112). However, when this gorilla moves in the darkness to shake hands with an unsuspecting couple on a bench, both reject the hulking image and flee separately into the night. The last reference to Enoch occurs with a description of his wounds from the fracas to become the gorilla, and the last sight of the surprised gorilla is looking over "the uneven skyline of the city" (112).

This gorilla appropriately faces the city, which has by this point in the novel accumulated a variety of evil-seeming associations. After Haze's car has been destroyed by the redneck patrolman, Haze also sits down and stares, but his direction is away from the city and its affiliations. He looks "across the clearing and on beyond," his face reflecting "the blank grey sky that went on, depth after depth, into space" (118). Here in chapter 13, O'Connor repeats the language she uses to describe the sky no one is paying attention to in chapter 3. On both occasions, she elevates the vastness and the beauty of God's work by contrast to the gaudy city. As Enoch's comic wise blood spirals him toward his own empty center, Haze's unrelenting wise blood moves him to blind himself in order to pay for his earlier efforts to thwart the message of his grandfather: "Jesus would never let him forget he was redeemed. . . . Jesus would have him in the end!" (11).

When O'Connor wrote the note for the second edition of *Wise Blood,* she marveled that it was ten years old and "still alive" (1265). In all the O'Connor canon, this first novel and its protagonist are the subject of the most critical commentary and the most heated controversy. While most scholars see Haze's self-blinding as a moment of spiritual salvation, a few argue that Haze is the property of nihilistic control, a view represented most notably in the work of Josephine Hendin: "After losing his Essex, [Haze] is engulfed in a sense of nothingness, a mental emptiness broken by ambiguous, irrelevant symbols."[16] The difficulty of easy interpretation resides in Haze's lack of happiness in his response to life. The Christian commitment has not made his days brighter. John Desmond sees the situation of Hazel Motes as connected with history, and though the novel's action argues for a redemptive vision, O'Connor has chosen to present "Haze's quest obliquely as a *via negativa.*"[17] Perhaps it is precisely this negative way that so throws off balance the unsuspecting reader. O'Connor never did intend to write a conventional novel.

Notes

1. Flannery O'Connor, *Flannery O'Connor: Collected Works,* ed. Sally Fitzgerald (New York: Library of America, 1988) 1242. All parenthetical citations for *Wise Blood* are from this edition.

2. Stephen G. Driggers and Robert J. Dunn. *The Manuscripts of Flannery O'Connor at Georgia College* (Athens: U Georgia P, 1989) xii.

3. Flannery O'Connor, *The Habit of Being,* ed. Sally Fitzgerald (New York: Farrar, Straus and Giroux, 1979) 9.

4. William Goyen, "Unending Vengeance," *New York Times Book Review* 18 May 1952: 4.

5. Oliver LaFarge, "Manic Gloom," *Saturday Review* 24 May 1952: 22.

6. "Southern Dissonance," *Time* 9 June 1952: 110.

7. "Briefly Noted," *New Yorker* 14 June 1952: 118.

8. "To Win by Default," *New Republic* 7 July 1952: 19.

9. John W. Simons, "A Case of Possession," *Commonweal* 27 June 1952: 297.

10. O'Connor, *Habit* 473.

11. Flannery O'Connor, *Mystery and Manners,* ed. Sally and Robert Fitzgerald (New York: Farrar, Straus and Giroux, 1969) 72.

12. O'Connor, *Mystery* 32.

13. Louis D. Rubin, Jr., "Flannery O'Connor's Company of Southerners: Or 'The Artificial Nigger' Read as Fiction Rather Than Theology," *Flannery O'Connor Bulletin* 6 (1977): 47.

14. O'Connor, *Mystery* 44.

15. Frederick Asals, *Flannery O'Connor: The Imagination of Extremity* (Athens: U of Georgia P, 1982) 46.

16. Josephine Hendin, *The World of Flannery O'Connor* (Bloomington: Indiana UP, 1970) 54.

17. John F. Desmond, *Risen Sons: Flannery O'Connor's Vision of History* (Athens: U of Georgia P, 1987) 55.

CHAPTER THREE

A Good Man Is Hard to Find

From the title story of O'Connor's first collection of short stories, she has the Misfit deliver a line about the grandmother that proves all too true in a figurative sense about each story in this gathering: "She would of been a good woman . . . if it had been somebody there to shoot her every minute of her life."[1] O'Connor felt that only when that moment of ultimate violence is reached, that moment precisely and explicitly before death, are people their best selves. Ten characters die in these ten stories, six of them in the title story. Violence finds its way into every story because O'Connor's vision was directed by a spiritual taproot that ran deep: "The novelist with Christian concerns will find in modern life distortions which are repugnant to him, and his problem will be to make these appear as distortions to an audience which is used to seeing them as natural; and he may well be forced to take ever more violent means to get his vision across to this hostile audience."[2]

Harcourt, Brace published the collection on 6 June 1955; on May 31 O'Connor was interviewed on the television show, *Galley-Proof,* by host Harvey Breit, then assistant editor of the Book Section of the *New York Times.*[3] As she wrote in a letter to Robie Macauley two weeks before the broadcast, she was worried about this television appearance for fear she would not be able to think of anything to say but "Huh?" and "Ah dunno" and would have to do penance "in the chicken pen to counteract these evil influences."[4] Of the thirty-seven questions Breit asked

A GOOD MAN IS HARD TO FIND

O'Connor in the thirty-minute broadcast, which also featured a dramatization of "The Life You Save May Be Your Own," she returned answers to thirty-four of them and gave a simple "yes" or "no" eight times. The high point of the interview occurred when Breit wanted O'Connor to summarize the story that was being dramatized because there was not time to reenact the whole of it: "Flannery, would you like to tell our audience what happens in that story?" Her response was characteristically blunt: "No, I certainly would not. I don't think you can paraphrase a story like that. I think there's only one way to tell it and that's the way it is told in the story."[5] O'Connor's integrity concerning her art cut short queries she found insipid. Upon her return to Milledgeville, she wrote to a friend that the show had been "mildly ghastly," and she was pleased "to be back with the chickens" who were indifferent to her published book.[6]

Contemporary reviewers were intrigued by what they read, but still uncertain as to how to write about it, how to respond to it. *Saturday Review*'s John Cook Wyllie was reduced to such banality as "the gal can really write." In a demonstration of how talent cannot necessarily be easily distinguished, how difficult it is to know the one that will be around a half century later, Wyllie places O'Connor's writing in "the first rank of this country's younger women writers, alongside Nancy Hale and Frances Gray Patton."[7] Sylvia Stallings, who wondered in her review of *Wise Blood* three years earlier "where, after an opening performance like this one, she has left herself to go,"[8] answers her own question when she delights in the "fresh evidence" of O'Connor's "strong and original gifts." Stallings praises her ability to "lay hold of the significant detail . . . in a reality [that] is generally not pleasant."[9] The reviewer from *Time* is another who could not see anything beyond or beneath these stories, although this reviewer finds the ten stories "witheringly sarcastic" and written with "a brutal irony, a slam-bang humor and a style of writing as balefully direct as a death sentence." Noting O'Connor's attempt in "The Displaced Person" to grope for "a symbolic second-story meaning . . . something about salvation," *Time* reduces the effort to "arty fumbling," the same flaw that "marred" *Wise Blood.*[10] In a letter to a friend, O'Connor said that when she read this review, "it nearly gave [her] apoplexy."[11]

In the *New Yorker,* O'Connor gets brief notice for her ability to depict the language and manners of her characters but is berated for tales that, ultimately, are meaningless and without depth.[12] When O'Connor saw the note, she commented to a friend, "I can see now why those things are anonymous."[13] At this point in her career, even the Catholic press did not understand her orthodoxy, although they noted her "relentless vision."[14] *Catholic World* reports that she delivers a "fiery rejection of Bible Beltism, of small, mean minds and small, mean ways," but then despairs with "The Displaced Person," a "marvelous parable, one not entirely clear of course."[15]

Something grotesque yet powerful was going on, but reviewers were having difficulty seeing into the fiction. Gone from these reviews is the dismissive attitude that permeated the reviews of *Wise Blood* in 1952, where her characters were allocated to a less-than-human species. Critical praise centered on her ability to capture the Southern voice and her keen awareness for detail, but, for the most part, the reviewers found that the work terminated in the grotesque. Reviewers could see the ludicrous distortions she employed, the marked departures from the natural, the expected, and the typical, but the reasons for such repetitive hybrid composites, the movement from the ridiculous to absurd comic ugliness left them mystified. O'Connor herself would have to explain and defend her use of the grotesque. Her interest was in combining what she saw in the concrete world around her with what existed "in a point not visible to the naked eye," which embodied the mystery of human existence.[16] First, she wanted the attention of the reader. Her use of the grotesque was an effective way to command it, but for many early readers, the grotesque became an end in itself.

Orville Prescott, book reviewer for the daily *New York Times,* called O'Connor an "extraordinarily accomplished short story writer." He praised her originality, her indifference to the "literary sachem of Oxford, Miss," but, he, like the majority, saw the stories concluding on "a note of grotesque horror." He is, however, among the first to hint at what would become a growing popular response to O'Connor's characters: "Their stupid remarks, their wretched thoughts, their miserable conduct haunt the mind." O'Connor was a writer that many readers were beginning to respond to with a passionate zeal, precisely because she had the power to "haunt the mind." Prescott concluded his response with a knowing awareness that readers would perceive her work the way he had: "Obviously, 'A Good Man Is Hard to Find' is not a dish to set before most readers. Those who are attracted by it will admire it immensely."[17] When O'Connor read his review, she repeated to her former editor, Robert Giroux, what she had been told: "[Harcourt] sent me the Orville Prescott review and said it was as near as he ever came to ecstasy and that on that day they sold 300 copies."[18]

Two days later, in the Sunday *Times Book Review,* Caroline Gordon, a friend of O'Connor's whom she often consulted about her progress on a story, had a distinctive assessment. Here was the first review to indicate not only that, but how, O'Connor differed from her contemporaries: "Miss O'Connor, for all her apparent preoccupation with the visible scene, is also fiercely concerned with moral, even theological, problems. In these stories the rural South is, for the first time, viewed by a writer whose orthodoxy matches her talent. The results are revolutionary." Gordon uses Henry James's response to Guy de Maupassant as an analogy to explain how the cumbersome reviewer's grasp faltered with the unexpected new young talent of this American writer. He may feel, Gordon conjectures "that a lioness has strayed across his path."[19] Although O'Connor was "not worried" that *A Good Man Is Hard to Find* would sell too many copies,[20] the collection sold surprisingly well—three printings by September 1955 sent 4,000 copies to the marketplace.[21] The following year, the English publisher, Neville Spearman, bought the rights for the collection. When it was published two years later, the name had been changed to *The Artificial Nigger and Other Tales*. When O'Connor saw the edition, she was outraged, for without permission the English publisher had made the title change and "featured a big black African, apparently in agony, granite agony" on the cover.[22]

O'Connor redefines the family unit in each of these ten stories; for example, granddaughter-grandfather; grandfather-grandson; grandmother-son-children's mother-children; however, she repeats four times a mother-daughter situation with hired help. Many of her important characters have no names, but, rather, are referred to by the roles they assume in their stories. In each of the stories, a visitor or a visit irrevocably alters the home scene and whatever prevailing view had existed. These visitors take various shapes—an unborn child, a one-armed tramp, three juvenile arsonists, a deranged escaped convict. As a result of some interaction, the protagonist and/or the visitor learns something that he or she had not considered before the experience. The narrative form appears direct and mildly uncomplicated. Yet, each of these stories shouts a wake-up call to the complacent reader, for at some identifiable specific point, O'Connor pushes the familiar world to the side while literal and figurative action race parallel to an exhausting end.

For every story, O'Connor places an action or gesture with a character that strikes the reader as strangely different; at the least, it is unexpected. At this moment, the story moves to a new level, one that transcends "any neat allegory that might have been intended or any pat moral categories a reader could make"; one that makes "contact with mystery."[23] O'Connor's use of the grotesque joins with mystery in these violent moments. Aware of the modern audience who did not share her driven vision, she reached them this way: "Violence is strangely capable of returning my characters to reality and preparing them to accept their moment of grace. . . . This idea, that reality is something to which we must be returned at considerable cost, is one which is seldom understood by the casual reader, but it is one which is implicit in the Christian view of the world."[24] All of O'Connor's stories, ultimately, turn on this point, and somebody learns something hitherto unknown.

"A Good Man Is Hard to Find"

The title story, previously published in *Modern Writing I* in 1953, is the most violent in the collection. Elizabeth Hardwick, remembering O'Connor at the time of her death, called the story "funny . . . even though six people are killed in it."[25] A nuclear family, with grandmother attached, leaves Atlanta for a three-day vacation in Florida. The grandmother asks her son, Bailey, to make a side trip down a dirt road to see an old mansion. When she suddenly remembers that the mansion she wanted them all to see is actually located in another state, her foot accidentally kicks her basket. The cat she has hidden in that basket jumps on Bailey's shoulder, causing him to lose control, resulting in their car turning over. The Misfit, about whom the grandmother warns her son Bailey in the first paragraph, coincidentally is the first to arrive at the scene of their accident. Never letting his Southern manners slip, the Misfit systematically does away with each member of the family, shooting them himself or having his henchmen, Bobby Lee and Hiram, do the job. On this literal level, the story is horrifying. Because of the specificity of detail of dress and family interaction, the story is also funny in a grotesque way.

In a region known for its hospitality, the members of this family treat one another with hostile deference. Southern manners are undermined in comic reversals. The grandmother is virtually ignored each time she speaks; the children, John Wesley and June Star, are openly antagonistic to their elders, both to their kin and to the proprietors of Red Sammy Butts's Barbecue Tower. When the disrespectful June Star demonstrates her tap dance, she rejects the offer to be Red Sam's wife's "little girl" with slashing honesty: "I wouldn't live in a broken-down place like this for a million bucks!" (141). She also has no interest in her grandmother's coming with them on their trip. O'Connor provides June Star with a popular radio show for an allusion: "She wouldn't stay home to be queen for a day" nor "for a million bucks" (137). Although the overemotional television show "Queen

A GOOD MAN IS HARD TO FIND

for a Day" premiered in 1956, a radio show with the same format began in 1945.[26] Women would tell stories about their lives generated to evoke sympathy from the audience who would applaud for the woman they deemed most worthy of prizes and the title, "Queen for a Day." Inevitably, the winner was the one who could deliver the thickest sentimental mush. The show was ripe for parody. June Star knows her radio, but she seems ignorant of the tales and stereotypes of her region. When the grandmother tells the watermelon story, John Wesley catches on immediately, realizing that the story is "funny" because it highlights the white Southerner's popular belief that the black Southerner loves watermelon. June Star, on the other hand, is certain she would have no interest in a man who "just brought her a watermelon on Saturday" (140). She is outside the loop of Southern myths and assumptions, a younger version of Joy/Hulga from "Good Country People."

The children's mother, who has no name and no idea of proper dress or cleanliness, wears slacks and "a green head-kerchief" (137, 138) two days in a row. According to the grandmother's worldview, the children's mother pales beside her own understanding of how to dress as a lady. She is known exclusively by her role in the story as "the children's mother," and is referred to sixteen times by that moniker; she is never "Bailey's wife" nor anybody's in-law. The role confines and undermines her possibilities. She never disciplines her children, not when they are rude to their grandmother or to strangers. She holds a place, but she says little, remembering her own manners only when she is about to go to her death. When she is asked if she would like to join her husband, the reply is "yes, thank you" (151).

Bailey offers his only kind words to his mother when he is being escorted to the woods to die: "I'll be back in a minute, Mamma, wait on me!" (148). However, the conversation central to the deeper meaning of the story is the exchange between the Misfit and the grandmother because here O'Connor delivers her "moment of grace." The Misfit and the grandmother have both cut through and yet linger in the Southern manners routine: "I know you're a good man. . . . You're not a bit common!" (148), and have complicated the conversation with talk of Jesus. For the grandmother, the talk of Jesus is part of manners, how strangers make polite, yet desperate, discourse. For the Misfit, the words hang heavy. Like Hazel Motes in *Wise Blood,* who knows he is not clean, the Misfit knows he "ain't a good man" (148). He is perplexed by Jesus who has "thown everything off balance" (151). The grandmother's words of conversation offer wisdom and hope, but they emanate from a source that does not grasp the deep significance of their meaning. When she suggests that he pray and ask Jesus for help, his sidekicks have just moments earlier killed both Bailey and her grandson, John Wesley. While she tries to find her voice through her trembling, Hiram and Bobby Lee are marching the children's mother, the baby, and June Star off to join the resting dead. When her words do surface, all that is audible comes through the narrator: " 'Jesus, Jesus,' meaning, Jesus will help you, but the way she was saying it, it sounded as if she might be cursing" (151).

When the grandmother hears the shots ring out from the woods, she instantly reverts to the only hold she has on life, the recordings in her mind that control outward behavior in a region consumed by appearances: "Jesus! . . . You've got good blood! I know you wouldn't shoot a lady! I know you come from nice people! Pray! Jesus, you ought not to shoot a lady" (151–52). O'Connor's placement of the word "Jesus" is ambiguous. It could be a way of speaking for the grandmother, perhaps as her ace in the hole, because "Jesus" is what she has been taught, what she has grown up with, what is proper to use in this wretched situation in which she finds herself. It could just as likely be a curse word. Even though she has presented herself as a "lady," she does not hesitate to call attention to a "cute little pickaninny" (139) or tell a story about a "nigger boy" stealing her watermelon (140). However, the Misfit keeps responding to the "Jesus" in her pleas. He wants to ponder the seriousness of Jesus' actions: "If He did what He said, then it's nothing for you to do but thow away everything and follow Him, and if He didn't, then it's nothing for you to do but enjoy the few minutes you got left the best way you can—by killing somebody or burning down his house" (152). No middle ground exists for the Misfit.

As the grandmother sinks into the ditch, the Misfit, toting a gun and wearing her dead son Bailey's shirt, continues talking about Jesus. The grandmother experiences a head clearing and reaches out to the Misfit: "Why you're one of my babies. You're one of my own children!" (152). The grandmother, to this point in the story, has not said anything that could be mistaken as seriously thoughtful. One reading of this moment is that the grandmother sees the charade that her own life has been in this split second before her existence is blown away. The system of people in a class structure that Southern manners has imposed on her thinking gives way to an insightful collapsing of that artificial hierarchy—the grandmother acknowledges that she is no better than the Misfit. He could indeed be her son; he could indeed be good enough to be her son. On a literal level, he is wearing

Bailey's shirt. If the story did not warrant a deeper reading, then the grandmother would stay in character and simply be confused by the Misfit's appearance, thinking him to be her son. The Misfit's instantaneous murder of her would scream nihilism. The story would only be grotesque.

Instantly upon hearing her words, the Misfit, "as if a snake had bitten him" (152), shoots her three times. In this sentence, O'Connor couples a reference to a "snake," fraught with links to the devil from the biblical Garden of Eden, with "three," a number that O'Connor repeatedly uses to elicit the Christian Trinity. In an allegorical reading, the devil is destroyed by Christ's goodness. However, the "snake" is associated with the grandmother, ungrasping yet innocent, and the "three" with the Misfit, full of meanness. The Misfit's words are a reminder as well of Christ's words to Peter, "Get behind me, Satan!" (Matthew 16:23, Mark 8:33), which suggest that one who has seen the truth can also be poisoned by the devil's venom and betray that truth. Because the Misfit struggles with the Jesus question, and because the grandmother acknowledges a bond with the Misfit, both characters demonstrate that "good" that is "so hard to find." The story ends with the grandmother dead, but wiser as she goes into that next life. The Misfit's life has been forever changed as well, for in his closing statement to the grandmother about his belief system, he acknowledges that there is "no pleasure but meanness" (152). After the grandmother acknowledges her connection with the Misfit and he kills her, he concludes: "It's no real pleasure in life" (153). The movement from a deliberate desire to seek meanness as pleasure to an understanding that meanness is not a pleasure is a discernible difference. With the grandmother's death, the Misfit has been offered a "moment of grace" as well.

A GOOD MAN IS HARD TO FIND

"The River"

Published for the first time in the summer 1953 issue of the *Sewanee Review,* A. R. Coulthard called "The River" O'Connor's "most theologically puzzling" story.[27] For here she places the weight of credibility on a small boy who is "four or five" (155). The premise is that Harry/Bevel's parents' lifestyle has created such a wasteland for him that he is irrevocably altered after one day with the babysitter, Mrs. Connin, and his baptism in the river. On the next day, he drowns himself in search of the Kingdom of Christ in that river. As unimaginative as the title is, the river not only serves as the setting of the all important action in the story, but it also looms large as a symbol. This is a story of baptism, a Christian sacrament not to be taken lightly or casually. The young preacher, the Reverend Bevel Summers, explains the symbolic importance of the river: "There ain't but one river and that's the River of Life, made out of Jesus' blood" (162). The river where the healing takes place is also literally full of "old red water" (162). Harry/Bevel asks Mrs. Connin on the way to her place if the preacher will heal him. When she wants to know what he has, the response is "I'm hungry" (156), which she interprets literally and promises breakfast on their arrival, but which also suggests a spiritual hunger that Harry/Bevel is, on some mysterious level he cannot understand, making contact with.

When the no-nonsense Mrs. Connin arrives at the Ashfields' to pick up young Harry, she remarks on a living-room stench of "dead cigarette butts" and a watercolor that has "black lines crossing into broken planes of violent color" (154). She does not understand this taste, for, by contrast, her own "tan paper brick" two-room, two-porch home (157) is decorated with pictures and calendars, all rooted in a reality she can see with her own eyes.

UNDERSTANDING FLANNERY O'CONNOR

Hers is not a world of modern, abstract art. Rather, in a prominent location, hangs a picture of a man, with "long hair and a gold circle around his head . . . sawing on a board while some children stood watching him" (157–58). She gives the child his first lesson in Christian education and the facts of life. Before they leave for the river, Harry/Bevel learns he "had been made by a carpenter named Jesus Christ"; he had thought "Jesus Christ was a word like 'oh' or 'damn' or 'God,' or maybe somebody who had cheated them out of something sometime" (160).

A biblical name changing often occurs accompanied by a kind of violence, most notably the example of Saul's blinding on the road to Damascus, the return of his sight, and the acceptance of the name Paul. "Harry" becomes "Bevel" on his own road to a different understanding of the world. Something works inside Harry, for "he had never thought at any time before of changing [his name]" (156), but when asked, "Bevel" is the reply. He takes the name of the young preacher, but he has no idea why. The first act of violence comes his way when Mrs. Connin's sons take him out to the hog pen and convince him to lift off the bottom rotten board to see the pigs, which he knows from his story books are "small fat pink animals with curly tails and round grinning faces and bow ties" (158). When the real pig snorts in his face and knocks him down, Harry/Bevel begins the scream that even when he is safe with Mrs. Connin lasts "five minutes" (159). The pig serves as an example of the gaping difference between Harry/Bevel's notions of the world and the reality of the world. Mrs. Connin reads him "The Life of Jesus Christ for Readers Under Twelve" (160), her valuable 1832 antique book. In it, Harry/Bevel notes a picture of "the carpenter driving a crowd of pigs out of a man," to which Mrs. Connin explains that all the pigs had come from one man. The pigs in this illustration, unlike his storybook pigs, look exactly like the ones he has just seen in the yard moments earlier. O'Connor has Mrs. Connin take liberty with the Luke 8:32 account, where Jesus drives the demons out of one man called "Legion" into the herd of swine and then sends the entire herd over the bank to drown in a lake.

As Harry/Bevel makes his way to the river with Mrs. Connin and her brood, his head is full of new information: Jesus Christ, a carpenter, made him; this same person makes pigs come out of a man; a pig has just rolled him backward and snorted in his face; a man named Mr. Paradise, with a cancer on his ear, looks like the pig that came after him. And Harry/Bevel, at "four or five," is too young to make sense of any of this, but his worldview has expanded. When it is his turn for baptism, Harry/Bevel has a feeling "that this was not a joke" (165), and he learns that now he counts; he "didn't even count before" (165). Upon his return home, the only report he can give to his mother, who is more interested in what the preacher has said about her, is that he counts.

Even to a boy so young, the preference for the richness of experience and growth on his day at the river to his routine life in the city with drinking and joking parents occurs to him. He makes the decision instantaneously: he is going to find "the Kingdom of Christ in the river" (170). His "moment of grace" comes precisely at his despair of suddenly realizing that this, like most things in his life to this point, is "another joke" (171). When he sees a "giant pig bounding after him," he is taken in by a gentle current and knows he is "getting somewhere" (171). O'Connor plays on the irony of Mr. Paradise's name; in an effort to swim away from Paradise, the child finds himself pulled toward the paradise he is seeking. Mr. Paradise, who never misses a healing, who comes faithfully, "to show he ain't been healed" (159), has his life touched at the mystery he watches. Mr. Paradise had been present when Harry/Bevel was baptized, and now he spots the determined child moving quickly toward the river, follows him, tries to save him, and, by his account, fails. The reader, like Paradise himself, who stares "with his dull eyes as far down the river line as he could see" (171), and like *Wise Blood*'s Mrs. Flood, is left with no conclusion. But the question that must come back to haunt Mr. Paradise is the mystery of why this child deliberately walked into the river. O'Connor pushes her resolve, as she has her preacher cry: "Believe Jesus or the devil! . . . Testify to one or the other!" (163). To demonstrate there is no middle ground, even the likes of the very young must choose.

"The Life You Save May Be Your Own"

Tom T. Shiftlet, the one-armed tramp with carpenter skills who ambles into Lucynell Crater's life one evening at sunset, is the protagonist of O'Connor's most productive revenue-garnering story. Originally appearing in the spring 1953 *Kenyon Review,* reprinted in the 1954 *O. Henry Prize Stories,* and eventually sold to General Electric Playhouse, the story was aired on the *Schlitz Playhouse* on 1 February 1956, as a vehicle for Gene Kelly. Before O'Connor, who did not own a television, imagined what would be its fate: "Mr. Shiftlet and the idiot daughter will no doubt go off in a Chrysler and live happily ever after. Anyway, on account of this, I am buying my mother a new refrigerator. While they make hash out of my story, she and me will make ice in the new refrigerator."[28]

Early working titles for the story, "Personal Interest" and "The World Is Almost Rotten," were changed to "The Life You Save May Be Your Own," a 1950s slogan for highway safety. In

A GOOD MAN IS HARD TO FIND

using this title, O'Connor directs renewed attention to the words of that once-popular roadside marker: Shiftlet's life is morally bankrupt and in order to save himself, he indeed must drive carefully. After abandoning at The Hot Spot the idiot girl he has just married, Shiftlet drives on toward Mobile, no more certain of that "moral intelligence" (176) he had earlier claimed for himself. When the honeymooning couple does not return from the two-day trip, Lucynell Crater will begin to question her own corruption, her need to save her own life, but the story ends before this dilemma is presented. All O'Connor gives is a suggestion of Shiftlet's uncomfortable feeling.

As soon as Shiftlet enters the story, he dominates it. Though Lucynell Crater identifies him immediately as a "tramp," she is mainly interested in procuring a handyman for her run-down place and a husband for her daughter, also named Lucynell. She is depicted as ruler of her roost, but O'Connor's hyperbole shows the superficiality of her vision—how she watches Shiftlet, "as if she were the owner of the sun" (173), how she sits with him in the evening when her "three mountains were black against the dark blue sky and were visited off and on by various planets and by the moon after it had left the chickens" (177). Lucynell's conversation with Shiftlet is directed for her own purposes, designed to generate answers that speed her toward her own end: "You from around here?" (173), when she knows already he is not; "What you carry in that tin box, Mr. Shiftlet?" (175), having already sized up his possibilities as a fix-it man; and, to the point, "Are you married or are you single?" (175), because, after all, she is "ravenous for a son-in-law" (177).

On the other hand, Shiftlet's conversation is more intricate, more probing, yet disconnected. He makes allusions that are lost on his conversation partner; his mind has been places hers will never go. As he appreciates the sunset, extending his arm and stub, he becomes a "crooked cross" (173), a man physically bereft, which in O'Connor's world indicates a corresponding spiritual deficiency. Evidence of his efforts to look closely at the world in which he exists appears in his disturbance over the Atlanta doctor who has "taken a knife and cut the human heart" and "studied it like it was a day-old chicken" (174). Shiftlet is convinced that the doctor does not understand the human heart any more than he does, an obvious reference to the mystery embedded in human feelings that flow from the heart. When he is told he may sleep in the car, his answer is an analogy to "the monks of old" who "slept in their coffins!" (176). James Joyce also alludes to these same monks who never speak, rise at two in the morning, and sleep in their coffins in his story "The Dead."[29] Just because Lucynell has not the faintest idea what he is talking about, she is not in the least prohibited from remarking that "they wasn't as advanced as we are" (176).

The car becomes symbolically more for Shiftlet—it is a place to be, a shelter at night, a way to get away from where he is to some other place he is not sure he wants to be. The car is the spirit part of a man, "always on the move" (179), so the green color he paints the car is reflective of that movement; and his destination, Mobile, is a pun on his need to propel elsewhere. To the boy behind the counter, he identifies his goal as Tuscaloosa, a city about a three to four hours' drive north of Mobile, in the opposite direction of where he is heading. His fixing the car is serious business, equivalent to "rais[ing] the dead" (178). He does not have to be like a "monk" any longer; he has turned his "coffin" into spirit.

The time has come to move on, for Shiftlet is a restless man, one who can begin a garden house roof, patch the steps, build a hog pen, restore a fence, and teach a deaf girl to say her first word—the symbolically laden "bird" which can fly away, just as he is about to do—all within one week. He is a man—while questioning "what is a man?" (175)—who is not satisfied. When he tells Lucynell after the marriage at the Ordinary's office that he is not satisfied, O'Connor moves the language on two levels: To Lucynell the ceremony literally "satisfied the law"; to Shiftlet, "it's the law that don't satisfy [him]" (180). He means something other than the laws of people; he is a twenty-eight-year-old carpenter, who can hang like a "crooked cross," and has done time as a gospel singer.

Shiftlet identifies Lucynell as a "hitch-hiker" to the boy who works the counter at The Hot Spot, who notes that "she looks like an angel of Gawd" (181). That image sticks in Shiftlet's mind as he repeats those very words in a description of his mother during the conversation that deepens the story. Depressed after his desertion of Lucynell, he looks for a real hitchhiker to lift his spirits. Once again, he falls short of the real thing; he settles for a young boy who has a "cardboard suitcase" and is standing by the road, with no thumb out, not saying he did or did not want a ride (182). However, he does get into the car, but only to hear a minisermon from Shiftlet on the sainthood of mothers. After the boy curses both his own mother and Shiftlet's, he abandons the car, jumping out into a ditch, offering Shiftlet an opportunity for grace. He has seen through Shiftlet; he has spoken the words that needed to be heard. Shiftlet feels the despair sink over him, hears the thunder "guffaw" at him, while the turnip-shaped cloud dumps "tin-can tops" of rain on his getaway car (183). What O'Connor suggests Shiftlet now knows is that he is the subject of his own prayer: "Oh Lord! . . . Break forth and wash the slime from this earth!" (183).

The story emphasizes Shiftlet's depressing thoughts and feelings, not his actions to do right by the abandoned Lucynell. By ending the story where she does and the way she does, O'Connor leaves room for speculation about Lucynell's mother, for she has never been without Lucynell before. Both the tramp and the mother must face their culpability in their own figurative hot spots, while the "angel of Gawd" rests easily at the literal Hot Spot.

"A Stroke of Good Fortune"

The material of what would become "A Stroke of Good Fortune" was part of the drafting process for *Wise Blood.* An early version titled "The Woman on the Stairs" appeared in the August 1949 issue of *Tomorrow.* Rufus, younger brother of Ruby Hill, is the character who became Hazel Motes. The apartment neighbor, Laverne Watts, who is interested in Ruby's size nine B feet and young Rufus, is an earlier try at Leora Watts, the too-large prostitute who services Motes. As rejected matter from the novel, "A Stroke of Good Fortune" was published as a story in the spring 1953 issue of *Shenandoah.* Later revised for the collection, Ruby, a jewel in the shape of a "funeral urn" (184), is a pregnant woman who denies her condition. Instead of visiting a doctor for what she decides is only a sickness, she chooses a palmist, Madam Zoleeda, who makes the pronouncement that after a "long illness, . . . it will bring [her] a stroke of good fortune!" (185), giving a literal reading to the title. Ruby, whose last name corresponds to the growing shape of her body, interprets that good fortune to be "moving" (185), for she is tired of all those steps it takes to reach home. Even grocery shopping becomes an exercise in denial, for she purchases four cans of beans to be able to excuse the kicks of the baby as gas pains. In fact, Ruby herself is portrayed as more food than human: "Her head [is] balanced like a big florid vegetable," surrounded by hair that is "stacked in sausage rolls" (184). And her mother as well is depicted as food: "She had looked like a puckered-up old yellow apple" (186).

The story is a collection of obvious life signs placed in a context of death images as Ruby mounts the four flights to her city apartment, a setting that O'Connor usually associates with evil. Freudian images abound—Hartley Gilfeet's pistol, "nine inches of treacherous tin!" (187), which she sits on and then has to pull out from under her, later his double pistols, "leveled and galloping" (195) toward her, and the reference to Hartley's begetting from "Rodman" (187). And deliberately placed reminders of the female menses—there "were twenty-eight steps in each flight" (187)—scream from the story's details to announce this baby to everyone but the mother, the one who most needs to understand what is happening. As the "funeral urn" Ruby struggles upward, she remembers that her mother had had eight children by the time she was Ruby's age, thirty-four. Four of those children died early, and the last one, her brother Rufus, for whom she has made the arduous trip to the grocery store and at whose special request she unwillingly purchases collards, had caused her mother to scream all night long, turning her into an old woman.

To counter Ruby's immense fear of aging, O'Connor places seventy-eight-year-old Mr. Jerger on the second floor to spring from his room to remind Ruby of Florida's birthday, and founder Ponce de Leon, who was in search of the Fountain of Youth. Even though Jerger looks as if his face "had mildew on it" (188), he had found that fountain, drank from it, and did so by going into his heart. Uncomprehending Ruby moves on to the third floor where, finally, Laverne Watts overtly delivers the message "in a loud guttural voice . . . 'Put them all together, they spell MOTHER! MOTHER!'" (193). Ever denying Ruby defends her position: Rufus is just an "enfant" (193), she is just fat, and Bill Hill, as the one responsible for birth control and seller of Miracle Products, would not slip up, even though lately "he was just more happy and didn't know why" (194).

At the end of the story O'Connor places the "moment of grace." Ruby hears what she wants to hear, not what she has been told; physical violence must bring her to her senses and prepare her to deal with reality. Ruby, stunned by "Little Mr. Good Fortune" (187) Hartley's striking into her, giving the title yet another literal meaning, but this time with figurative implications, lets the words "Good Fortune" and "Baby" echo three times into the "dark hole" (196) of the hallway. On her part, this physical jolt has caused her to begin, albeit feebly, to put together the clues of the trip upstairs. The echoes "leer" (196) at her, and her response to Rufus's birth comes at her again in rejoinder to her own pain that feels "out nowhere in nothing" (196). She is not quite at total understanding or acceptance, but also, sitting on the step, she has not yet reached home.

"A Temple of the Holy Ghost"

Published originally in the May 1954 issue of *Harper's Bazaar,* "A Temple of the Holy Ghost" is one of two stories in the collection to highlight the Roman Catholic experience and the only one to privilege it over other denominations or religious perspectives. Two fourteen-year-old cousins, Susan and Joanne, spend a weekend away from their convent school in the country with their unnamed twelve-year-old cousin, referred to throughout the story as "the child." The title comes from the line the girls have learned from Sister Perpetua; when they are in a state of arousal caused by the activity of being with a boy in the back seat of an automobile, they are simply to state: "Stop sir! I am a Temple of the Holy Ghost!" (199). The girls find this line hysterical and can hardly say it without breaking into frenzied laughter. The child does not see this as funny. The vastly different responses the visiting cousins and the child have to the same language and activity provide the tension and the humor in the story. What each side thinks is funny or not and why or how or at what point it becomes funny contributes to O'Connor's goal: The focus is the child's realization through the course of the weekend that being "a temple of the Holy Ghost" is serious business, full of mystery beyond her comprehension.

When the local boys, Wendell and Cory, who serve as dates to the county fair for the visiting girls, serenade them—and the hiding child—with Protestant hymns, the girls try to control their giggling. Youthful awkwardness in dealing with the opposite sex only serve to move the boys to "The Old Rugged Cross." The girls counter with a Latin response from Mass, "Tantum Ergo," which Wendell, not recognizing what he has heard, identifies as "Jew singing" (202). The hidden child screams her frustration at the "big dumb Church of God ox" (202) and falls off her barrel in the bushes.

The child oscillates from a moderate interest in attending the county fair to an obsessive imaginative involvement with the mysteries of the Roman Catholic Church, spurred by the fair's return. Upon visiting the fair the previous year, she had been curious about those closed tents with faded pictures of assorted freaks, whom she had compared to "martyrs waiting to have their tongues cut out" (203). Because she had imagined that what was inside the tent had something to do with medicine, she had decided to become a doctor when she grew up. In her mind, then, if she were a doctor and the subject inside those closed tents for adults only was medicine, she could legitimately enter those tents and satisfy her curiosity. However, because the pictures on the tent bring into her mind an image of the Christian martyrs of old, she, over the course of the year since last visiting the fair, realizes that being a doctor would not be enough. In her mind, she rapidly moves from doctor to engineer to saint and finally to martyr. The possibilities of whatever is inside those tents at the fair pale beside the richness of her imagination with the idea of martyrs "burn[ing] in oil," being "torn to pieces by lions" (204).

The powerful effects of the mysteries of the Roman Catholic Church direct the routines of her life. When she goes to bed the night that her cousins and their dates are at the fair, she forgets to say her prayers; however, the calliope's song keeps her awake and she remembers to get out of her bed, kneel beside it, and repeat the prayers that she has rotely learned from the church. At random times, her imagination leaps to the graphic image of "Christ on the long journey to Calvary, crushed three times under the rough cross" (205), and then, just as abruptly, her mind empties of the thought. On this night, the child relishes in the delight that she is not Protestant: "Lord, Lord, thank You that I'm not in the Church of God, thank You Lord, thank You!" (205). Although the obsession with Christ is reiterated throughout O'Connor's fiction, it is usually characterized by an overtly crazed backwoods fundamentalist Protestant. This strong grip that the Catholic Church has on the child's imagination is unparalleled in the O'Connor canon.

The story of the hermaphrodite the cousins report in exchange for learning how a rabbit gives birth is the key factor in the child's "moment of grace," where she begins anew to plumb the enormity of life's mysteries. When she learns that God can make a person both woman and man, without two heads, she is forced to think literally below the belt, although she has no clue how to begin imagining what this means as indicated by her half-dreamt, half-imagined conversation between the hermaphrodite and the audience in the tent. On a deeper and more disturbing level she understands something about the power and mystery of God. The child, however, remains a child; she cannot quite yet fathom what male and female genitals are all about. In her promise to explain how a rabbit has its young, she reverts to the comfort of a secure childlike version of the world; the rabbit simply "spit them out of its mouth" (207).

The words the cousins have quoted to the child from the hermaphrodite, "I don't dispute hit. This is the way He wanted me to be" (209), hang in the child's mind and fall into the commotion of returning the cousins to their convent. They arrive in time for benediction, and the child's mind goes through its usual ugliness to a moment of serious repentance, and just as quickly moves to the freak at the fair as the priest raises "the monstrance with the Host" (208). As they leave, the nun tightly embraces the child, "mashing the side of her face into the crucifix hitched onto her belt" (209). On the return home, the child, thus marked, hears the story from their driver, fat-necked, piglike Alonzo, that the fair has been closed down by the preachers because of what is in those tents. Once again, the image of the Host rises in front of her, this time emanating from the sun.

The child knows more than she did before her cousins came to visit, but she is not able to put together the pieces: The body is "a temple of the Holy Ghost," God can make one person both man and woman, these freaks do not have to have two heads, the Host is both in the Church and in the world. If God can do all this, what will God do to her? Being "a temple of the Holy Ghost" is not something to laugh at or take lightly, not even for a minute.

"The Artificial Nigger"

On the rural roadsides throughout the South, the traveler can still purchase concrete statues to which the title of this story is a reference. Many proprietors sell representations of Jesus, Mary, deer, and different male versions, what O'Connor's uncle called "nigger statuary."[30] The molds for each concrete piece assure a sameness in position and form. Though the colors may vary, the people statues are usually painted brown or black, with red and white clothes. The statues are about one to three feet in height and thirty to fifty pounds in weight. The "artificial nigger" that O'Connor depicts in the story, however, is not the jockey most often associated with this concrete genre, but rather a variant holding "a piece of brown watermelon" (229). O'Connor's decision for this title came from a story her mother told her about needing directions when she got lost trying to buy a cow: "Well, you go into this town and you can't miss it 'cause it's the only house in town with a artificial nigger in front of it." O'Connor knew she had to find a story to fit that expression.[31]

When the story was published for the first time in the spring 1955 *Kenyon Review,* coinciding with the bus boycott in Montgomery, Alabama, the editor, John Crowe Ransom, wanted to change the title. According to O'Connor, he said, "Well, we'd better not use this title. You know, it's a tense situation. We don't want to hurt anybody's feelings."[32] O'Connor was firm in her stand, however, for as she reports in a letter, what she "had in mind to suggest with the artificial nigger was the redemptive quality of the Negro's suffering for us all."[33] And O'Connor uses the "plaster figure" (229) as the medium through which grace is delivered to Mr. Head and Nelson. "The Artificial Nigger," at least as long as several years afterward, was her own "favorite and probably the best thing" she thought she would ever write.[34] The story also appeared in *The Best American Short Stories of 1956.*

O'Connor was charmed with her own story because it contained more than she thought she understood. Critics have debated whether the ending is deserved, organically growing out of the story's action, or whether it is contrived, deliberately plastered on top of the conclusion. Mr. Head, who cannot speak with depth or insight, by story's end manages to understand mercy beyond his ability to articulate it. The narrator gives Mr. Head comprehension—as clear and free from irony as O'Connor ever is—in the concluding narrative tract on the healing power of mercy. The message has close links with both the story's literal action and the deeper point that O'Connor wishes to drive home: Only God's mercy can burn away pride.

The story begins and ends in the middle of night with a moon altered by the growth of the characters in the course of the day they spend in the city. Before the trip, O'Connor gives Mr. Head power to control that moon and to speak with it: the moon, with its "grave" face, pauses, "as if it were waiting for his permission to enter," and Mr. Head could have explained to that moon how age was a "choice blessing" and what makes one a "suitable guide for the young" (210). After the trip, however, Mr. Head has been humbled; O'Connor has restored the moon to its own "full splendor," out of the control of Mr. Head, who now has "no words in the world" that could speak to the moon or explain his new understanding (230).

At the beginning, not only can Mr. Head give counsel to the moon, but he measures himself against figures of significant proportion—"Vergil summoned in the middle of the night to go to Dante, or better, Raphael, awakened by a blast of God's light to fly to the side of Tobias" (210). The grandfather wants to take young Nelson to the city so that the lad will understand he "ain't as smart" (211) as he thinks he is. The contrast between O'Connor's plot—a grandfather with a "moral mission" (211) to reduce a grandson's boastful pride—and the significantly loftier aims of Dante's *Divine Comedy* and the *Apocrypha*'s "Tobit" quickly establish the comic veneer. Virgil appears before Dante to conduct him through Hell, Purgatory, and blissful Paradise; he will be the guide, the one with the answers as they maneuver through the circles of hell, descending lower and lower, making their way across rivers, through locked gates, around various monsters to new knowledge. And, indeed, the reader can see many parodic allusions to the work of Dante in the O'Connor story. In the second reference, the angel Raphael, disguised as Azarias, is sent by God to guide Tobias to retrieve a sum of money for his father Tobit. While on the errand, the good angel also arranges a meeting and marriage between Tobias and Sarah, whose seven previous husbands have all died in the bridal chamber. While this latter tale has little connection to O'Connor's story, she needs the allusion to emphasize the role of the guide.

A GOOD MAN IS HARD TO FIND

Mr. Head sees himself first as a man like Virgil, and "better" as an angel like Raphael, "one of seven holy angels who present the prayers of the saints and enter into the presence of the glory of the Holy One" (Tobit 12:15). Deflating Mr. Head's image of himself as the good angel guide for Nelson is the slop jar that, with the moonlight's help, appears to "stand guard over [Nelson] like a small personal angel" (211).

Mr. Head and ten-year-old Nelson live without women in a small home in a rural place. Nelson has been cared for exclusively by his grandfather since his mother died when he was a year old. The trip to Atlanta, Nelson's birthplace, has become necessary for Mr. Head, with his "youthful expression by daylight." He feels his authority and wisdom challenged, and needs to keep Nelson in his place, who has an "ancient" look, "as if he knew everything already and would be pleased to forget it" (212). In searching for some area of expertise where he has the advantage over Nelson, Mr. Head realizes that Nelson has never "seen a nigger" (212). After the first mention of what appears to be a revelation for Mr. Head, he repeats this discovery until it becomes the locus of the trip, inflating his own pride with each repetition. Because Mr. Head has helped to "run" one out of the county before Nelson was born (212), he discerns that he has arrived at one certain point where his knowledge outshines Nelson's.

Once on the train, Mr. Head asks Nelson to identify a "huge coffee-colored man" (215). When Nelson can only reply, "a man," and then amend it to "a fat man" and "an old man" (216), Mr. Head is delighted in his triumph and Nelson's ignorance. He must tell a fellow passenger, "That's his first nigger" (216). When Nelson hates "with a fierce raw fresh hate" (216) just because the man has walked up the aisle, O'Connor delivers her interpretation of one of the ways the South has treated its own. Blacks merely have to exist to be despised. When they see the same man again in the dining car, behind "a saffron-colored curtain," it never dawns on Nelson that the man is eating hot food while he is not, but rather, he is persuaded by his guide's position: "They rope them off" (217). When Mr. Head's smart retort to the "black waiter" who wants to steer them out of the kitchen makes the passengers laugh, Nelson begins to feel "a sudden keen pride," and realizes that he "would be entirely alone in the world if he were ever lost from his grandfather" (218). At this point, Mr. Head has Nelson exactly where he wants him.

As the twosome make their way on foot around Atlanta, O'Connor volleys the control from one to the other. Nelson has but to delight—"This is where I come from!" (220)—in the mysteries of the city, for Mr. Head to show him its sewers and deflate him: "Yes, . . . this is where you were born—right here with all these niggers" (221). When he has the strange immediate affection for the "large colored woman" (222), Mr. Head steps in to rescue him, and in return Nelson "took hold of the old man's hand, a sign of dependence that he seldom showed" (223). Sensing that Nelson would be rested after his nap on the pavement and ready once more to assert his affection for the city, Mr. Head decides to leave the boy to wake up to no one he knows. His cruel joke panics Nelson into dashing down the street "like a wild maddened pony" (225) and crashing into a woman, knocking down both of them. This moment sets the scene for the "moment of grace," which is yet to come. When Nelson sees his grandfather and flings himself at the old man's legs, Mr. Head, scared of the policeman who has appeared at the scene of Nelson's accident, betrays Nelson: "I never seen him before" (226). For this brief interlude, Mr. Head becomes like Peter, who denies Christ. And the volley is over; Mr. Head has the last proud word, but Nelson wins when he is able to turn his back to his grandfather "with a dignity he had never shown before" (227) in rejection of the offer of getting a Coca-Cola.

Mr. Head feels "the depth of his denial" (227), which continues to deepen as Nelson ignores the invitation of cleansing from a symbolic Eucharist, drinking from the water spigot his grandfather almost trips over. Driven to despair and abandoning his proud role as guide, Mr. Head screams his desperation to a passing stranger: "Oh Gawd I'm lost! Oh hep me Gawd I'm lost!" On the literal level of action, Mr. Head wants to know how to find the train that will take him home, but on a deeper level Mr. Head articulates an agony that comes from his denial of Nelson. As the stranger tells them where to catch the train, and with the blank expression still planted on Nelson's face, a "plaster figure of a Negro" appears in their path (229). After a few minutes, Mr. Head realizes that for the first time since his denial of Nelson, the two of them are standing in front of the statue, staring together. It is one of those moments of grace that is charged with the necessity for some utterly profound words that are beyond Mr. Head's capability. "An artificial nigger" (229) is all he says, but the significant factor is that Nelson, who is depicted as Mr. Head's twin—"necks forward," "shoulders curved," and "hands trembling identically in their pockets" (230)—repeats his grandfather's words: "An artificial nigger!" (229). By way of a concrete statue, O'Connor provides the medium through which both old and young feel their differences dissolving "like an action of mercy" (230).

Mr. Head has pointed to blacks throughout the day as a means to show Nelson the ugliness of the city; and he has insulted them, firmly indicating through repetition a lesson in the Southern class hierarchy. But as the two stand together staring at yet another one, this one artificial, the reader understands that it is the black who triumphs. Mr. Head's final comment to Nelson on this subject pulls in opposite directions; it could be easily dismissed as callous or hailed as deliberately sensitive: "They ain't got enough real ones here. They got to have an artificial one" (230). On the property of the white homeowner, there must be a symbol of how the black man continues to serve the white man, a throwback to a bygone era, a reminder of a time when slavery, locked in by law and supported by Christian teachings, reigned supreme. Mr. Head speaks a deeper truth than he is capable of realizing, but the moment has provided him the opportunity to feel mercy.

When the two changed people arrive home from their day in the city, both are irrevocably altered. For Nelson, the transformation is simply stated. He knows now that he has been to the city "once," not twice as he argued en route, counting his being born there as his first trip. For Mr. Head, there is no more proud talk slotting blacks into a specific place, only a gigantic awareness of "monstrous" (231) sin, a deeper understanding of Paradise, and a readiness to enter it humbly.

"A Circle in the Fire"

Like three other stories in this collection, "A Circle in the Fire" includes a farm woman who has a solitary daughter. Mrs. Cope must assume the chief responsibility of coping with her

A GOOD MAN IS HARD TO FIND

obsession for work, countering the modern miracle-dazed Mrs. Pritchard, the wife of the hired hand, and tolerating the rudeness of her abrasive child, Sally Virginia. Published earlier in the spring 1954 *Kenyon Review,* this was the first O'Connor story to claim a prize in the O. Henry Awards, winning second place in 1955. The story was included in *The Best American Short Stories of 1955.* The story's end provides that necessary twist that makes it a natural for O. Henry recognition, for the three juvenile arsonists that have invaded Mrs. Cope's property and set fire to her woods are shrieking with "joy, as if the prophets were dancing in the fiery furnace, in the circle the angel had cleared for them" (251). The presence of Powell Boyd, W. T. Harper, and Garfield Smith on her land and in their activity is a subtle allusion to Shadrach, Meshach, and Abednego's visit to the fiery furnace in Daniel 3. The fire the boys set is reminiscent of the biblical tale in the similarity of response from both Mrs. Cope and King Nebuchadnezzar. The king understands that there is a God more powerful than the golden image he was demanding his people worship; Mrs. Cope feels anew the old misery that she cannot comprehend.

Mrs. Cope has her priorities out of kilter; the property has become her life's purpose. She is deathly afraid of fire—worrying that the barn is full of hay, that the woods are very dry, that a dropped cigarette butt will set everything on fire. She mistakenly shouts for "Ashfield" to pick up his cigarette butt; he quickly corrects her—"Gawfield! . . . Gawfield" (238). She listens to W. T.'s taunt that Powell had once "locked his little brother in a box and set it on fire" (241). She is beside herself with concern about the damage these three boys are likely to do to her land. Her ability to be ever thankful is being severely tested. Next to these boys, the irritations she receives from "her Negroes," who are "as destructive and impersonal as the nut grass" (233), from Mrs. Pritchard, who is fascinated with how a woman in an iron lung can conceive and deliver a baby, and from her daughter, who remains mostly aloof, hidden, and defiant when addressed, are relatively minor. The visiting boys provide Mrs. Cope's opportunity to see more clearly; their perpetration of the fire is her moment of grace.

Until the boys' arrival, Mrs. Cope manages her world evenly. She has a single focus: Work hard and be thankful. She knows how to control the challenges of everyday life. When Mrs. Pritchard, a good country person, interrupts Mrs. Cope's sermonette on the importance of saying daily prayers of thanksgiving with speculative chatter about the intimate details of her distant kin in the iron lung, it is as though Mrs. Cope does not hear her. She has no response to sex in an iron lung; this is beyond what she can fathom. But when Mrs. Pritchard says all she has are "four abscess teeth," Mrs. Cope can handle this one: "Well, be thankful you don't have five" (234).

Her daughter, referred to over two dozen times in the course of the story by the narrative voice as "the child," has an awkward place in this world. At the beginning, she is antagonistic toward her self-righteous mother. In response to her mother's suggestion to look at a "gorgeous" sunset, Sally Virginia would "scowl," "glare up," and mutter in "meanness, 'It looks like a fire. You better get up and smell around and see if the woods ain't on fire'" (233). When the boys arrive, she views most of the action from an upstairs window in the house. By this point, she softens slightly. Offering somewhat clumsy support to her mother, she bellows out the window, "Ugggghhrhh," grimaces "as if she were going to vomit," and threatens to "beat the daylight out of [Garfield]" (242). Mrs. Cope's weak response emanates from her training in Southern manners; she knows only that "ladies don't beat the daylight out of people" (242). At the time of the fire, Sally Virginia tightly grips a tree, which leaves the print of the bark on her cheek. Clinging to a tree on the property her mother values above all, she feels "weighted down with some new unplaced misery" (250).

By the time Mrs. Cope faces the fire she had so long dreaded, Sally Virginia has found her way to her side. Like twins, the two stand before their mutual horror, with the "new misery" the child felt and its "old" look on her mother's face (250). Mrs. Cope is not saying a prayer of thanksgiving now. The situation is too complicated for her former ways of doing. The black character Culver and Mr. Pritchard move, as in slow motion, with shovels in their hands to throw dirt on the fire, but Mrs. Cope is helpless. The God she had earlier and consistently resorted to, and the rules of Southern manners that she had used to entertain and deal with her young guests are insufficient for the moment. The boys and their fire have profoundly affected the way Mrs. Cope will view the world from this point on. She is forced to face a mystery that escapes her understanding.

"A Late Encounter with the Enemy"

"A Late Encounter with the Enemy" is O'Connor's only story to overtly refer to the Civil War. O'Connor believed that with the loss of that war, the Southerner has "gone into the modern world with an inburnt knowledge of human limitations and with a sense of mystery which could not have developed in our first state of innocence—as it has not sufficiently developed in the rest of our country."[35] Through the medium of the Civil War she expresses a deeper, more personal issue—the individual's own contact with the essence of his or her true self. A picture of General and Mrs. William Jordan Bush on the first page of the *Milledgeville Union-Recorder* in August 1951 was the suggestion for Sally Poker and her grandfather George Poker Sash.[36] Altering the relationship from husband-wife to grandfather-granddaughter, O'Connor also adds a Boy Scout nephew, young John Wesley, "a fat blond boy of ten with an executive expression" (258).

Both major characters in this story have a late encounter with the enemy, and both learn something not entirely articulated but suggested by the author. For Sally Poker Sash, 62-year-old about-to-be college graduate, the adversary is pride. For her 104-year-old grandfather, George Poker Sash, the literal enemy is history and his stubborn refusal to understand its importance; but for him, as well, the enemy is his own sense of inflated self. After twenty summers of continuing education at the state teachers' college, Sally Poker will receive her degree, which pales in its importance to having her grandfather sit on the stage so that the people in the audience can see her rich heritage, "what all was behind her" (252). She lives for the moment of walking across that stage with the old man on display behind her. He, on the other hand, is interested in parades, beautiful "guls" (256), and having the crowd "see him" (252). Both characters use one another to move the self into a superior position. At the precise instant of her brief time onstage, a moment of grace occurs for each of them. This late encounter is realized instantly and finally for the old man and beyond the end of the story for the new graduate.

A GOOD MAN IS HARD TO FIND

One of the earlier stories of the collection, O'Connor finished "A Late Encounter with the Enemy" in the summer of 1952 and sold it to *Harper's Bazaar*. It was published in September 1953, representing the first placement of a story in the collection in a popular magazine, rather than a literary journal. The appeal to a popular audience is clear in the story's many references to popular culture: parades with "floats full of Miss Americas and Miss Daytona Beaches and Miss Queen Cotton Products" (252), "the premiere" in Atlanta "twelve years ago" (253–54), the twice-mentioned group of "UDC members" (255), Sally Poker's concern with her "Girl Scout oxfords" (256), and "the big red Coca-Cola machine" (259). The beauty contests represent the most prestigious in the country to something considerably less, the Southern penchant for having its product line represented by the charms of a Southern belle. The premiere, though not identified in the story, is a reference to the 1939 opening night of *Gone with the Wind,* in Atlanta, Georgia. The "twelve years ago" reminder from an early 1950s publication date places the premiere in contemporary time. The "UDC" is an abbreviation for the United Daughters of the Confederacy, an elite organization founded in 1874 for women descendants of Confederate veterans of the Civil War. "Girl Scout" shoes, which appear with some regularity in O'Connor's fiction, are a sturdy saddle oxford, worn for support by girls and older women who prefer comfort to fashion. Atlanta was and is the world headquarters for the soft drink, Coca-Cola, the most popular drink in the South. Its red machines have become icons in both Southern literature and art.

When O'Connor has the General's head fill with the words "Chickamauga, Shiloh, Johnston, Lee" (260), she is suggesting more than a reference to the Civil War. The fact that she places generals and war battles together and out of order is indicative of the General's denial of the importance of history and his own place in it. Shiloh was fought in April 1862, the site of the death of Confederate General Albert Sidney Johnston, who was hit in the leg and bled to death. Chickamauga occurred in late September 1863 and General Robert E. Lee was not present. The General, who was never really a General but "had probably been a foot soldier" (253), does not remember anything about it. That war becomes one small piece of his life, and as he sits on the stage, in the midst of a stroke, listening to the speaker's talk, words and images from his own life swirl around him, confusing him, "dogging" (261) him. The "black procession" of college graduates, whom he had earlier deemed as "deadly as the River Styx" (252) and outwardly cursed them all: "God damn every goddam thing to hell" (258), was now upon him. O'Connor suggests that the General comes to a new understanding in this precise moment before he dies, for he "recognize[s]" (261) his past, that he cannot keep living it, and in a "desperate effort to see over it," he meets his death when his "hand clenche[s] the sword until the blade touche[s] bone" (261). The General's obsession with the premiere, when he became the fictional "General Tennessee Flintrock Sash of the Confederacy" (255), his delight in the attention paid to him by a temporary, adoring public is not enough in the end to redeem him. The past is over, suggests O'Connor, and old George Poker Sash, who according to Sally Poker "had only been a major" (255), is all he stands on to meet his future. The fact that he is making a "desperate effort" at the end to understand that he must reach beyond his past is to his credit.

The slower learner of the two is the granddaughter. It takes three specific events for her to learn finally the place of pride, and at the end of the story, the reader is not sure she yet understands.

Sally Poker Sash, who began teaching before a B.S. or certification was necessary, has devoted her career to a kind of revenge—teaching "in the exact way she had been taught not to teach" (252). She may have spent twenty years finishing the degree, but the process has been meaningless to her teaching. The premiere has been an occasion for her as well because she escorted her grandfather onstage in an outfit she had purchased for the milestone—"long black crepe dinner dress with a rhinestone buckle and a bolero" (255). The silver slippers that would adorn her feet, however, never make it to the stage. She is so full of herself and her own moment in the spotlight that she forgets to change out of her Girl Scout shoes. Even though she is horrified to discover the fashion faux pas, she does not appear to learn anything of humility. At the graduation ceremony, she accepts the degree not from an internal sense of satisfaction but as an external physical display of her heritage. She walks across that stage with her head "a perceptible degree higher" after staring into the "fixed and fierce" (261) eyes of the unknown-to-her imminently deceased old man. The story ends without any reference to Sally Poker's knowledge that her grandfather is now a "corpse" (262) in line with John Wesley, the ever thirsty Boy Scout, at the Coca-Cola machine. O'Connor suggests it will take the old man's death to point out to Sally Poker her own prideful ways. What she does with the new knowledge will be her call.

"Good Country People"

The contents of the collection had already been decided when O'Connor finished "Good Country People" and wanted to add it at the last moment. It was published in *Harper's Bazaar* in June 1955, the same month the collection was available. At the end of the magazine story, an editor's note calls attention to the collection: "Allen Tate, the distinguished American poet and critic, considers 'Good Country People' 'the most powerful story of maimed souls by a contemporary writer.'"[37] It is in this story that O'Connor makes most clear her leitmotif of matching a physical deformity to a spiritual affliction: Joy/Hulga's wooden leg corresponds to her "maimed soul."

The four major characters have similarities to others in the collection: Mrs. Freeman, the farm's good country person, has an affinity for the bizarre: "Mrs. Freeman had a special fondness for the details of secret infections, hidden deformities, assaults upon children" (267). Mrs. Hopewell must handle the responsibilities of single parenting and managing her farm with unreliable help: "Mrs. Hopewell had no bad qualities of her own but she was able to use other people's in such a constructive way that she never felt the lack" (264). Even though Joy/Hulga is thirty-two years old, with a Ph.D. in philosophy, her wooden leg has deprived her of "*normal* good times" (266); her mother sees her "as a child" (266). Manley Pointer is a con artist and humbles a female character who acts confidently within her belief system.

Mrs. Freeman and Mrs. Hopewell serve as foils to one another. Each of them operates from the presumption that each understands the foibles of the other. Mrs. Hopewell, queen of the often-turned cliché, knows that she depends on the labor of her "good country people" to handle the demands of the farm. She is pleased they are not "trash," but her level of conversation with Mrs. Freeman is always superficial and pragmatic. Mrs. Freeman meets Mrs. Hopewell's clichés with the message that she already has arrived at her own conclusions: "I always said it did myself" (265).

Joy/Hulga plays the two women against each other so that attention will not fall on her. Her mind is overdeveloped, but her emotions, governed by her weak heart, are without exercise until the two days in which the story takes place. Mrs. Freeman's daughters, never seen but referred to in the kitchen banter of the two women, serve as the foil for Joy/Hulga: sticky to dry, sexually aware to naive, visceral to intellectual. Glycerin and Caramel, the supplanted names that Joy/Hulga uses for Glynese and Carramae, are both substances of sticky sweetness, whereas Joy's renaming herself "Hulga" suggests to Mrs. Hopewell "the broad blank hull of a battleship" (266) and to Joy/Hulga "the ugly sweating Vulcan who stayed in the furnace" (266–67). Just as the names indicate a polar opposition, the activities follow suit: fifteen-year-old Carramae is married, pregnant, and always vomiting; eighteen-year-old Glynese is dating a young man in "chiropracter school" (273), who can pop her neck to remove her sty. Carramae spends an entire day and does not "do nothing but ramble in the bureau drawer" (269), while Joy/Hulga reads philosophy all day and out of the blue screams at her mother: "Malebranche was right: we are not our own light" (268). Joy/Hulga is citing Nicolas Malebranche (1638–1715), a French philosopher whose most enduring work is *The Search after Truth.*[38] Mrs. Freeman diagnoses Carramae's morning sickness as a pregnancy "in the tube" (274), and, by contrast, in the next sentence Joy/Hulga cracks "her two eggs into a saucer" (274). Joy/Hulga, with her advanced degrees, is more than twice Carramae's age, yet her sexual experience is nil.

Before the story ends, however, O'Connor develops the most romantic scene in all of her fiction. Bible salesman Manley Pointer, with his phallic name, and Joy/Hulga will try to seduce each other on a picnic with no food. In Manley, Joy/Hulga finds someone new to grace with her philosophical view of "nothing," but she also finds a person to kiss and the ultimate intimate encounter—someone she could trust with her leg, which she guarded as another would the "soul" (281). When she lets him remove it, "it was like surrendering to him completely" (281). During the kissing scene, he has already removed her glasses, now he has her leg, but Manley is not the simple innocent she thought. He displays the contents of the valise he carries with him: A hollow Bible with whisky flask, a pack of cards with obscene pictures, and a blue box of condoms. When he wants to have "a good time" (282), Hulga instantly reverts to what her mother has taught her, imploring him with "aren't you just good country people?" (282) and then attacking his Christian status: "You're a fine Christian!" (283). Once the innocent Hulga finds herself in a jam, all the advanced degrees and the philosophical pondering of nothing are of no help to her. In this moment, she becomes the mother she has so often belittled.

Her moment of grace occurs when she is marooned in the barn loft while Manley leaves with her literal leg and figurative soul. He never returns the glasses, so her vision is faulty, but spiritually insightful: "His blue figure struggling successfully over the green speckled lake" (283), a reminder of Jesus, who walked on water. Manley's words and his departure with the hollow part of her have left her chastened. She has to get back home without her leg, past her mother and Mrs. Freeman who have already noted the Bible salesman's distant figure, and more importantly, without the belief system that has permitted her to function to this point. She can get another leg, but how she thinks about the world in which she dwells has been forever altered by the Bible salesman's words and actions.

A GOOD MAN IS HARD TO FIND

"The Displaced Person"

O'Connor published a short version of "The Displaced Person" in the fall 1954 *Sewanee Review*. The rewritten and expanded final rendering in the collection is in three parts, with the first part substantively changed. The powerful description of Mrs. Shortley's physical stature, for example, was dropped: "It was the kind of stomach that the faces of Washington, Jefferson, and Lee might have been carved on, or a sign splashed that said, DAMNATION TO THE EVIL-DOER. YOU WILL BE UN-COVERED."[39] Mrs. Shortley and her husband are the seventh in a line of good country people that have passed through Mrs. McIntyre's property, helping out and then stealing something when they leave. The Shortleys are different, "not quite trash" (305), but in Mrs. McIntyre's assessment, they can be sacrificed ahead of blacks or Mr. Guizac, the Polish miracle worker and displaced person.

Part 1 establishes the relationships among these three workers and their boss, Mrs. McIntyre. Their lots are cast in the social dictates of the South: The black laborers have been on the property as long as Mrs. McIntyre; they are expected to steal—"Mrs. McIntyre . . . was a long time explaining to the Pole that all Negroes would steal" (293). Mrs. Shortley spends the most time with Mrs. McIntyre, walking the property and talking, but they keep the class distinction by calling each other by their respective last names. The Shortleys have amiable feelings toward blacks because they know that they are the one group of people who keep them from the bottom of the social status ladder: "When the time comes, ... I'll stand up for the niggers and that's that" (298). Mr. Guizac is the odd man out. He is "extra" (316). The black laborers and the Shortleys perceive him as a veiled threat because he is different; except for the language, he looks like the Shortleys, only he works harder and more efficiently.

At the beginning, Mrs. Shortley is "the giant wife of the countryside" (285), able to ignore "the white afternoon sun" (285) in order to direct her gaze on the arrival of the displaced intruder. At the end of part 1, Mrs. Shortley's eyes are "like blue-painted glass" (305) and in death she "seemed to contemplate for the first time the tremendous frontiers of her true country" (305). O'Connor borrows this line from a prayer to St. Raphael: "The prayer asks St. Raphael to guide us to the province of joy so that we may not be ignorant of the concerns of our true country."[40] Mrs. Shortley's myopic vision in the first part yields in the split second before death—expressed on her face immediately in death—to a larger understanding that in life she would not have been able to articulate. Mrs. Shortley is not blinded by the brilliance of the afternoon sun, and her description of the peacock's "tail full of suns" as "nothing but a peachicken" (289) staggers the old priest. This is evidence that her comprehension of the mystery and wonder that exists in the world is crushed by her encapsulation in a code of manners that has long dictated her responses to life.

The conversation of Mrs. McIntyre and Father Flynn—O'Connor's only named priest in the collection—deepens the meaning of the peacock's presence. Many years ago, there had been many more peacocks and Mrs. McIntyre had allowed the number to diminish. Like Mrs. Shortley, Mrs. McIntyre sees them as an expense; she, too, misses their symbolic significance. Mrs. McIntyre attempts to tell the priest that she can no longer use Mr. Guizac, but his mind is elsewhere. Staring at the full display of the peacock, the priest exclaims: "Christ will come like that!"

(317). In the ensuing discussion, Mrs. McIntyre issues a diatribe against the displaced person while each of Father Flynn's comments are about Jesus Christ: "The Transfiguration" and "He came to redeem us" (317). Neither character is responding to the other, but Mrs. McIntyre is increasingly agitated. By the time she explodes at the priest, Mr. Guizac and Christ have merged in her mind: "Christ was just another D. P." (320).

Mr. Guizac's presence on her property has made a major difference. She has begun to see him as her savior, one unlike the others who have paraded through her land over the years. He must go because he has dared to violate the sacred code of Southern honor: He wants to bring his cousin from a concentration camp to marry one of Mrs. McIntyre's black workers. When she hears word of this plan, she is incredulous in her rage and confronts Mr. Guizac without hesitation: "You would bring this poor innocent child over here and try to marry her to a half-witted thieving black stinking nigger! What kind of a monster are you!" (313). Mr. Guizac knows only the hellish world from which he has escaped and wants to bring his family members into a life of freedom. Mrs. McIntyre is obstinate in her position. The two cannot understand or listen to each other any more than she and the priest do.

Failing to secure the priest's assistance in Mr. Guizac's termination, Mrs. McIntyre must issue the notice on her own. Taunted and encouraged by Mr. Shortley, she is determined to do the task. While she waits for the opportune moment when Mr. Guizac will crawl out from under the tractor, Mr. Shortley's bigger tractor, left unattended briefly, makes its way toward the hapless mechanic. In a symbolic image of the South against the rest of the world, Mr. Shortley, the black farmhand, and Mrs.

McIntyre lock eyes "in one look that froze them in collusion forever" (326). Not one of them shouts a warning; Mr. Guizac is crushed to death. In this moment of grace, Mrs. McIntyre learns something that changes her forever. If she chooses ultimately to understand the moment is a matter beyond the story's end. Symbolically, Mrs. McIntyre has crucified her savior. She participates unwittingly because she, like Mrs. Shortley, cannot see the "frontiers of her true country" (305); in the doing, she is as "expressionless as the rest of the countryside" (326). Mrs. McIntyre is abandoned by Mr. Shortley and the black farmhands, and the property passes into a stranger's hands. She is left in a deteriorating state of health with only the old priest to "explain the doctrines of the Church" (327). She has not yet arrived at seeing the peacock's splendor.

Notes

1. Flannery O'Connor, *Flannery O'Connor: Collected Works,* ed. Sally Fitzgerald (New York: Library of America, 1988) 153. All parenthetical citations from the stories in *A Good Man Is Hard to Find* are from this edition.

2. Flannery O'Connor, *Mystery and Manners,* ed. Sally and Robert Fitzgerald (New York: Farrar, Straus and Giroux, 1969) 33–34.

3. A tape of the *Galley-Proof* show featuring O'Connor is housed in the O'Connor Collection in the Ina Dillard Russell Library at Georgia College in Milledgeville. This tape makes available the only extant means to see O'Connor and hear her talk.

4. Flannery O'Connor, *The Habit of Being,* ed. Sally Fitzgerald (New York: Farrar, Straus and Giroux, 1979) 81.

5. Rosemary M. Magee, ed., *Conversations with Flannery O'Connor* (Jackson: UP of Mississippi, 1987) 8.

6. O'Connor, *Habit* 84.

7. John Cook Wyllie, "The Unscented South," *Saturday Review* 4 June 1955: 15.

8. Sylvia Stallings, "Young Writer with a Bizarre Tale to Tell," *New York Herald Tribune Book Review* 18 May 1952: 3.

9. Sylvia Stallings, "Flannery O'Connor: A New, Shining Talent among Our Storytellers," *New York Herald Tribune Book Review* 5 June 1955: 1.

10. "Such Nice People," *Time* 6 June 1955: 114.

11. O'Connor, *Habit* 89.

12. "Briefly Noted," *New Yorker* 18 June 1955: 105.

13. O'Connor, *Habit* 88.

14. James Greene, "The Comic and the Sad," *Commonweal* 22 July 1955: 404.

15. In "New Books," *Catholic World* 182 (Oct. 1955): 66.

16. O'Connor, *Mystery* 42.

17. Orville Prescott, "Books of the Times," *New York Times* 10 June 1955: 23.

18. O'Connor, *Habit* 87.

19. Caroline Gordon, "With a Glitter of Evil," *New York Times Book Review* 12 June 1955: 5.

20. O'Connor, *Habit* 87.

21. Sally Fitzgerald, ed., "Chronology," *Collected Works* 1248.

22. O'Connor, *Habit* 249.

23. O'Connor, *Mystery* 111.

24. O'Connor, *Mystery* 112.

25. Elizabeth Hardwick, "Flannery O'Connor, 1925–1964," *New York Review of Books* 8 Oct. 1964: 21.

26. Alex McNeil, *Total Television: A Comprehensive Guide to Programming from 1948 to the Present,* 3rd ed. (New York: Penguin, 1991) 621.

27. A. R. Coulthard, "Flannery O'Connor's Deadly Conversions," *Flannery O'Connor Bulletin* 13 (1984): 90.

28. O'Connor, *Habit* 174.

29. I would like to acknowledge Hyman Datz for reminding me of this similar reference.

30. O'Connor, *Habit* 101.

31. Magee, ed., *Conversations* 20.

32. Magee, ed., *Conversations* 21.

33. O'Connor, *Habit* 78.

34. O'Connor, *Habit* 209.

35. O'Connor, *Mystery* 59.

36. See J. O. Tate, "O'Connor's Confederate General: A Late Encounter," *Flannery O'Connor Bulletin* 8 (1979): 45–53, for a full exploration of the connection, and reprints of the newspaper pictures.

37. O'Connor, "Good Country People," *Harper's Bazaar* June 1955: 130.

38. See Nicolas Malebranche, *The Search after Truth.* Trans. Thomas M. Lennon and Paul J. Olscamp (Columbus: Ohio UP, 1980) to note discrepancies between what Malebranche is saying and Joy/Hulga's misinterpretation of him.

39. O'Connor, "The Displaced Person," *Sewanee Review* 62 (Autumn 1954): 634.

40. O'Connor, *Habit* 132.

CHAPTER FOUR

The Violent Bear It Away

Her second novel, *The Violent Bear It Away,* is O'Connor's last. Farrar, Straus and Cudahy published it on 8 February 1960, the culmination of a writing activity that had occupied O'Connor intermittently since 1952. She included the first chapter, entitled "You Can't Be Any Poorer than Dead," as part of her successful application for the *Kenyon Review* Fellowship in the fall of 1952, and it was published as a story in *New World Writing* in October 1955. In 1954, she wrote to the Robert Lowells, "I'm writing a novel but it's so bad at present that I'm writing a lot of stories so as not to have to look at it."[1] When the novel finally did appear, O'Connor already knew "hints of things to come."[2] An early response in *Library Journal* notes the novel's lack of "convincing action" that would carry the "macabre tale to a successful conclusion." However, what is worth noting in the review is the librarian's recognition, for O'Connor, of a future still worth considering; she adds to her response: "Recommended only for those libraries that want a complete collection of all potentially important young American writers."[3]

O'Connor's tale, so long in the spinning, is a short novel of just over 200 pages. As in her previous fiction, it is the subject matter that perplexes her reviewers: This is a book about prophets and baptism. Among others, the characters include a fourteen-year-old would-be prophet, Francis Marion Tarwater, who fights the promised call and its coming certainty; a voice that is "stranger" and becomes "friend," who bedevils Tarwater's

UNDERSTANDING FLANNERY O'CONNOR

thoughts and directs his actions; the deceased great-uncle old Mason Tarwater, who spends his life as a proclaimed prophet; the schoolteacher-uncle Rayber, who actively denies the past and future prophets their due; and Rayber's idiot child Bishop, who is the focus of the novel's action. Young Tarwater must baptize the child because old Tarwater has failed to do so. The relationship of these characters to each other as they would look on a genealogical chart is illustrated below.

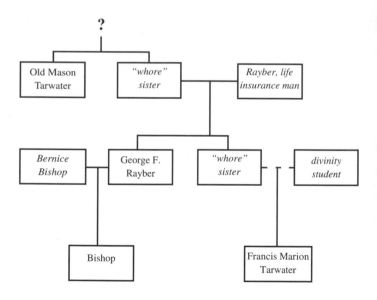

Early reviewers sensed the grotesque was being intricately confounded, but, as with *Wise Blood* and her first stories, they drove their reviews to dead ends that often doomed the teller along with the tale. *Time* depicted a "retiring, bookish spinster who dabble[d] in the variants of sin and salvation like some self-tutored backwoods theologian," made references to her lupus, suggested that the disease caused her to "visit remote and dreadful places of the human spirit," and concluded that the novel was the work of a "secure believer" who "pok[ed] bitter fun at the confused and bedeviled."[4]

The *New Yorker* hurled a two-sentence paragraph her way, calling the novel a "dark, ingrown Gothic tale,"[5] while the *Times Literary Supplement* broke off midway in its review with a determination that O'Connor's "sophisticated pessimism creates a number of unrewarding moral culs-de-sac."[6] Both comments showed no awareness of the title's importance to the novel's action. On the other hand, the *New Republic*'s Frank Warnke decided that O'Connor's primary concern was with "the misery of man without God," but he, too, did not pursue the title's implications. He limited his reading, seeing O'Connor's characters Tarwater and the idiot Bishop as an allegorical rendering of "a mad and murderous John the Baptist baptizing an idiot Christ." Though he praised her "stylistic felicity," which can "penetrate the tortured minds of her characters with sympathy and, occasionally, even rueful humor," he concluded the book "is one of crankiness and provincialism," and asked a question that would have been unnecessary had he pursued the title's meaning: "Does it have something to do with a national conviction that only violent actions performed by ignorant and underprivileged people are 'real' enough to write about?"[7]

UNDERSTANDING FLANNERY O'CONNOR

In a letter to a friend, O'Connor reports that she has taken the title "from the Douay, also Confraternity versions"[8] of the Bible.[9] The Douay or the Rheims-Douay Version was translated from the Latin Vulgate, with serious efforts to compare the Latin with Hebrew and Greek at the English College at Douay in 1609 for the Old Testament and at the English College at Rheims in 1582 for the New Testament. O'Connor's title comes from the last portion of Matthew 11:12: "And from the days of John the Baptist until now, the kingdom of heaven suffereth violence, and the violent bear it away." Notes to the verse in the 1850 Douay state: "[The kingdom of heaven] is not to be obtained but by main force, by using violence upon ourselves, by mortification and penance, and resisting our perverse inclinations. . . . That is, the kingdom of heaven is to be obtained by mortification, penance, poverty, and those practices of austerity which John, by word and example, pointed out."[10] The note indicates that the only means of entering the kingdom of heaven is by "main force," but the source of the violence is not clear in the note. The violence could be self-induced, a possibility suggested in the note, or it could be inherent within the kingdom itself, which results in something perceivable as self-induced violence. In the case of the latter, the violence is cast upon the violent, intimating those who would be predisposed to or prepared for receiving violence. These people would then bear or tolerate the violence necessary to enter the kingdom of heaven. Tarwater is such an example. Further, the chosen person need not be violent, as exampled in the calls to the Old Testament prophets where violence comes down from above, and is not self-induced; rather, the kingdom of heaven suffers or permits this violence to happen. Rayber has not had the ongoing exposure to violence for the Lord's sake or preparation to receive more violence, but he cannot shake conclusively its low murmur.

THE VIOLENT BEAR IT AWAY

O'Connor connects her fictional characters to biblical figures early on when she establishes the identity of old Mason Tarwater and details his preparation of Francis Marion Tarwater to receive the call: "He was let free for the pursuit of wisdom, the companions of his spirit Abel and Enoch and Noah and Job, Abraham and Moses, King David and Solomon, and all the prophets, from Elijah who escaped death, to John whose severed head struck terror from a dish."[11] The violence that O'Connor dwells on in this novel is far removed from any "national conviction" that "violent action" of the poor is worthy of her consideration; rather, she deals with an older, far more provocative violence, and her source, repeatedly, is biblical.

Tarwater knows what his great-uncle looks like when he has been making "his peace with the Lord": "He would look as if he had been wrestling a wildcat, as if his head were still full of the visions he had seen in its eyes, wheels of light and strange beasts with giant wings of fire and four heads turned to the four points of the universe" (334). The wheels of light, the beasts with wings of fire, and the four heads in each direction are a description of Ezekiel's vision. The biblical prophet saw a beast with four heads each of man, lion, ox, and eagle, connected by wings, and all afire: "Their appearance was like that of burning coals of fire . . . a bright fire" (Ezekiel 1:13). When the rage of the old man's vision is noticeable to Tarwater, he is satisfied with being a prophet himself; in fact, he eagerly would say: "Here I am, Lord, ready!" (334). What Tarwater cannot comprehend or tolerate from the old man or from his God is the length of time between those rages, when life goes on placidly or routinely, when no visible sign of the call exists.

Old Tarwater identifies the "Elijah and Elisha" (356) relationship he has with his grandnephew, so when Tarwater is setting fire to the property and house, the reference to the old man's ascension is the first of several blatant Elijah references: "[Tarwater] could hear [the body] moving up through the black night like a whirling chariot" (361), and when Tarwater arrives at Rayber's and reports the old man's death, the uncle asks, "Did the Lord arrive for him in a chariot of fire?" (386). When Elijah departed this planet, he had been walking beside Elisha, to whom he had thrown his mantle: "They went on, talking as they went, and suddenly there appeared chariots of fire and horses of fire which separated them one from the other, and Elijah was carried up in the whirlwind to heaven" (2 Kings 2:11).

Upon his great-uncle's death, Tarwater must go through the stages of doubt and rejection. He debates fiercely with "the voice," succumbing to its diabolical urging to dismiss the three essential requests of old Mason Tarwater: to bury him in the ground, to put the sign of the cross over his head, and to baptize Bishop, the idiot boy. Tarwater cannot, however, simply ignore those directions; he is driven to annihilate them. Tarwater is stock O'Connor material, the kind of character that most interests her: if he does not believe in the whole Christian orthodox message, then he has no choice but to deny it fervently and fight it indefatigably. Thus, Tarwater burns the grounds and the house, believing he has burnt the old man as well. Without a physical 200-pound body to put in the ground, a cross need not be erected. The young Tarwater can then go to the city to visit the uncle whom the old man has spent the youth's lifetime denigrating. He can go see the idiot Bishop that he has no intention of baptizing. By showing up and standing firm, Tarwater can laugh in the face of the old man's belief, the old man's prophecy, and his own predicted destiny.

THE VIOLENT BEAR IT AWAY

Tarwater's stay in the city with his relatives is brief, and with calculation and callousness he rebuffs every gesture from Rayber. He ignores the new clothes, eats disinterestedly, follows along on the tours of the city distantly. When he chooses to explore independently, he seeks out the evangelical Carmody family, who reaffirm what Tarwater struggles with as he begins to see he cannot deny the message that Rayber continues to disavow. After all, Lucette Carmody chooses Rayber as the fallen one, not Tarwater. The day following the revival meeting is Tarwater's first opportunity to avoid baptizing Bishop, as he planned in coming to the city. Bishop runs toward a fountain filled with water in the park; at the same time, Tarwater's eyes begin to burn "as if he beheld some terrible compelling vision" (421). This is Tarwater's chance to stare the deed in the face, to resist doing what the old man had prepared him for, but Tarwater moves under some power greater than his own will: "He seemed to be drawn toward the child in the water but to be pulling back, exerting an almost equal pressure away from what attracted him" (421). Rayber snatches the child out of what he perceives to be harm's way, away from the rushing waters of the stone lion's mouth, away from the "enormous indignity" (421) of baptism by his crazed nephew.

Several days later, after Rayber delivers a lecture on baptism as an "empty act" (450), Tarwater takes Bishop for a boat ride. Here, with Rayber resting inside the Cherokee Lodge, the two of them are physically alone when the drowning and the baptism occur: Bishop climbs onto Tarwater's back and hangs on "like a large crab," while Tarwater sinks "backwards into the water as if the whole bank were pulling him down" (462). Whether Tarwater frees himself from Bishop's grasp who then sinks into the water by accident, or whether he deliberately drowns Bishop is not stated in the narrative, but up to this point Tarwater has followed the advice of "the voice" who is present with him in the boat and strongly encouraged him to drown the boy. As Bishop goes under water, "in a high raw voice the defeated boy cried out the words of baptism, shuddered, and opened his eyes" (463). O'Connor chooses the word "defeated" to describe the now broken Tarwater; he has capitulated to a power he cannot understand. He has done the deed that the old man ordained him to do. And violence is inherent in both the action, the drowning, and in the actor, who delivers the words of baptism. The crux of the novel resides in this moment of baptism.

O'Connor was aware that baptism did not carry the weight of importance for a majority of her readers, so she had to distort the event: "I have to see that this baptism carries enough awe and mystery to jar the reader into some kind of emotional recognition of its significance. To this end I have to bend the whole novel— its language, its structure, its action."[12] For O'Connor, the distortion and the exaggeration of this central Christian sacrament exist in the novel because of her belief. O'Connor makes no bones about her position, about what matters; readers are left to ponder what matters that much for them.

While Tarwater is in the city, he also begins to experience a "strangeness in his stomach, a peculiar hunger" (430). Rayber notices it from the beginning, but he does not associate it with anything spiritual: "Something in [Tarwater's] very look, something starved in it, seemed to feed on [Rayber]" (402). Tarwater records the cost of what he considers each meal to be worth (but he never asks the actual cost), so he can repay Rayber, not wanting to be "beholden" to him (403). When Tarwater stops and stares through a bakery window, Rayber notices once again that he has "the face of someone starving who sees a meal he can't reach laid out before him" (406), but Rayber is disappointed to discover that it is only a solitary loaf of bread. To Rayber, this is "a false alarm" (407), but to Tarwater, the bread is a reminder of his great-uncle's message that "Jesus is the bread of life" (342), which echoes Jesus' own words: "And Jesus said to them: I am the bread of life: he that cometh to me shall not hunger: and he that believeth in me shall never thirst" (John 6:35).

Tarwater wants to negate this spiritual hunger, but it clearly grips him. He cannot be satiated with literal food anymore than he can avoid baptizing Bishop. Each literal meal that Tarwater eats from this point on is almost painful to him and less than satisfying. He remains hungry, ravenous. After the baptism, when the driver of the lavender and cream-colored car offers him some whisky, Tarwater's response is that it is "better than the Bread of Life!" (471). The acceptance of the Bread of Life and his full spiritual awareness of hunger do not come until his moment of violence back at Powderhead: "He felt his hunger no longer as a pain but as a tide. He felt it rising in himself through time and darkness, rising through the centuries, and he knew that it rose in a line of men whose lives were chosen to sustain it, who would wander in the world, strangers from that violent country where the silence is never broken except to shout the truth" (478). That moment for Tarwater—when he sees the "red-gold tree of fire" and knows that it is the same fire that had "encircled Daniel, . . . raised Elijah, . . . spoken to Moses" (478)—finally arrived when he could freely say "Here I am, Lord, ready!" (334).

O'Connor's choice of the name "Tarwater" suggests some of the difficulties the character encounters. Tar and water do not mix. Tarwater's struggle is to accept ultimately his destiny, to integrate his resistant dark tar with the healing water of baptism, so that he may heed the command: "GO WARN THE CHILDREN OF GOD OF THE TERRIBLE SPEED OF MERCY" (478), spoken to him in capital letters. His first and middle names are those of Brigadier General Francis "Swamp Fox" Marion, whose contributions to history were three major military operations of the American Revolution, one of them the assault against Savannah, O'Connor's birthplace. Similarities between the historic and fictional figures include a small stature, limited patience, oversensitivity, and a propensity toward deep and black moods. For such a minor historical figure, Marion has twenty-nine towns, seventeen counties, and a college named after him; Marion was also a popular name for male children throughout the South in the first part of the century.[13] The story of how the local hero Marion acquired his nickname would have been well known in Savannah elementary schools, and the story matches O'Connor's theme in *The Violent Bear It Away*. Lt. Col. Banastre Tarleton, in pursuit of Marion and his men, chased him for seven hours, through twenty-six miles of swamp; on giving up he said: "Come my Boys! Let us go back, and we will find the Gamecock [General Thomas Sumter], [b]ut as for this damned old fox, the Devil himself could not catch him."[14] Tarwater is under the spell of the devil when "the voice" begins to assert influence, but it, at length, does not prevail.

"The voice" appears for the first time early in chapter 1: "The voice sounded like a stranger's voice" (336). Almost immediately, it becomes "the loud stranger's disagreeable voice" (337), and then the word "voice" appears seldom and is most often replaced with "the stranger" (352) and "his friend" (353). Although "stranger" dominates in the first chapter, O'Connor occasionally interchanges "friend" or "kind friend" (359). The "stranger" "laughs," "pants," and "hisses," among other verbs, to indicate its position. The voice's role is to concur with Tarwater about his crazy deceased great-uncle: "He was crazy! That's the long and short of it, he was crazy!" (357). "The voice" becomes a support for Tarwater in denying his anticipated call to be a prophet. After the novel was published, speculation abounded on the identity of "the voice." In a letter to John Hawkes, O'Connor makes clear her position: "I certainly do mean Tarwater's friend to be the Devil."[15]

Tarwater's first message from the voice is to bury the old man "and get it over with" (337), in support of what old Tarwater requested of his grandnephew, but the voice switches quickly. While Tarwater hacks away at the hard earth, the voice in a "kind of restrained fury" scoffs at Tarwater's task: "You got to bury him whole and completely by hand and that schoolteacher would burn him in a minute" (345). Next, the voice nags about the placement of the cross on the grave: "Don't you think any cross you set up in the year 1952 would be rotted out by the year the Day of Judgment comes in?" (352). The date of old Tarwater's death corresponds to the year O'Connor first began to write this novel. Further, the voice reinterprets the great-uncle's message. Tarwater knows he has to choose—"Jesus or the devil" (354)—but the voice rewrites that script: "No no no, the stranger said, there ain't no such thing as a devil. . . . It ain't Jesus or the devil. It's Jesus or *you*" (354). The voice's suggestion that Tarwater choose the self is synonymous with selecting the devil that exists within him and contradicts the old man's instructions. Finally, the voice is with him and Bishop in the boat and converts the old man's decree of baptizing Bishop into drowning Bishop: "Be a man, his friend counseled, be a man. It's only one dimwit you have to drown" (462). As the drowning occurs, Tarwater cannot prevent himself from baptizing Bishop. At this moment, the voice disappears, who has "counseled [Tarwater] in both country and city" (461). As soon as Tarwater issues the words of baptism, his first blatant disregard of the voice's instructions, he hears "the sibilant oaths of his friend fading away on the darkness" (463). In the desert, Jesus told the devil to be gone, and so the devil left him (Matthew 4:10–11). Tarwater does not dismiss his "friend," and although his appearance in the incorporeal realm vanishes with Tarwater's rejection of his advice, he makes one final horrifying incarnate appearance.

The first incarnate appearance of the "friend" early in the novel is T. Fawcett Meeks, the copper flue salesman, who drives young Tarwater into town and offers him advice on love, work, and the pursuit of happiness. His middle name suggests a progressive connection to his career, for a faucet controls the flow of water, and a flue is a passage for smoke or gas in a chimney. Symbolically, he is capable of controlling how much hot air he emits into the atmosphere. The last name O'Connor borrows from one of the eight beatitudes: "Blessed are the meek: for they shall possess the land" (Matthew 5:4). The name is used ironically, however, for Meeks wants to exploit the boy for earthly purposes: "[Young Tarwater] was just enough off in the head and just ignorant enough to be a very hard worker, and he wanted a very ignorant energetic boy to work for him" (364). Meeks encourages Tarwater toward "running to doom" in town with the common masses (381), a similar line of encouragement that he has heard from the voice prior to burning Powderhead and leaving for the city. Meeks is "meek" indeed, though, compared to the unnamed stranger Tarwater meets as he leaves town. The driver of the lavender and cream-colored car is a horrific intensification of Meeks.

After Tarwater has had several exchanges with the stranger, he is able to describe him without looking at him: "He didn't search out the stranger's face but he knew by now that it was sharp and friendly and wise, shadowed under a stiff broad-brimmed panama hat that obscured the color of his eyes" (352). When Tarwater is able to see those eyes, in the boat with Bishop, they are "violet-colored, very close and intense" (461). Within eight miles of Powderhead, a lavender and cream-colored car stops to pick up Tarwater. The driver fits the earlier description of the stranger: "The person who had picked him up was a pale, lean, old-looking young man with deep hollows under his cheekbones. He had on a lavender shirt and thin black suit and a panama hat" (469). His eyes are also lavender, a shade lighter than the violet eyes of the voice. The old man had warned Tarwater of taking up with the devil who would offer "a smoke or a drink or a ride" and inquire about "your bidnis" (367); the driver of the lavender and cream-colored car does each of these things. Further, he rapes Tarwater, leaving him naked in the woods. This ultimate form of human violence Tarwater now bears causes him to set the "evil ground" on fire, purifying "every spot the stranger could have touched" (472). Tarwater awaits the supernatural power that lies just ahead for him: "He knew that he could not turn back now. He knew that his destiny forced him on to a final revelation. [His scorched eyes] would never be used for ordinary sights again" (473). The devil is defeated at last by the end of chapter 11; it vanished in the form of the voice and "refreshed . . . on blood . . . , sped away" (472) in its corporeal form. The dismissal of the devil, however, does not dismiss the violence that Tarwater must bear away in his work for the kingdom of heaven, which is just beginning as the novel ends.

At the beginning of the novel, old Mason Tarwater is dead, yet he remains a central character throughout the text. A prophet, his call had come "in his early youth" (332), and he had gone to the city "to proclaim the destruction awaiting a world that had abandoned its Saviour" (332). The modern world is no more ready for a prophet today than the ancient world was in the times of Jonah, Daniel, and Ezekiel. However, biblical prophets were at length understood and acknowledged for their warnings, while modern prophets, such as old Mason Tarwater, are considered crazed and need to be institutionalized. As a young prophet, his "whore" sister (355) has him committed to an asylum. Old Tarwater, after four years, learns that the way out is "to stop prophesying on the ward" (369).

The old man learns caution while in the asylum, which helps him execute his plan to baptize seven-year-old Rayber, but he does not get smarter in the ways of the world as the years pass. His vision remains unchanged for the baptism of his family members. After the wreck, when Rayber took in his dead sister's child, young Tarwater, the old man appears at Rayber's home. Living three months at his nephew's house, old Tarwater wakes to the discovery that Rayber has been "creeping into his soul by the back door" (331). The article on his uncle that Rayber writes for his schoolteacher magazine so infuriates the old man that he is never forgiven. Most especially, old Tarwater is dumbfounded that Rayber would so miss the concept of the prophet and how one comes to be called. Rayber assigns the vocation to the would-be prophet himself. O'Connor's repetition of Rayber's folly is paramount in understanding the mystery that is essential to the book. That a prophet could or would call himself is beyond ludicrous to the old man: "Called myself. I called myself. I, Mason Tarwater, called myself! Called myself to be beaten and tied up. Called myself to be spit on and snickered at. Called myself to be struck down in my pride. Called myself to be torn by the Lord's eye" (341–42). O'Connor makes her point well; no one chooses to be a prophet.

O'Connor's choice for Tarwater's first name, "Mason," suggests the organization of men who bond in the name of the fatherhood of God. No one is invited to join, but Masons enter the brotherhood by requesting members to sponsor them. Ironically, to become a Mason, then, a person would call himself. A "mason" is also a craftsman, who creates with stone, brick, concrete block, or some other substantive building material. To old Mason Tarwater, the prophecies he speaks are as solid a medium as exists anywhere.

Old Mason possesses that clarity of conviction and inner coherence that remains a mystery to the rest of the world. The old man and the idiot child are flat characters; they grow, change, and behave in predictable ways. Both are directed by forces outside and beyond their comprehension. Mason Tarwater's impetus for action is divinely guided; he is the agent of tasks to be accomplished, and the wisdom by which he succeeds is as enigmatic to him as the insights, interpretations, and interrogations of his biblical counterparts Ezekiel, Daniel, and Jonah. When the old man feels himself locked inside the head of his nephew, the context within which O'Connor places the character is these three prophets: "Jonah, Ezekiel, Daniel, he was at that moment all of them—the swallowed, the lowered, the enclosed" (378). Jonah is swallowed by a whale (Jonah 1:17); Ezekiel is tied with ropes and lowered to the ground in order to bear Israel's iniquity (Ezekiel 4:4–8); Daniel is enclosed in the lions' den (Daniel 6:16–17).

O'Connor creates a world in *The Violent Bear It Away* in which, in the end, only Rayber, representative of the modern world, sees the prophet as expendable, insane, or obsessed. He assumes a modern everyman role and becomes the most vehement of antagonists. On the other hand, young Tarwater and pertinent minor characters serve to validate the old man's position. First among the minor characters, Buford Munson, the black neighbor, stops by for some liquor on the day the old man dies and does the job that Tarwater is supposed to do: "[He] had to finish [digging the hole] and drag the body from the breakfast table where it was still sitting and bury it in a decent and Christian way, with the sign of its Saviour at the head of the grave and enough dirt on top to keep the dogs from digging it up" (331). Munson accepts the old man as prophet, as though there was nothing out of the ordinary in his behavior. When he tries to rouse the drunken young Tarwater, he implores for the old man's sake: "He deserves to lie in a grave that fits him. . . . He was deep in this life, he was deep in Jesus' misery" (360). Munson's daughter, who worked for Rayber's mother at the old man's suggestion, cooperated with his scheme of spiriting away the young Rayber to Powderhead.

Munson is akin to Faulkner's Dilsey in that he understands the power and mystery of the orthodox Christian faith, and he is willing to do right in honoring a man's life at death. When young Tarwater returns to Powderhead after his violation, he discovers for the first time that he did not burn his uncle's body when he set fire to the property under the influence of the voice and left for the city. Only at the end of the novel does Tarwater realize the service that Munson has rendered. Munson himself tells Tarwater: "It's owing to me he's resting there. I buried him while you were laid out drunk. It's owing to me his corn has been plowed. It's owing to me the sign of his Saviour is over his head" (477). O'Connor presents in Buford Munson a character that contributes a directive, that models human decency in taking care of the business of the dead.

The Violent Bear It Away is divided into three parts and twelve chapters, numbers suggestive of the Trinity and the disciples of Jesus. Part 1, with three chapters, focuses on Tarwater's beginning denial of the old man's plan for him and on his departure for the city to seek out his uncle Rayber, let him know of the old man's death, and measure what the old man has said about Rayber to the man himself. Part 3, with three chapters, has Tarwater handling the aftermath of emotion in dealing with Bishop's drowning and baptism, the rape by the driver of the lavender and cream-colored car, and the return to Powderhead where he is ready to receive the call, ready to be burned cleaned by God Almighty. Parts 1 and 3 move backward and forward in time and end similarly; in each, Tarwater prepares to depart for the city. While at first he goes intent on resisting baptism, at the end he returns to the city in order to carry the message to the sleeping "children of God" (379).

Part 2 takes place entirely during the intervening week that occurs between the first and last parts. In six chapters, O'Connor guides the reader through six days of Rayber and Tarwater's coexistence. Rayber is locked into real time and its passage; he sees things as they are, for their own sakes. Tarwater, because of the influence of the old man, sees nothing as worthy of consideration for its literal self. In chapter 5, while Rayber is listening to the preaching of the young Lucette Carmody, who appears to have the ability to make others, like Rayber, spiritual Lucite, he rhapsodizes about a conversation he had with the old man when his father, the life insurance salesman, had come to pick him up from his uncle's house. Rayber sees himself as the recently baptized child, understanding literally where his father was going to take him. The old man tells Rayber he cannot go back where he was before: "He can't take me back to town?" Rayber inquires, and his uncle replies, "I never said nothing about town" (409). Old Tarwater understands time and place in terms of all eternity; for him, baptism provides a second life. Rayber's literal child's mind becomes his literal adult's mind; he grows intellectually, but he does not flourish spiritually.

In chapter 4, O'Connor covers the first four days, moving Rayber from enthusiasm to determination in his efforts with Tarwater. Rayber leads Tarwater through the city sights—an art gallery, the movies, department stores and their escalators, supermarkets, the water works, the post office, railroad yards, and city hall. On the whole of the tour, Tarwater is struck by only one place. He recognizes the spot where he lost his first hat when he had been on the legal mission with his great-uncle. His reaction to seeing the spot again is to rush away, "as if he could not stand to be near it" (398). When Tarwater lost the first hat, it had been brand new. He had been on his first visit to the city, aside from being born there in a wreck; the hat represents his innocent self. When the hat drifted away, Tarwater made three references to it, but neither the lawyer nor the great-uncle responded. As they continue to visit lawyers, Tarwater counted "eleven men who might have had on his hat or might not" (348). The reference to eleven is suggestive of the twelve apostles of Christ, who never asked to be called, minus one. Tarwater sees himself as the twelfth man, the one who one day will be called. His second hat, the one he wears with Rayber in the city, never leaves his head, and Rayber identifies the hat with Tarwater's character, "as if its shape had been formed over the years by his personality" (405). When Tarwater jumps overboard and swims to shore, abandoning Rayber in the boat, he strips himself of all but the hat, which he pulls "tight down on his head so that it would not possibly come off" (439). He takes caution to preserve the hat when he is in the process of drowning/baptizing Bishop, removing the hat and placing it in one of his shoes, which he has also removed. He does not lose the hat until it is stolen by the unnamed, lavender-eyed rapist. The hat and Rayber's gift of the corkscrew–bottle opener are the last two vestiges of his former life; Tarwater, through no choice of his own, leaves behind the old self as he is prepared to be burned clean in the sight of God.

On Rayber's city tours, one other incident commands Tarwater's pause. On this occasion, Tarwater reads a paper banner that issues this John 3:3 promise: "UNLESS YE BE BORN AGAIN YE SHALL NOT HAVE EVERLASTING LIFE" (398). The banner advertises the appearance of the Carmodys for Christ. O'Connor's choice of this name, "Carmody," is a blend of "comedy" and "harmony." The traveling trio has circled the globe so that the story of Jesus' love may be told out of the "mouths of babes" (408), their little girl with the "thin legs twisted from the knees" (411). While O'Connor uses comic dress and exaggerated language and gestures in the young girl's delivery and style: "Listen you people!" (413), her message is allegedly one of Christian harmony. The harmony she preaches, however, is not the harmony that either Tarwater or Rayber feels in his life. Tarwater listens uncomfortably from inside the tabernacle, and Rayber, who has followed Tarwater through the night to the revival meeting, hovers outside a window. The disenchanted Rayber knows she is "not a fraud" (411), but when Lucette identifies Rayber as a "damned soul . . . deaf to the Holy Word!" (415), he blocks that message by literally making himself deaf to her words by turning off his hearing aid. Tarwater's initiative takes him to the meeting, but O'Connor chooses to focus on Rayber's resistance.

Rayber has left the house on this night without shoes and with only a coat over his pajama shirt. A "knot of small boys" (406) make fun of Rayber's appearance as his rage hurls him in pursuit of Tarwater. O'Connor plays on the signature close of the popular radio and later television show (1949–1957) the *Lone Ranger*. Each episode concluded with the Lone Ranger exchanging clever repartee with his sidekick, the American Indian Tonto, and then his horse, Silver, reared backward while the Lone Ranger exclaimed as he rode into the sunset: "Hi Ho, Silver; away!" The street urchins' gibe at the comic Rayber—"Hi yo Silverwear, Tonto's lost his underwear! What in the heck do we care?" (406)—is a contemporary allusion, indicating the popularity of television to the city youth. O'Connor has depicted Rayber in such a way that he would be oblivious to the context of the jeer.

Chapter 6 covers the fifth day of Tarwater's stay—a visit to the natural history museum and the baptism attempt. The final day of Tarwater's visit is the subject of the remaining three chapters of part 2. Rayber takes both boys to the country, to a run-down place called the Cherokee Lodge, about thirty miles from Powderhead. While no Powderhead exists on a Tennessee map, the state's Grainger County contains a populated place called Powder Springs located easily within thirty miles of Cherokee Lake, north of Knoxville. The Cherokee Lodge itself is painted white and green; the state flower of Georgia is the Cherokee Rose, a wild white waxy rose with velvet petals among excessive thorns and bright green leaves. The Cherokee Indians have historical ties to Southern states, specifically Georgia and Tennessee. The Southern milieu and its history present a backdrop against which to depict the themes and plot of the novel. The attention to details in the naming of people and places indicates how O'Connor bends the whole of the story line to carry out her dictum that "the longer you look at one object, the more of the world you see in it."[16]

Back in the country, Rayber returns with Bishop to the site of his own baptism thirty-one years earlier. Powderhead represents rejected salvation to Rayber, who was baptized here at seven, returned at fourteen to repudiate the old man, attempted at twenty-four to reclaim young Tarwater and was shot in the leg and ear, and ventured a final visit at thirty-eight to stare into the face of his "dreaded sense of loss" (445). On this final visit, Rayber realizes that the land is legally his, and the initial response is a momentary euphoria as his literal mind, functioning in real time, converts his property into a "college education for the boy" (445). Rayber, however, is never free from the faces of the past that haunt his present. As he surveys the land and feels the pull of Bishop's hand in his, the old man's face returns in the midst of the two denuded chimneys, the property young Tarwater burned before his departure. Rayber knows he cannot return here again. As Tarwater's life is depicted as a spiritual choice between Jesus

UNDERSTANDING FLANNERY O'CONNOR

or the devil, Rayber's life is more narrowly defined. Rayber rejects every spiritual or eternal consequence for the momentary salvation of intellectual inquiry. Because the latter ultimately fails him, he comes full circle at the end of chapter 9 staring in the face of nothing.

Rayber's memory of his parents' reactions to him is malevolent neglect. During Lucette Carmody's castigation of him, he reflects on his father's words to his uncle: "His mother wants him back, Mason. I don't know why. For my part you could have him but you know how she is," to which old Mason can only spew: "A drunken whore" (410). So when Rayber's wife, "twice his age" (334) Bernice Bishop, deserts him and her idiot child namesake, Bishop, Rayber opts not to follow his own parents' lead. Instead, he sacrifices himself and his worldly luxuries for the life of the modern ascetic and would-be scholar. Mystery does not exist in his world, for education makes all things understood. The name O'Connor selects for him is a corruption of "rabbi," which means teacher, Rayber's calling, one to which he does call himself. By virtue of its nature, mystery must be a part of the prophet's life; Rayber cannot accept this perspective.

Rayber's love for Bishop is "love without reason" and as such marks the beginning of a more intense, uncontrolled love that is "like an avalanche [which] covered everything his reason hated" (401). In a letter to a student, O'Connor explains what she means by this passage: "He had the idea that his love could be contained in Bishop but that if Bishop were gone, there would be nothing to contain it and he would then love everything and specifically Christ."[17] When Tarwater drowns Bishop, according to O'Connor, Rayber makes the "Satanic choice."[18] Rayber, who is not present at the drowning, but knows instinctively that

Tarwater has baptized Bishop even as he drowns him, waits for the pain to begin, but nothing happens, "and it was not until he realized there would be no pain that he collapsed" (456). Rayber's response is beyond despair—his collapse signals that he knows his life does not work, all his book knowledge is of no assistance to him at this point. O'Connor leaves Rayber at this crossroad in the novel, but she hints in a letter that "his collapse then may indicate that he is not going to be able to sustain his choice—but that is another book maybe."[19] Frederick Asals is content with letting Rayber be trapped in "the nothing of his emancipated ego."[20] O'Connor's forceful position maintains that mystery and a belief in it must exist in the world, for without it, and with only nothing, life is unbearable.

The Violent Bear It Away delivers two symbolic alternatives for the reader: choose the way of Tarwater, which is less choice than a violence racked upon its chosen, or the way of Rayber, the ultimate torture because it yields only nothing disguised as free will. Richard Giannone sums it up this way: "The Lamb of God, not the laboratory, . . . takes away the sins of the world. To suffer in the O'Connor world means to suffer because of God or to live in absurdity."[21]

Notes

1. Flannery O'Connor, *The Habit of Being,* ed. Sally Fitzgerald (New York: Farrar, Straus and Giroux, 1979) 65.

2. O'Connor, *Habit* 370.

3. Dorothy Nyren, "Review of *The Violent Bear It Away,*" *Library Journal* 1 Jan. 1960: 146.

4. "God-Intoxicated Hillbillies," *Time* 29 Feb. 1960: 118–19.

5. Review, *New Yorker* 19 Mar. 1960: 179.

6. Review, *Times Literary Supplement* 14 Oct. 1960: 666.

7. Frank J. Warnke, "A Vision Deep and Narrow," *New Republic* 14 Mar. 1960: 18–19.

8. O'Connor, *Habit* 532.

9. The Douay (Rheims-Douay) Version of the Bible is the one most commonly used by Catholics in English-speaking countries, according to the *Catholic Encyclopedia Dictionary* (New York: The Gilmary Society, 1941) 308.

10. The Holy Bible, Douay Version (New York: G. Virtue, 1850) 18. The first part of this useful note appears in the 1989 Rheims-Douay version as well. The second note has been dropped. It is likely O'Connor would have had knowledge of both notes.

11. Flannery O'Connor, *Flannery O'Connor: Collected Works,* ed. Sally Fitzgerald (New York: Library of America, 1988) 340. All parenthetical citations for *The Violent Bear It Away* are from this edition.

12. Flannery O'Connor, *Mystery and Manners,* ed. Sally and Robert Fitzgerald (New York: Farrar, Straus and Giroux, 1969) 162.

13. Hugh F. Rankin, *Francis Marion: The Swamp Fox* (New York: Thomas Crowell Co., 1973) 1.

14. Rankin, *Marion* 113.

15. O'Connor, *Habit* 367.

16. O'Connor, *Mystery* 77.

17. O'Connor, *Habit* 484.

18. O'Connor, *Habit* 484.

19. O'Connor, *Habit* 484.

20. Frederick Asals, *Flannery O'Connor: The Imagination of Extremity* (Athens: U of Georgia P, 1982) 186.

21. Richard Giannone, *Flannery O'Connor and the Mystery of Love* (Urbana: U of Illinois P, 1989) 253.

CHAPTER FIVE

Everything That Rises Must Converge

In the fall of 1962, O'Connor refers to a second collection of short stories in a letter to Robert Giroux, her chief editor throughout her writing career. At this time, she had seven stories, but she was not convinced of a satisfactory variety. Further, she was "not in any hurry."[1] When the collection appeared, published by Farrar, Straus and Giroux, in the spring of 1965, O'Connor had been dead for over half a year. The preparation of the final manuscript occupied those last months of her life. She signed the contract in May of 1964 and continued to write and rewrite through the end of July; she died 3 August 1964.

In that 1962 letter to Giroux, she had selected her title: "I still want to call the book *Everything That Rises Must Converge*."[2] An earlier reference exists, however, in a letter to a friend in the fall of 1961: "I'm much taken . . . with Père Teilhard. . . . I've even taken a little from him—'Everything That Rises Must Converge' and am going to put it on my next collection of stories."[3] The short story with this title had appeared in the October 1961 issue of *New World Writing,* and the title's significance and importance to her soared beyond that particular story's activity. By May 1964, however, she is less committed to the title, for in a letter to her agent, Elizabeth McKee, O'Connor lists her stories for possible inclusion and indicates that she will leave the order to Giroux, and "which story I'll use for title."[4] Two weeks later, in a follow-up letter to McKee, O'Connor acknowledges her acceptance of the title, with somewhat less excitement than she evidenced in the early 1960s: "I forgot to tell Giroux that the title *Everything That Rises Must Converge* is all right with me if he thinks that is what it ought to be."[5]

Representing the only title she ever chose from a serious piece of prose without explicit or literal reference to it within the story itself, the phrase "everything that rises must converge" comes from Pierre Teilhard de Chardin, a French Jesuit paleontologist. In 1956, O'Connor began reviewing books for the Georgia Catholic diocesan periodical the *Bulletin.* Teilhard's death in 1955 made it possible to begin the publication of his writings and their subsequent translation into English, for the Society of Jesus had forbade his doing so during his lifetime. O'Connor reviewed *The Phenomenon of Man* (20 February 1960), *The Divine Milieu* (4 February 1961), and *Letters from a Traveler* (27 April 1963). She also reviewed three books about Teilhard: Nicolas Corte's *Pierre Teilhard de Chardin: His Life and Spirit* (15 October 1960), Oliver Rabut's *Teilhard de Chardin: A Critical Study* (23 December 1961), and Claude Tresmontant's *Pierre Teilhard de Chardin: His Thought* (20 February 1960, simultaneous review with *The Phenomenon of Man*).[6]

O'Connor's response to Teilhard was so positive that when she was invited "among a number of distinguished writers, scholars and critics" by the editors of the *American Scholar* for their thirtieth anniversary issue to name "the outstanding books" of the past three decades, 1931–1961, her choice was Teilhard's *The Phenomenon of Man.* She called the book "a scientific expression of what the poet attempts to do: penetrate matter until spirit is revealed in it."[7] Since she had a similar penchant in her own writing vision, she considered him a kindred spirit. She was willing to do battle for him when a friend took issue with his position: "This is a scientific age and Teilhard's direction is to face it toward Christ. . . . Talk about this man after you know something about him."[8] She calls Teilhard "dangerous" in the last review she writes of one of his books,[9] but clarifies that word choice in a letter: "If they are good, they are dangerous."[10]

Particularly important to her was Teilhard's concept of the Omega Point, a scientific explanation of human evolution as "an ascent towards consciousness" that would "culminate forwards in some sort of supreme consciousness."[11] In a complicated exegesis, Teilhard suggests that this human evolution, which brings the outside universal world in tandem with the inside personal world, finds its convergence in Christ. Teilhard believes that no human remains static and that to be human is to be continually evolving toward a point that is simultaneously autonomous, actual, irreversible, and transcendent.[12] O'Connor admits to not understanding the depth of his argument, but, nevertheless, finds it "very stimulating to the imagination."[13] The context of the title comes from the explanation of the Omega Point: "Remain true to yourselves, but move ever upward toward greater consciousness and greater love! At the summit you will find yourselves united with all those who, from every direction, have made the same ascent. *For everything that rises must converge.*"[14] Thematically, most of the nine stories in the collection have characters that are in evolution toward some "supreme consciousness," but their full arrival at the Omega Point is beyond the end of the story; rather, the story suggests a projection toward that eventual arrival.

The reviewers of *Everything That Rises Must Converge* were more thorough in dealing with her stories than those who had written about her earlier fiction. This is the volume that has the most in-depth reviews. For example, the *New Yorker,* which had granted her one less-than-flattering paragraph for each of her earlier three works, gives her more than a page. Here, when she can write no more, the reviewer is willing to say that several of the stories are "just about as good as short stories can be."[15] In fact, O'Connor's death is a part of every review of this book; some blend the review with obituary, rambling commentary on the lupus that killed her, and attempts at understanding her religious fixation. All come out, in part, in high praise for an author that has died too soon. In *Christian Century,* Robert Drake suggests that "her vision of the fallen world seemed to be growing sharper and her perception more deadly: most of these stories have the lethal immediacy of a loaded shotgun."[16] Granville Hicks, in *Saturday Review,* places the violence inherent in these nine stories, where seven people die in six of the stories, in a position that is not gratuitous: "Violence is an integral part of the world Miss O'Connor is describing, an inevitable consequence of the evil she portrays." Hicks also establishes her religious vision as concomitant with the violence: "I am not saying that Miss O'Connor's Catholicism was responsible for the harshness of her judgments; but the harshness, which probably had many causes, was compatible with her religion as she conceived it." Concluding with a testimony to her artistic integrity, he hallows her not as a "saint," but as "one of the best writers of short stories this era has seen."[17]

For Richard Poirier, in the *New York Times Book Review,* her "particular genius [is] to make us believe that there are Christian mysteries in things irreducibly banal," and she is capable of producing "as much violence from a quiet conversation as can other writers from the confrontations of gangsters or fanatics." No review eliminates O'Connor's "limitations"; Poirier states it this way: "Caring almost nothing for secular destinies, which are altogether more various than religious ones, she propels her characters toward the cataclysms where alone they can have a tortured glimpse of the need and chance of redemption."[18] Webster Schott expresses her limitations bluntly: "She had only a few ideas, but messianic feelings about them."[19] Upon her death, the religious entanglements of her writing were popularly perceived as its weakness.

Finally, there were reviewers who wanted to revisit history and alter its pronouncements. The *Newsweek* reviewer serves as such an example: "With her first novel, 'Wise Blood,' it was clear that a major writer had arrived; and this conviction was confirmed by her first collection of stories, 'A Good Man Is Hard to Find.' With her second novel, 'The Violent Bear It Away,' nearly all doubters were converted to passionate belief."[20] The fact remains that critics did have a difficult time with her harsh vision, bizarre humor, and, what seemed at the time, mysterious grotesque. *Newsweek* did not review her first three publications. Actually, Irving Howe, in the *New York Review of Books,* most closely predicts O'Connor's future with the critics: "On and off these last months I have been fussing in my mind with Miss O'Connor's stories." He does not wish to jump quickly on the bandwagon of acclaim, if at all, but he thinks closely about what is missing in the stories and what eventually is present, assessing the stories chronologically, coming to the determination that O'Connor's work matured and ripened as she herself did. The highest praise goes to that on which critics are in general agreement—that "Revelation" is her crowning achievement.

Howe does not mince his words in his concluding statement: "It is intolerable that a woman who could write ["Revelation"] should have died at the age of thirty-nine."[21]

In an unprecedented achievement, O'Connor's last collection of stories contains three first-prize winners from the O. Henry Awards: "Greenleaf" in 1957, "Everything That Rises Must Converge" in 1963, and "Revelation" in 1965. Only Stephen Vincent Benét in 1932, 1937, and 1940; Eudora Welty in 1942, 1943, and 1968; and Cynthia Ozick in 1981, 1984, and 1992 have won the first-place O. Henry Award three times, and O'Connor is the only writer to have all three award-winning stories appear in the same collection. Of the nine stories, all but the last one, "Judgment Day," a rewrite of the first story of her M.A. thesis, "The Geranium," appeared in periodicals from the summer of 1956 until April 1965.

In *A Good Man Is Hard to Find,* O'Connor uses the mother-daughter family unit four times as a means of exploring a tension in their relationship. In this compilation, she avoids completely any mother-daughter dynamics, but rather switches on four occasions to the mother-son family unit. Three stories have a couple, but only one story places any emphasis on their relationship. The remaining two stories offer a son and father, and a daughter and father in difficult alliance with each other. O'Connor's family units are spiritually broken, physically flawed, or intellectually limited. For many of these characters, home, usually thought of as a place of sustenance and nurturing, becomes a place of hostile endurance. Even though O'Connor pits characters against each other, the significant focus, as in every piece of O'Connor fiction, is a vertical relationship, the individual with his or her Maker, rather than a horizontal involvement, individuals in community with each other. In *Everything That Rises Must Converge,* most characters find themselves moving toward some consciousness that is beyond a human exchange. Except for the title story, which is placed first, a reminder of the Teilhardian evolution toward something higher, the stories appear in the collection in chronological order according to when O'Connor wrote them. All stories are set in the South but the last one, which nonetheless has a character with a desire to return to the South.

"Everything That Rises Must Converge"

The title story appeared in the October 1961 issue of *New World Writing.* First-place winner in the O. Henry competition in 1963, this story contains an O. Henry twist involving the relationship between Julian and his mother. Julian's task is to deliver his mother to a weight-reducing class at the downtown Y; the story begins on the bus on the way to class and ends with the bus's downtown arrival and Julian's mother's death on the sidewalk. The end has little to do with Julian's expectations—or the readers'.

On the literal level, "Everything That Rises Must Converge" is the only story that gives a nod to the Civil Rights Movement that was ongoing during the time O'Connor was writing. The setting is a bus in a Southern city where blacks only recently had been granted a legal right to sit wherever they chose. Julian's mother is part of the "Old South," where relationships, names, home, tradition, and history all shape a person's life and livelihood. She is embarrassed enough to be on the bus in the first place, and she makes conversation after noting that only white people are fellow passengers: "I see we have the bus to our-selves."[22] The question is open to anyone to respond to or not and the woman across from her relays: "I come on one the other day and they were thick as fleas—up front and all through" (490). For a white person to report that a black person would sit "up front" indicates the information is still current enough news to bring to the attention of the others. By contrast, Julian belongs to the "New South," represented by liberated youth who hold little stock in the former racist ways of their parents' generation. Whenever Julian's mother makes a comment that appears to him as retrograde, he counters her old ways with one of his more modern views. She is an embarrassment to him.

The story, however, is far more tangled than Old vs. New, and Julian's mother is not the all-racist, white supremist that Julian may suggest she is. Julian, on the other hand, is not the totally liberated, farseeing man of reality he thinks he is. From the first paragraph in the story, O'Connor shows the reader that both characters are to be simultaneously pitied and laughed at. Julian's mother has no name of her own; she is known throughout the story by her role in relationship to him. Going to the reducing class is one of "her few pleasures" (485), and Julian has to "consider all she [does] for him" and "brace himself" (485) to escort her. His mother holds out hope for him in her mind: "You've only been out of school a year. Rome wasn't built in a day" (486), but he knows he is a failure. O'Connor likens him to Saint Sebastian, a third-century Roman martyr. The cliché that his mother spouts about Rome is thus connected to the image of her son as a martyr of that city, left for dead, full of arrows from archers who were hired to slay him. Sebastian miraculously rallied and was later clubbed to death. Sebastian is usually pictured full of arrows, and Julian's manner of carriage displays a heavy burden of despair. He walks with "his head down and thrust forward" (486), and to confuse the image of Sebastian, O'Connor writes that Julian is "saturated in depression, as if in the midst of his martyrdom he lost his faith" (486). He is impotent to affect his mother's attitude or to understand how to change his own. While Julian maintains his superiority to his mother, the reader senses that he is the one to be more pitied.

Julian's mother is the stereotypical Southern lady. She knows what she is supposed to espouse, but her feelings indicate something to the contrary. She has been reared well connected: her grandfather is a former governor of the state, her father is a prosperous landowner, and her mother, a Godhigh. Political position, land, and name all carry importance and have become her means of identifying herself. She knows the line about blacks that is part of her high-class rhetoric: "They should rise, yes, but on their own side of the fence" (488). The message is in the kind of language she has heard all her life. It works well enough when the black race has no specific face, no name, no personal connection. However, it has no place in the reality of what matters deeply to her on a personal level, for when she remembers her nurse, Caroline, she gushes with affection: "There was no better person in the world" (488), and her last line on the sidewalk is also connected to the past from which she cannot remove herself: "Tell Caroline to come get me" (500).

The Southern lady also cares about her dress. Proper dress for a trip to town would include matching heels, hat, and gloves. Julian's mother wears hat and gloves to her reducing class, and she is accompanied by a college-educated son who wears a tie. She can be embarrassed by surface appearances. When Julian takes off his tie on the bus, she stiffens: "Why must you look like *that* when you take me to town? . . . Why must you deliberately embarrass me?" (489). Julian, on the other hand, is likely to be mortified by her words, her actions, and how he perceives they appear to the watching world. Mother's and son's responses to her velvet purple and green hat exemplify their basic differences. In her reduced status, living in an apartment in one of the "bulbous liver-colored monstrosities" that had been "a fashionable neighborhood forty years ago" (486), she has splurged $7.50 on a new hat. She displays genuine tentativeness about the purchase—remembering that she can pay the gas bill with that money, but finding some satisfaction in knowing that the extra cost would prevent her from meeting herself "coming and going" (486). To Julian's mother the hat is necessary to complete her outfit and vital to her self-image, reflective of good taste and indicative of who she is. In contrast, to Julian the hat is "hideous," "jaunty and pathetic," and he finds himself disturbed by her desire for the hat: "Everything that gave her pleasure was small and depressed him" (485). He has the final word in her decision to keep the hat: "Shut up and enjoy it" (487). For Julian, the hat is a ridiculous outward and visible reminder of his mother's foolish and outmoded views of the world.

When the "gaily dressed, sullen-looking colored woman" (495) gets on the bus with her small son Carver, the hat becomes a convergence point in the story, both literally and figuratively. For Carver's mother has on the identical purple and green hat that Julian's mother is wearing. Coming and going, they have met themselves. Julian has spent the bus ride "withdrawing into the inner compartment of his mind" where he could "see out and judge," but be "safe from any kind of penetration from without" (491). Mentally, he conjures up a series of personal involvements with black people that would drive his mother wild, but not quite to the point "of making her have a stroke" (494). The black woman's giant presence in reality becomes an opportunity for him to see one of his fantasies played out. He hopes that she will place herself beside his mother, but Carver takes that seat and Julian finds himself annoyed that the woman has "squeezed herself" (495) into the seat beside him. Then Julian reads the scene symbolically, for the two mothers have, "in a sense, swapped sons" (495). Black and white stare into the faces of white and black—mother to mother, noticing each other's hat. While son faces mother across the aisle, Julian's mother smiles at Carver.

Julian's mother lumps "all children, black and white, into the common category, 'cute,' and she [thinks] little Negroes [are] on the whole cuter than little white children" (495). O'Connor uses this instance as an example of how general platitudes of white Southern racist hatred are negated by the reality of specific faces and incidents. Julian's mother comments to Carver's mother: "I think he likes me" (497). Julian notes the smile on her face, however, as one his mother "[uses] when she [is] being particularly gracious to an inferior" (497). Julian's mother, oblivious of Julian's interpretation of her smile to Carver's mother, plays peekaboo with Carver. Julian's mother has accepted the other woman's son as well as the hat on the other woman's head on some honest level, one that comes from "the heart," not "the mind," as Julian has insisted is the mark of "true culture" (489), while Julian despairs that his mother has not learned a "permanent lesson": he had hoped that she—her pettiness, her joy in the hat—would be punished by having to sit across from a black woman with the same hat.

Carver's mother, meanwhile, functions alongside the main story line—Julian and his mother mired in the inability to understand the other. She sees her hat on Julian's mother's head and, as Julian distractedly notes, she mutters "something unintelligible," bristles, growls like "an angry cat," and rumbles "like a volcano about to become active" (496). The hat becomes symbol of all white oppression she has known. She wants no part of young Carver's association with Julian's mother, and in a defiant and hostile act, she snatches Carver to her side, slaps his hand from his face, and demands his cooperation: "Quit yo' foolishness . . . before I knock the living Jesus out of you!" (497). Though the line is a cliché, to knock out the living Jesus is literally to terminate what O'Connor sees as the source of goodness. Carver's mother gives him a message as steeped in the old ways of Southern tradition as Julian's mother has been given in her early days—keep a healthy distance from the other race.

Carver's mother and Julian's mother read each other as poorly as Julian and his own mother read each other. As both prepare to leave the bus at the same stop, Julian's mother wants to give the boy a coin because it is a gesture "as natural to her as breathing" (497). Carver's mother's response is "to explode like a piece of machinery" (498) and to let her "black fist swing out with the red pocketbook . . . 'He don't take nobody's pennies!'" (498). Julian's mother, sprawled on the sidewalk, does not gain sympathy nor help from Julian; rather she receives a lesson, a symbolic interpretation of what has happened: "That was the whole colored race which will no longer take your condescending pennies. . . . What all this means . . . is that the old world is gone. The old manners are obsolete and your graciousness is not worth a damn" (499).

In "Everything That Rises Must Converge," O'Connor is writing a story about race relations, about the Old South up against the New, and about a son and a mother who do not understand each other. On a deeper level, she is writing a story about love, and it is in love that all three of the literal stories converge. As O'Connor states in an interview: "The Georgia writer's true country is not Georgia, but Georgia is an entrance to it for him. . . . One uses the region in order to suggest what transcends it."[23] The full seating integration of Southern buses is the vehicle that O'Connor uses for a more substantive theological projection. Julian's mother cries out for the unconditional love and acceptance she found as a child from her nurse Caroline; Julian's arrogant and timely message pales in significance to her deeper need for a home, not to be found in this life. With one final raking with her eye on Julian's face, finding nothing, she is able to transcend this moment for something elsewhere. Julian must watch his mother die—from a stroke he had not wanted to "push her to" (494)—before he can surmount his own pettiness and find the love he actually does have for her, before he can affectionately call out to her "Darling, sweetheart, wait!" (500). At story's end, he is moving toward the "cluster of lights . . . in the distance" (500), but he is neither going to see the light yet nor understand his full dependence on love. First he must dwell in the "tide of darkness" and then spend time in the "world of guilt and sorrow" (500). He has awareness, but full consciousness lies ahead.

"Greenleaf"

"Greenleaf" is the earliest story of the collection and her first top-award recipient for the O. Henry. It was published first in the summer 1956 issue of the *Kenyon Review,* appearing a year after the publication of *A Good Man Is Hard to Find.* The story was also included in *The Best American Short Stories of 1957.*

"Greenleaf" joins three earlier stories in featuring a lone woman who seeks to protect her farm property and to control the people who live on it. Mrs. May has hired some "good country people" to assist in working the land, whose irritating ways irk the stubborn landowner. "Greenleaf" is O'Connor's last story that features a hard-working farm-owning woman who has problems of control with both the hired help and her children. As a transition story, it is the first of four stories that O'Connor writes about a single mother struggling with an adult still-at-home son.

All of the single threads of the story line—Mrs. May's struggling dynamics with her sons, their constant comparisons to the more successful Greenleaf boys, the striking contrast of Mrs. May's and Mrs. Greenleaf's responses to religion—converge in the momentary dilemma of this story: the scrub bull that has come to court Mrs. May and to invade her property and her herd of cows. This bull has connections with the myth in which Zeus disguises himself as a white bull and carries off Europa to Crete,[24] as well as biblical connections to the holy hunt of the unicorn, where the courting animal becomes a symbolic Christ figure that pierces Mrs. May through the heart with a deeper understanding of Christian reality.[25] Before the bull and Mrs. May have a final and fatal meeting, O'Connor makes clear the limited perspective with which Mrs. May views the world.

Mrs. May, "a small woman with pale near-sighted eyes and grey hair that [rises] on top like the crest of some disturbed bird" (503), has sole responsibility for the success of her farm. Her two adult sons—thirty-six-year-old Scofield, the "nigger-insurance salesman" (504), and Wesley, the younger intellectual—have one thing in common, "neither of them care[s] what happen[s] on the place" (504). Both sons verbally abuse their mother at every opportunity. Scofield suggests that she can easily be replaced by some "nice fat farm girl" wife that he will choose upon her death (505). Wesley, who causes her "real anxiety" (509), "wouldn't milk a cow to save [her] soul from hell" (510). As a final blow in this daily barrage, he also strips his mother of parenthood; to Scofield, he taunts: "Neither you nor me is her boy" (517). Mrs. May, on the other hand, remains foremost a Southern mother. She feels a duty to her sons and takes whatever treatment they offer. Although she does not eat breakfast with them, she sits "with them to see that they [have] what they wanted" (504). She makes sure that Wesley maintains his salt-free diet. Mrs. May's downfall, however, is that she constantly reminds her sons how great her own sacrifice has been, and she stands at the ready with plenty of good advice about how they could improve their lives. For example, if Scofield would sell "decent insurance, some *nice* girl would be willing to marry [him]. What nice girl wants to marry a nigger-insurance man?" (505). Mrs. May does not hear her racist comments. Her simplistic worldview extends to every aspect of her life and beyond: "I'll die when I get good and ready" (511).

Mrs. May's relationship with her sons is complicated by the success of her hired people's twin sons, a few years younger than her own. Mr. Greenleaf, her employee for fifteen years, is always quick to point out what his sons would do by comparison. Because of the rigid class structure that so permeated the South of O'Connor's day, the upper-class land-owning Mrs. May has to endure the comeuppance from a lower class that refuses to adhere to old rules: "As scrub-human as the Greenleafs were, [Mr. Greenleaf] never hesitated to let her know that in any like circumstance in which his own boys might have been involved—

UNDERSTANDING FLANNERY O'CONNOR

O. T. and E. T. Greenleaf—would have acted to better advantage" (507). Mrs. May is prepared to credit anything outside and beyond the boys with their elevated place in the world: the war that sent them to Europe, where they could "disguise" themselves in uniform (507), court and marry French women who do not realize they are "murder[ing] the king's English" (508), and "manage" to get wounded and receive a pension (508). She takes credit as well for her contribution to their rise and wants to hold it over them when she discovers the scrub bull on her property belongs to O. T. and E. T. She reminds Mr. Greenleaf, with a repetition of the first person possessive pronoun, that his boys "wore my boys' old clothes and played with my boys' old toys and hunted with my boys' old guns"; further, for Mrs. May, those twins had access to "my pond . . . , my birds . . . , my stream" (518). Mrs. May is without subtlety or nuance; her only deficiency is that she is a woman: "You can get away with anything when you're dealing with a woman. If there were a man running this place . . ." (519). She tolerates her own sons' fighting: "Nobody feels sorry for a lousy bastard like you" (517), shouts one to the other before the dishes crash, the table is overturned, and the boys are grabbing each other's shirtfronts. Because her own boys fight, Mrs. May is sure the Greenleafs do, but according to their hired help, "they never quarls. . . . They like one man in two skins" (516). Mrs. May and her sons are denied the superiority she feels is the privilege of her class.

Mrs. May carries her superficial thinking into matters of religion as well. She has reduced religion to attending church, a "proper" place for her boys to "meet some nice girls" (510). Mrs. Greenleaf, by contrast, takes religion to the "preoccupation" of "prayer healing" (505). By clipping appropriate stories from the paper—rape, burned children, escaped criminals, train wrecks, plane crashes, and movie star divorces—burying them in the ground, and praying over them, she is in direct communication with the healing power of her Jesus: "Oh Jesus, stab me in the heart!" (506). Mrs. May is shocked at her first encounter with Mrs. Greenleaf's ritual, for her Jesus is a practical man. She knows that Jesus would be *"ashamed"* of Mrs. Greenleaf and tell her to "get up from there this instant and go wash [her] children's clothes!" (507). Mrs. Greenleaf, with her backwoods fundamentalist perspective, values the mystery of Jesus as deity, accepting his power to right the wrongs of the day. Mrs. May understands the language of the Christian religion where it fits in society, and how she might work it to her advantage, but "she [does] not, of course, believe any of it [is] true" (506).

Into the melee of these relationships comes the bull, an "uncouth country suitor" (502). The May boys have the advantage over their mother as Scofield knows it is the Greenleaf boys' bull. The Greenleaf boys have no intention of reclaiming the bull and are willing to let Mrs. May assume the responsibility of having their father kill it. As O'Connor closes in on the activity of the killing scene, she advances the bull to symbol. From the opening scene with his Christlike hedge wreath "caught in the tips of his horns" (501), his presumptuous invasion of her property, until the end when he picks up the pace of his wooing, no longer the "patient god" (501), the bull, as an image of Christ, crosses at a "slow gallop" and then, suddenly, is "racing toward her" (523). Until this point in the story, Mrs. May has set her own schedule and controlled her world, but now the bull changes everything. Mrs. May moves from "freezing unbelief" (523), not just her response to the bull's charge but her response to religion's role in her life, to "the look of a person whose sight has been suddenly restored but who finds the light unbearable" (523). O'Connor uses repetition of language and image to draw the parallel between Mrs. May's response to the earlier scene of Mrs. Greenleaf in her prayer healing and the charging bull. With Mrs. Greenleaf, Mrs. May stops still: "The sound was so piercing that she felt as if some violent unleashed force had broken out of the ground and was charging toward her" (506). Facing the bull, Mrs. May remains perfectly still: "She stared at the violent black streak bounding toward her as if she had no sense of distance" until his horn "sank until it pierced her heart" (523). Mrs. Greenleaf's figurative chant for Jesus to stab her in the heart takes on a literal action as the bull stabs Mrs. May through her heart. O'Connor has set up the scene of the "last discovery" of Mrs. May, as she whispers "into the animal's ear" (524), to be the beginning of understanding her own limitations. O'Connor suggests that Mrs. May reaches the Teilhardian Omega Point of God in the "unbearable" light.

"A View of the Woods"

O'Connor completed "A View of the Woods" by the fall of 1956 and sent it to *Harper's Bazaar*. She doubted they would accept it, thinking it "may be a little grim for the dryer set."[26] And she was correct. The story was published in the fall 1957 issue of *Partisan Review,* and also was included in *The Best American Short Stories of 1958.* In a letter to a friend about this story, she indicates her idea of art—"impressing an idea on matter" or using "reality to make a different kind of reality."[27] Several years later, when O'Connor had read Teilhard, she used similar language to note the scientist's effort: "penetrate matter until spirit is revealed in it."[28] In "A View of the Woods," O'Connor impresses her idea on the woods—that they represent a Christ figure—and gives life to the idea through a central character, the young Mary Fortune Pitts. In this story, what matters is that the characters hold onto "a view of the woods."

In the first paragraph, O'Connor gives the woods symbolic weight, for their appearance has a Christlike power: "a black line of woods which appeared at both ends of the view to walk across the water and continue along the edge of the fields" (525). In spite of the fact that the grandfather, Mark Fortune, plans to sell the lawn that will end the family's view of the woods, the persistence of the woods and their symbolic Christlike weight never falters. As the old man is dying, "he saw that the gaunt trees had thickened into mysterious dark files that were marching across the water and away into the distance" (546). At the beginning and ending of the story, these woods appear to walk on water. O'Connor alludes to the story in Matthew where Jesus moves toward his disciples in a boat across a storm-tossed sea: "And in the fourth watch of the night, [Jesus] came to them walking upon the sea" (Matthew 14:25, Rheims-Douay Version).

On a literal level, this story is a candidate for one of O'Connor's darkest, most violent escapades, for in it a seventy-nine-year-old grandfather and his nine-year-old favorite grand-child grip, claw, and pound each other to death in the midst of those woods. The issue is the old man's tedious desire to sell his land by lots, in the name of progress, to spite his resident son-in-law, Pitts. This recurring activity has been fine with his grand-daughter until the day he announces one more plan: "I'm going to sell the lot right in front of the house for a gas station" (531).

To him, it is just another lot with no special significance. To her, however, it is the "lawn . . . where we play . . . , see the woods across the road" and where "my daddy grazes his calves" (532). It is the loss of the view of the woods, repeated three times in their conversation, that most alarms the old man. He cannot understand her position. Mark Fortune is representative of modern materialists; he wants the easy accessibility of convenience. When he looks at those woods for the first time with Mary Fortune's concern in mind, he sees only woods where a "pine trunk is a pine trunk"; however, on the third glance, the trees have a different look and he is aware of being "held there in the midst of an uncomfortable mystery that he had not apprehended before" (538). He feels the "mystery" but shuts his eyes to it. Mary Fortune does not want this land sold, and she is willing to fight to their mutual deaths to defend her position. If the woods are only woods, whether engagingly pretty or horrifyingly ominous, the story is bleak and its vision is sullen, which is why this story cannot rest on its bizarre surface level.

For O'Connor, the vision that piloted her stories was never lighthearted and easy. Integrity to her vision meant characters had to yield, to suffer, to die, if necessary, so that an essential Christian point could be driven home. During the Christmas of 1956, she sent a copy of the story to the Fitzgeralds with a message that suggests her earnestness: "I enclose a little morality play of mine for your Christmas cheer but as it is not very cheerful, I'd advise you to leave off reading it until after the season."[29] What O'Connor means to underline is, as she tells a friend, "one is saved and the other is damned. . . . One has to die first because one kills the other."[30] Mark Fortune is the intended damned. He thinks of the Pittses as fools, for they would "let a cow pasture interfere with progress" (525) and "with the future" (528). He prefers the selling of his land to a man who allows an outside display of "old used-car bodies . . . , stone cranes and chickens, urns, jardinieres, whirligigs" (535). Mary Fortune Pitts is the planned saved. She values the view of the land, preferring the "profusion of pink and yellow and purple weeds, and on across the red road, to the sullen line of black pine woods fringed on top with green" (537). Mary Fortune, however, is by no means a Christian advocate in the story, so as O'Connor's "saved," she is a pawn in a role that is larger than her comprehension.

In a story where primary colors abound, Mary Fortune, in her yellow dress, follows with interest the desecration of the red clay by the giant yellow machines, that, monsterlike, "gorge" themselves and "with the sound of a deep sustained nausea and a slow mechanical revulsion, turn and spit [the clay] up" (525). At the story's beginning, Mary Fortune watches the scene intently with her grandfather, who sees in her his own fascination. In spite of the seventy years that separate them, they have converged as doubles, one for the other, outside and inside, and, in his mind, they view the world the same way. What the old man cannot fathom is her seeming complicity with her father, the idiot Pitts, in allowing him to beat her. While Mary Fortune denies those beatings, claiming five times that "nobody has ever beat me, . . . and if anybody tries it, I'd kill him" (544 with slight variations on 530, 530–31, 533, 541). The old man is proud of his heritage as "PURE Fortune" (541) and wants his granddaughter to follow suit.

Mark Fortune's decision to sell the lawn splits the perceived convergence at the story's beginning. The middle of the story exposes the old man's path toward inevitable destruction as he does not heed his granddaughter's warning not to sell the land and not to beat her. The prospective buyer of the land, Tilman, has a name that suggests a till keeper, a man who would care about money, a modern materialist, like Fortune himself. Tilman, who advertises in "dazzling red letters" (535), is described as the devil incarnate, reminiscent of the serpent that deceives Eve in the temptation scene in the Garden of Eden (Genesis 3). He inhabits a "dark store"; he is a man of "quick action and few words," with an "insignificant head weaving snake-fashion above [his folded arms]," containing narrow eyes and a "tongue [that is] always exposed in his partly opened mouth" (542). At the moment of closure on the land transaction, Mary Fortune hurls the first of many bottles across the store at this devil who would destroy her view of the woods. This retaliation on her part, this defense of her view, is the stunt that causes the old man to beat her.

The five death threats that she has issued him if he attempts to lay hands on her mean nothing to him. Both prepare for serious warfare as she removes her glasses and causes his to fly to the side. Whenever glasses are removed in an O'Connor story, outward physical sight is symbolically replaced by inward spiritual clarity. On a figurative level, she is fighting to protect her view of the woods, that through the Christ image inherent in them is also the "uncomfortable mystery" (538). On the literal level, she lights into him for all she is worth, clawing his arms, battering his knees, pounding his chest, and biting the side of his jaw. His appeal to her to stop reverts to the language of Southern manners. She should not abuse "an old man" and especially one who is related: "I'm your grandfather!" (545). The physical torment yields to her resounding blow with language; she abandons him forever in her declaration that she is "PURE Pitts" (545). In saying this, Fortune responds as though he has heard a rallying cry. He must blot out what is not "Fortune" and what does not see the world Fortune's way: "With his hands still tight around her neck, he lifted her head and brought it down once hard against the rock that happened to be under it. Then he brought it down twice more" (545). On the symbolic level, the modern materialist denies his Christ, elevating convenience above spiritual mystery. On the literal level, he kills his granddaughter, sacrificing her to his own greed and pride.

This exertion, however, brings about his hallucination and a fatal stroke. The ending converges in his perceived self-discovery of that "uncomfortable mystery" of the woods; he is not the master of this land, the controller of its destiny. The woods, which "march across the water" (546) oblivious to his human designs, overpower him. He is alone with only the "yellow monster" to his side (546), the gorging tractor, unmoving. To his side, as well, is Mary Fortune, a smaller monster also dressed in yellow who, likewise, does not move. The two characters converge in death at the end of the story. The younger of the two has defended her cause and died in pursuit of her belief that the view of the woods must prevail.

"The Enduring Chill"

Published the first time in the July 1958 *Harper's Bazaar,* "The Enduring Chill" pairs Mrs. Fox, a Southern mother, with her returning adult son, Asbury, who has allegedly come home from New York to die. Mrs. Fox owns a dairy farm and has a couple of hired hands to assist her. She is present to serve her son, do his bidding, and assess his situation. Asbury, an aspiring writer, after anguishing in New York with chills and fever, returns home to Timberboro, Georgia, to await his death. On the occasion of this event, his mother is instructed to open a sealed envelope containing a letter to her "which filled two notebooks" (554), and which, he is sure, will leave her with an "enduring chill" (555). This is the title's literal presence in the story, but the figurative emphasis of the title falls on Asbury himself as he begins to understand what life includes this side of death. The animosity between mother and son operates on a surface level in the story. A more significant aspect of the story is Asbury's unrequited movement toward the Teilhardian Omega Point. What Asbury needs to learn about life and death can take place in the humble setting of his origin, and New York, with its expansive cultural eclectic charm, pales by comparison.

At the beginning, the story is ripe with wondrous overlays that add mystery to the setting of an ordinary country town in middle Georgia; the sun is like "some strange potentate" and the light it casts could turn flat roofs into "mounting turrets of some exotic temple" (547). Asbury has been in New York and his imagination has been fed by a world of people who see things differently from the provincial folks of his native town. Containing the most allusions to world religions of any O'Connor stories, "The Enduring Chill" explores the meaning of Asbury's eventual death through references to Buddhism, Hinduism, existentialism, and the Christianity of Roman Catholicism. Mrs. Fox, on the other hand, represents everything from which Asbury has tried to remove himself. Yet, in the end, O'Connor elevates Mrs. Fox's position; she is the kind of character that lets her intellectual son have his say, but not necessarily his way. She might not know much of the world beyond Timberboro, but she knows how to survive at home, indifferent to a desire for enlightenment.

While Asbury is still in New York, his friend Goetz explores and rejects Buddhism with this simple denial: "Although the Bodhisattva leads an infinite number of creatures into nirvana, in reality there are neither any Bodhisattvas to do the leading nor any creatures to be led" (549–50). In Buddhism, the Bodhisattva is an enlightened being who has arrived at perfect knowledge and acts as a guide for others toward nirvana, the attainment of disinterested wisdom and compassion. Goetz, an existential agnostic, believes that death is an illusion. Ironically, O'Connor has chosen a name for him of German derivation, which is "a pet form of Godizo (God)."[31] Goetz has a similar response to the lecture on Vedanta, which is a Hindu philosophy that affirms the identity of the individual human soul, *atman,* with Brahman, the holy power that is the source and sustainer of the universe. Asbury, who is bored by the lecture, finds a Roman Catholic priest among the disparate audience whose nonverbal gestures appear to match his own lack of appreciation. The Hindu references also provide a source of subtle humor, as the cow, a sacred animal to the Hindu, is later determined to be the source of Asbury's undulant fever.

This priest, Ignatius Vogle, S.J., serves as the vehicle through whom Asbury begins to read the symbolic world around him once he is home again. The priest's comment is pivotal in the story and is eventually what Asbury comes to understand about enlightenment: "There is . . . a real probability of the New Man, assisted of course . . . by the Third Person of the Trinity" (550). O'Connor has selected the priest's name carefully; *vogel* is the German word for bird, the symbol of the Holy Ghost, the third person of the Trinity, and "Ignatius" is the name of the founder of the Society of Jesus. When Asbury takes to his bed, whose name O'Connor has taken from the first bishop of the Methodist

Episcopal Church in America, Francis Asbury, he notes the water stains on his wall: "Descending from the top molding, long icicle shapes had been etched by leaks and, directly over his bed on the ceiling, another leak had made a fierce bird with spread wings" (555). Since his childhood, this bird has "irritated" and "frightened" him (555).

His name indicates a protestant family, and the story confirms this by Mrs. Fox's discomfort with his suggestion that a Jesuit priest provide the intellectual conversation he lacks in "this desert" (561): "What is the matter with you?" (561) and "You're not a member of that church" (562). The memory of Vogle encourages Asbury, who prepares for the priest's visit by rearranging his room and removing "a picture of a maiden chained to a rock" from his wall, which he knows would "make the Jesuit smile" (564). The best images of such a picture are Rubens's *Perseus and Andromeda* and Ingres's *Roger Freeing Angelica.* In each, a chained naked maiden at the foot of a cliff is being rescued from a threatening sea monster. Asbury's knowledge that the Jesuit would smile could be related to the maiden's lack of clothes, or to either the irony of Andromeda, which means "ruler of men," in chains, or the use of a magic ring and shield by the pagan champion Roger, who rides a hippogriff, to protect the fair Angelica. But Father Finn, with his own name bearing a relation to a sea animal, but hardly a monster, is not the kind of intellect Asbury wants. Father Finn does not know James Joyce, but he does know his catechism, a compendium of Christian doctrine for children. In Asbury, O'Connor suggests the possibility of knowing the work of one of the literary geniuses of the twentieth century, but being ignorant of a child's understanding of the Christian faith. Assuming the mother and son's Catholic training, Father Finn chides the mother for her shortcomings: "I should think you would have taught him to say his daily prayers. You have neglected your duty as his mother" (567). Like Ignatius Vogle, Father Finn also points out to him the importance of the Holy Ghost. When Asbury claims that the Holy Ghost "is the last thing [he's] looking for," the priest retorts: "And He may be the last thing you get," for the "Holy Ghost will not come until you see yourself as you are—a lazy ignorant conceited youth!" (567).

Asbury has been warned twice, once by each priest, of the Holy Ghost's importance, but his immediate response is to revert to the literal world around him. He confronts the simple Randall and Morgan—the two farm hands who have earlier rejected his effort to have "communion" by drinking warm cow's milk—who deny his own certainty that he is at death's door. He is chastised by his doubting mother, who refuses to believe that he is going to die: "Do you think for one minute . . . that I intend to sit here and let you die?" (562). From Doctor Block, the country physician whom Asbury knows is too unsophisticated to understand his disease and dilemma—"What's wrong with me . . . is way beyond Block" (550)—he learns the diagnosis of his chills and fever.

When Asbury understands that he is not going to die, he retrieves the key that opens the lock to the manuscript drawer that will destroy his mother. His eyes become "paler" (572) and the "white-gold sun" reminiscent of a "strange potentate" (547) becomes a "blinding red-gold sun" (572). The bird, the water stain on the wall, "which through the years of his childhood and the days of his illness had been poised over his head, waiting mysteriously, appeared all at once to be in motion" (572). Asbury can be the "New Man" that Father Vogle spoke of now that he realizes he is "a lazy ignorant conceited youth." He can travel to

New York, he can blame his mother for his failures, but his movement toward his Teilhardian Omega Point, in the end, wraps him "racked" and "frail" (572) in an "enduring chill."

"The Comforts of Home"

Flannery O'Connor placed more of her stories in the *Kenyon Review* than with any other publication. "The Comforts of Home," appearing in the autumn 1960 issue, is the fifth and last story that the *Kenyon Review* published. This is O'Connor's last story featuring an adult still-at-home writer son with his single parent mother, who provides for his comforts. Thomas, who writes history and serves as president of the local Historical Society, lives with his widowed mother, who exists, as Thomas sees it, to serve his needs. To the extent that Thomas is self-centered, his mother is other-centered, embracing society's down-trodden because "it [is] the *nice thing to do*" (575). She takes candy to one of society's miscreants, Sarah Ham, who calls herself Star Drake, and then cannot desert her, for she under-stands that this misguided unfortunate young woman could be her own daughter. Thomas's mother has no name of her own. Throughout the story, over fifty times, she is referred to only as his mother, a constant reminder of O'Connor's emphasis on the roles mother and son play for each other.

O'Connor's choice of the biblical name Thomas plays on the doubting apostle story as well as the meaning of Thomas, "twin" (John 11:16). When Jesus appears to his apostles the first time after his crucifixion, Thomas is not present to see his Master, so he does not believe. On the eighth day, Jesus appears to Thomas; then he believes: "Because thou hast seen me, Thomas, thou hast

believed: blessed are they that have not seen, and have believed"
(John 20:29, Rheims-Douay Version). In O'Connor's story, on
the eighth day Thomas shoots his mother. The sad extravagance
of his mother's death is essential to Thomas's beginning understanding of the potential comforts of an eternal home. Further,
Thomas as "twin" has doubling implications with literally every
character in the story. Thomas duplicates both mother and father
partially: "Thomas [has] inherited his father's reason without his
ruthlessness and his mother's love of good without her tendency
to pursue it" (577). Though he struggles with Sarah Ham's
intrusion into the quiet of his home, his mother sees her repeatedly as interchangeable with Thomas: she could be him. In fact,
the suggestion affects him so profoundly that the distance between them, the polar opposition each represents, fades as he
feels he is "slowly turning into the girl" (575). Farebrother, an
ironically suggestive literal name, is not only the double of
Thomas's father, but of Thomas as well. Sarah Ham thinks
Thomas looks like a cop she saw in a movie, and Farebrother asks
if Thomas "want[s] to swap jobs," since he knows how "it ought
to be done" (590).

Like his biblical namesake, O'Connor's Thomas does not
realize the cost and responsibility of Christian goodness, nor does
O'Connor's Thomas fully appreciate the power of the devil. As
a historian, Thomas would seek verifiable evidence when writing
about the past, just as the biblical Thomas needed tangible proof
before believing in the resurrection of Christ. Both overlook the
bigger issue—Christ's resurrection as a denial of the remaining
apostles' witness and Thomas's mother's self-denying attention
to an inconvenient other as a refusal to forego the amenities of a
comfortable existence: "[Thomas's mother] was counting on his

attachment to his electric blanket" (573). In a letter to a friend, O'Connor once stated: "What people don't realize is how much religion costs. They think faith is a big electric blanket, when of course it is the cross."[32] Thomas loves his mother; he wants to protect her from herself. However, his long deceased father, who has taken up "squatter's rights" in Thomas's head, serves as the tempting and directing devil. He is the one who gives the order to "Fire!" (593), and Thomas does so. Only when he stares into the face of the horror he has committed can he begin to understand the ultimate value of his mother's sacrifice.

Of all O'Connor's stories, "The Comforts of Home" lends itself most easily to both Freudian and Jungian analysis. Frederick Asals calls Thomas's attachment to his mother and his hatred of his father "thunderingly Oedipal."[33] Marshall Bruce Gentry suggests that "O'Connor's most overtly Freudian" scene is when Thomas puts the gun in Sarah Ham's red pocketbook.[34] The red pocketbook has a "skin-like feel" with "an unmistakable odor of the girl." He "thrust[s] in" the phallic gun and quickly "[draws] back," the excitement causing his face to burn "an ugly dull red" (592). In the midst of this heightened activity, Thomas is caught by his mother, who innocently asks: "What would Thomas want to put his pistol in your bag for?" (593). All of Sarah Ham's nymphomaniacal desires pour out in the next paragraph; in front of his mother, she fixes Thomas with an "intimate grin," "cock[s]" her head and declares he is "a case" (593).

His mother, in earnest astonishment, declares his behavior to be beyond reproach for he "wouldn't put a gun in [her] bag. . . . Thomas is a gentleman" (593). The gun works on a literal level, confirming the forthcoming violence, but the gun, in its seven repetitions, takes on heavier symbolic weight and becomes sexual. When Thomas fires it, he is a man spent, with the "echo [dying] away in waves" (593). Sheriff Farebrother, who has just come in the door, is left reading a scene that the literal Thomas never wrote: Farebrother sees the crafty man in the arms of the young slut. Thomas's unconsciousness, however, has made another scenario possible: he has shot his mother to erase his embarrassment in front of her. The self-centered Thomas, on the other hand, is devastated, for a horrible travesty has occurred. The "peace of perfect order" (593), alone again with his mother and all the "comforts of home," which to him are "home, workshop, church, as personal as the shell of a turtle and as necessary" (585) are lost forever. In this final moment of the story, Thomas has the opportunity to see the true value of his mother through his own pitiful shortcomings, and to begin the long upward route toward convergence at the Teilhardian Omega Point.

"The Lame Shall Enter First"

In "The Lame Shall Enter First," Rufus Johnson, a clubfoot delinquent with a high IQ, enters the lives of Sheppard, a widowed atheist do-gooder, and Norton, his sniveling ten-year-old son, who is still grieving for his dead mother. Andrew Lytle, editor of the *Sewanee Review,* published the story in the summer 1962 issue, along with two critical articles on O'Connor's fiction. One of these articles, John Hawkes's "Flannery O'Connor's Devil," provides the first serious challenge to O'Connor's position on evil. Since Rufus Johnson declares that "Satan . . . has [him] in his power" (600), Hawkes's commentary provided a deeper exploration of the story, and it remains today a significant entry in O'Connor criticism. The debate between O'Connor and Hawkes centers on the source or identity of the devil. O'Connor claims "explicit acceptance for the devil's existence"; her devil is Lucifer, a fallen angel. Hawkes, on the other hand, sees O'Connor using an "authorial-devil," which she employs as a "vehicle for satire," one that is a "subjective creation."[35]

Robert Fitzgerald suggests that O'Connor's development of Rufus, Sheppard, and Norton are "a second effort with the three figures of [*The Violent Bear It Away*], Tarwater, Rayber and Bishop."[36] In fact, earlier drafts of the novel's manuscript contain a "Florida Rufus Johnson," whom O'Connor removes from the novel's finalized version. Both Rayber and Sheppard attempt to convert Tarwater and Rufus, respectively, to their views; both fail to do so. Tarwater and Rufus each has an older fanatical relative who has reared him: old Tarwater, the great-uncle, has passed the mantle of prophecy onto the fourteen-year-old Francis Marion, and Rufus's grandfather has deserted his fourteen-year-old grandson to travel "with a remnant to the hills. . . . to bury some Bibles in a cave" and reenact the story of Noah, only this time with fire (607). Bishop, the idiot son, here becomes Norton, a "normal" child. Both are overlooked while more interesting young men come into their fathers' lives; both die, and at their fathers' final awareness of their indirect contributions to their respective fatalities, the fathers have the chance to reconsider former ways.

O'Connor was uneasy with the story, convinced that it did not work: "The story doesn't work because I don't know, don't sympathize, don't like Mr. Sheppard in the way that I know and like most of my other characters." Sheppard is a man who, according to O'Connor, "fills up his emptiness with good works," and of this type of character she has no "felt-knowledge."[37] The other-serving Sheppard, the name suggestive of one who would lead his flock responsibly, finds substitutes for the loss of his wife. The bedroom he shared with her stays intact, with all her clothes in the drawer and her accessories laid out on a linen runner, as though she herself would soon return. Sheppard has removed himself to another room, where an "ascetic-looking iron bed [stands] on the bare floor" (605), and he eats his breakfast out of the individual cardboard box it comes in. In his spare time, he coaches a little league baseball team on which his son does not play and volunteers his Saturday time to counseling wayward youths in whose lives he wants to make a difference. On one of these Saturdays, he meets Rufus and instantly assesses that his problem is his deformed clubfoot. Sheppard does not know that charity begins at home. He is bothered by his selfish son, certain that Norton will be able to overcome his too-long grief if he can "stop thinking about [himself] and think what [he] can do for somebody else" (597). Sheppard's involvement with Rufus Johnson is his attempt to follow his own advice to Norton.

Norton is a young child who has been left alone too much. Without guidance or direction, he is free to have ketchup, chocolate cake, and peanut butter for breakfast. His excessive and long-sustained grief for his mother indicates she must have been a superior parent to the one he has left. Sheppard's answer to Norton's grief—his howling, his unleashed tears—is to remind the child that his mother "isn't anywhere. . . . She just isn't" (611). Norton would prefer that she be in a penitentiary, as is Rufus's mother, so he could at least see her. Norton cannot understand or accept his father's response. Underdeveloped as a character throughout the story, Norton takes a back seat to Rufus, once the clubfooted Satan-enmeshed youngster comes to stay. Foreshadowing to Norton's suicide—in order, finally, to see his mother—appears early in the story as Norton is ignored. Sheppard wants Rufus to be able to reach for the stars, so he buys a telescope. In fact, he "would have given anything to be able to put a telescope in Johnson's hands" (601); Sheppard's cost becomes literally just that—the sacrifice of his son—as the telescope is the medium through which Norton, instructed by Rufus, can see his mother. In the time that Rufus and Norton spend together, the older youth instructs the younger in some distorted basic Christian education. From Rufus, Norton learns that his mother is "on high, . . . in the sky somewhere," and that "you got to be dead to get there" (612). Rufus teaches him about timing as well, for if Norton lives too long, he will go to hell, but "right now" he has his best chance to see his mother (613). When Sheppard takes Rufus for a fitting of the new shoe he wants to buy him, Norton, tagging along, sits across the room "trussed up in a rope he had found and wound around his legs from his ankles to his knees" (610). Norton's use of the rope foreshadows his hanging, but Norton's symbolic appearance of being bound is lost on Sheppard, whose focus is the pleasure that he presumes Rufus will receive from his new shoe. Sheppard has concluded that if he can replace Rufus's old shoe with a new one, he can repair the boy.

Rufus Johnson's character portrays O'Connor's best work. His foot deformity carries symbolic weight. Sheppard interprets the clubfoot literally, seeing it as the reason and motivation for Rufus's behavior. For Rufus, the outward heaviness of his lame foot corresponds to an inward clutch of Satan's power. A bright young lad, who clearly sees and feels this controlling force, Rufus cannot tolerate the supercilious Sheppard. To Norton, who attempts a defense of his father, Rufus responds in a series of protests: "I don't care if he's good or not. He ain't *right*!" (604); "God, kid, . . . how do you stand it? . . . He thinks he's Jesus Christ!" (609); "big tin Jesus! . . . He thinks he's God. I'd rather be in the reformatory than in his house, I'd rather be in the pen!" (630). Rufus knows he is in Satan's power, and what infuriates him is that he also knows Sheppard is in Satan's power, but Sheppard does not know it. As far as Rufus is concerned, Sheppard can save himself because "nobody can save [Rufus] but Jesus" (624). Rufus is O'Connor's spokesperson for her dogmatic stance on orthodox Christianity. He is no lukewarm contender: "If I do repent, I'll be a preacher. . . . If you're going to do it, it's no sense in doing it half way" (627). No decree in the O'Connor canon more overtly states her fervent position.

Rufus is a young man of much daredevil animosity toward Sheppard precisely because he knows the biblical story so well. He knows he is headed toward a Satan-run hell unless he repents. When he steals the Bible from the ten cent store, brings it to the dinner table, and is challenged by Sheppard, he emulates the prophet Ezekiel. Sheppard tries to remove the Bible from the table, but Rufus tears out a page and chews it, then tears another with his teeth and grinds it, making a reference to the behavior of Ezekiel: "I've eaten it . . . and it was honey to my mouth!" (628; see Ezekiel 3:1–3). O'Connor's message from Rufus to Sheppard in the story comes from the notes in the Rheims-Douay for this verse: "By this eating of the book was signified the diligent attention and affection with which we are to receive, and embrace the word of God; and to let it, as it were, sink into our interior by devout meditation."[38] Sheppard cannot hear the warning. O'Connor is not ready to relinquish him yet, however, for she has Rufus deliver a line with opposite meaning to his apparent intent: "He don't know his left hand from his right" (630), a reference to

Jonah 4:11 when God claims that the people of Nineveh are worth saving even though "they know not how to distinguish between their right hand and their left."

After four incidents with various police officers suspecting Rufus's crimes, the last where Rufus reports that Sheppard has made "immor'l suggestions" (630) to him, Sheppard attempts his defense: "I did more for him than I did for my own child" (630). The sexual misconduct that Rufus's comment hints at evaporates when Rufus defines what Sheppard has said: "He's a dirty atheist. . . . He said there wasn't no hell" (630). Sheppard's own defense hangs in his mind, and he repeats the line three times, at long last coming to grips with Satan's power over him. He is now a man "shrivelled," "paralyzed, aghast" (632). Almost simultaneously though, his physical move toward Norton is instant, he is speedy to rectify his wrong and to establish a new relationship founded in a nonselfish love toward his son. But Norton hangs from an attic beam, having just launched his flight to see his mother, and Sheppard "reel[s] back like a man on the edge of a pit" (632). O'Connor uses an image similar to one that Jonathan Edwards made famous in his 1741 "Sinners in the Hands of an Angry God," in describing a God who would hold the helpless human like a spider over the edge of a flaming pit. Edwards concludes with a God who salvages the human; Sheppard teeters on "the edge." He is in the best possible position to begin his return trip toward the Teilhardian Omega Point.

"Revelation"

"Revelation" appeared in the 1964 spring *Sewanee Review,* the last story published separately before O'Connor's death that summer. O'Connor's central character, Ruby Turpin, "just sort

EVERYTHING THAT RISES MUST CONVERGE

of springs to life," but a month later when O'Connor went to the doctor's office "Ruby and Claud were in there."[39] In a letter to a friend, ten days before her death, she mentions that "Revelation" has won first place in the O. Henry Award. Critics are in general agreement that "Revelation" is O'Connor's finest story, and, in many ways, it serves as the ultimate culmination of her vision.

The story falls structurally and symbolically in two parts: the first takes place in a small Southern town doctor's waiting room where virtually every representative of the South's class structure is present: the propertied white, the common white, the poor white trash, and a "colored boy" (639). Where these people sit and how they interact with each other while waiting for their respective turns with the doctor, who is enigmatically described as "young" (645), but "a thin grey-haired man" (646), foreshadows and predicts the second part of the story. The transition occurs about two-thirds of the way through: "Claud came limping out and the Turpins went home" (647). The revelation that Ruby Turpin has at the pig parlor echoes the collective gathering of the doctor's waiting room. Just as representatives from the various class groups wait to see the head man, the doctor, a cleaned up group of each class makes its way "climbing upward into the starry field and shouting hallelujah" (654) to see another head man in heaven.

Mrs. Turpin appears in the doctor's waiting room, dwarfing it by her size, and begins, in her mind, to peg each of the assembled white patients, and the black delivery boy, into a specific Southern class. She makes the assignments by their clothes, shoes, and manners. In the doctor's waiting room, however, Mrs. Turpin cannot separate herself from the common trash. She must sit with and among them, and wait with husband Claud, who has been kicked on his calf by a cow. Once Mrs.

Turpin is inside the waiting room, she starts dual conversations, one inside her head and one out loud. Outwardly, to the gathered seven who wait with her and Claud, Mrs. Turpin is a pleasant lady with "a good disposition," but her private thoughts contradict the cheerful facade. She notes an "ugly girl" with a "pitiful" face, "blue with acne," later identified as Mary Grace; a "leathery old woman," who wears a dress of the same print as the sacks that hold chicken feed in her own pump house; "dirty yellow hair" on one who appears to be the mother of the rude young boy whose nose runs unchecked (635). At this point, Mrs. Turpin's thoughts about the "white-trashy" trio divulge her racist side: "Worse than niggers any day" (635). Silently, she clashes with this "white-trash woman" (638) on hogs, "niggers," and green stamp redemption.

The green stamps that the "white-trash woman" brings into the conversation are a reference to a popular promotional activity that swept the country through the 1950s and early 1960s. Stores gave one trading stamp for each dime spent on merchandise. Customers collected the stamps, pasted them into books provided by the promotional company, and redeemed them for a wide assortment of quality goods, including clocks, "joo'ry" (637), and contour (fitted) sheets, at some 1600 centers throughout the country. O'Connor makes double use of the "redemption" process, calling attention to the secular materialistic exchange of stamps for things and Mrs. Turpin's need for a "redemption" process that operates on a sacred level: her soul is in need of some spiritual cleansing.

Occupied with figuring her place in a society long obsessed with putting people where a Southern code dictates, Mrs. Turpin spends both night and day on the question. At night, the intricacies of the dilemma—where to place the "colored dentist in town who has two red Lincolns and a swimming pool" (636)—causes her to have fitful dreams of being "crammed in together in a box car, being ridden off to be put in a gas oven" (636). O'Connor was aware of the human atrocities committed in Germany during the war. She uses this strong analogy to suggest that Southern tradition's history of locking people into class cages fosters continued stereotyping, denies cross-class interactions, and suffocates individuals' potential growth. By day, Mrs. Turpin carries the obsession with her into the doctor's waiting room. She communicates by looks that speak to members of her own class; for example, the well-dressed lady with "red and grey suede shoes" (635): "The look that Mrs. Turpin and the pleasant lady exchanged indicated they both understood that you had to *have* certain things before you could *know* certain things" (639).

Further, Mrs. Turpin extends this obsession of her own social place by bringing Jesus into her silent conversation as coparticipator. Asserting her strength, Mrs. Turpin controls Jesus' lines: "If Jesus had said, 'You can be high society and have all the money you want and be thin and svelte-like, but you can't be a good woman with it,' she would have had to say, 'Well don't make me that then'" (642). However, when Mrs. Turpin erupts verbally with praise to Jesus because she has remembered that she has Claud, she is struck by a book "directly over her left eye" (644). Her nemesis, surprisingly not the poor white trash woman but the ugly college girl with acne, has pronounced judgment. Mary Grace, who has been the not-so-subtle target of her mother and Mrs. Turpin's conversation, the "someone" who lacks a pleasant disposition, the one who "would like to hurl them all through the plate glass window" (643), does hurl the weighty, appropriately named *Human Development* at Mrs. Turpin's head. On the floor of the doctor's waiting room, with people emulating the "moiling and roiling" (636) of Mrs. Turpin's class status dream, Mrs. Turpin has her first revelation, one that sets the stage for the obvious literal revelation that will happen that afternoon at the pig parlor. With Mary Grace sedated on the floor beside her, Mrs. Turpin has a momentary head clearing and, looking directly into Mary Grace's eyes, "there was no doubt in her mind that the girl did know her, knew her in some intense and personal way, beyond time and place and condition" (645–46).

The message that Mary Grace gives her—"Go back to hell where you came from, you old wart hog" (646)—haunts her the rest of the day. She muses upon the pronouncement while napping, trying to deny its force, wondering why she had been "singled out for the message, though there was trash in the room" (647). She repeats the message to the truckload of workers who have come in from picking cotton, even though Mrs. Turpin knows "just exactly how much Negro flattery [is] worth" (650). The message has not permeated the ways in which Mrs. Turpin treats the help; to her they are still "niggers" with whom a routine must be maintained. Their responses to the "wart hog" comment are ones of mock horror: "I'll kill her! . . . She b'long in the sylum . . . You the sweetest white lady I know." These replies climax in two women speaking simultaneously, as though the race as a class is being represented as a collective, rather than as individuals: "She pretty too. . . . Stout as she can be and sweet. Jesus satisfied with her!" (650). Even though Mrs. Turpin has actually repeated out loud the bothersome phrase, she dismisses instantly their remarks: "You could never say anything intelligent to a nigger. You could talk at them but not with them" (650).

EVERYTHING THAT RISES MUST CONVERGE

Still irritated and with "the look of a woman going single-handed, weaponless, into battle" (651), she makes her way to the pig parlor, which had been part of the morning's conversation with the "white trash woman" at the doctor's office. The number of shoats in her parlor, seven, who await their hosing down is the same as the number of people who waited earlier with her at the doctor's; the shoats' behavior is similar to the way in which the people responded once she had been attacked by Mary Grace: "The shoats were running about shaking themselves like idiot children, their little slit pig eyes searching the floor for anything left" (651). Mrs. Turpin chooses to expunge her frustrations in the pig parlor. With a "knotted" fist and "fierce voice," she demands an explanation: "What do you send me a message like that for? . . . How am I a hog and me both? How am I saved and from hell too?" (652). Her free hand aims the stream of water directly "in and out of the eye of the old sow" (652), giving a graphic answer to her own questions. A popular expression, "not in a pig's eye," means "absolutely not; no chance; no way." Her comments and rage are not directed at the pigs, however, but beyond them to some larger force, some greater entity, who has ceased to be the Jesus in her morning conversation, the one she could control, speak for. In a letter to a friend, O'Connor praises her character: "You got to be a very big woman to shout at the Lord across a hogpen. She's a country female Jacob. And that vision is purgatorial."[40] The biblical Jacob also wrestled with the Lord (Genesis 32:24), until he was convinced of the power of divine assistance.

Mrs. Turpin does not control the answer she receives at the pig parlor. Instead, a revelation, as vivid and powerful in detail and color as any biblical revelation, comes her way. She receives a "visionary light" (653), into which all the classes of people are heading off to heaven, and all of them—"companies of white-trash," "black niggers," and "battalions of lunatics and freaks" (654)—are ahead of her and Claud. She sees for the first time a blurring of the Southern class system; on some scope of eternal magnitude, earthly virtues are "burned away" (654). Mrs. Turpin, unlike any other O'Connor character, has visible proof of the Teilhardian Omega Point. Her response is sobering; the loquacious Ruby Turpin is "immobile" (654). As she makes her way back home this night, earthly possessions and Southern status yield to a humbling spiritual insight.

"Parker's Back"

Mentioned in a letter as early as December 1960, initial work on "Parker's Back" was concurrent with O'Connor's reading of Teilhard's *The Divine Milieu,* his second published book in America. However, the writing was not going well; O'Connor observed that the story was "too funny to be as serious as it ought."[41] In her review of Teilhard's book she quotes an important question: "Where is the Catholic as passionately vowed (by conviction and not by convention) to spreading the hopes of the Incarnation . . . ?" Her own reply acknowledges her bewilderment: "It is a question depressing to answer today when the sense of expectation has largely disappeared from our religion."[42] O'Connor returned to "Parker's Back" a few months before her death in August 1964. In this story, she comically illustrates how that "sense of expectation" for the "hopes of the Incarnation" can come from the most surprising of places. O'Connor creates a frustrated, tattoo-covered O. E. Parker, who cannot understand the source of his "peculiar unease" (658) and ultimately addresses his lingering malaise with a tattoo of the Byzantine Christ on his back. The story appeared in the April 1965 *Esquire,* shortly before the publication of the posthumous collection.

The title of the story, "Parker's Back," refers to his physical back, where he will eventually place a Christ tattoo that will simultaneously correspond with the direction that Parker finds himself heading. He travels literally back home to be rejected, but his true destination becomes a spiritual movement back home. A play on the title, "Parker is back," makes this declaration.

The fourteen-year-old O. E. Parker sees his first tattooed man at a fair and is "filled with emotion, lifted up as some people are when the flag passes" (657–58). From this moment, the "ordinary as a loaf of bread" Parker feels the "peculiar unease" but does not realize that he has been turned "so gently in a different direction" (658). Obtaining tattoos becomes his reason for existence; like the man at the fair, Parker wants to be a "single intricate design of brilliant color" (657). The tattoos he acquires and the order of his preferences follow a Teilhardian path toward his own Omega Point.[43] He moves from the world of the inanimate to the animal kingdom to humans, to religious symbols and deities, and, ultimately, to Christ: an eagle perched on a cannon, his mother's name on a heart, anchors and crossed rifles, tiger and panther, a cobra coiled about a torch, hawks, obscene words, Elizabeth II and Philip, Buddha, peacocks, and the Byzantine Jesus. Along the way, the tattoos he selects only satisfy him "about a month" (659), but the sought-after "intricate arabesque of colors" does not emerge; instead he is "something haphazard and botched" (659).

Although he swears with each meeting that he will not return, Sarah Ruth, the woman he courts, becomes the wife he had vowed he "would have nothing further to do with" (663). Something else controls Parker. His names that he has revealed only to "government files" but never before to man or woman he divulges "in a low voice" to Sarah Ruth (662). "Obadiah" is a common Old Testament name, occurring at least a dozen times, and which means "servant of the Lord." The Book of Obadiah, a minor prophet, is a single chapter, foretelling the destruction of Edom and predicting the day of God's rule on earth. The tattoo that Sarah Ruth, when forced to choose, will say she likes the best is the "chicken," which Parker explains is an "eagle" (660). Part of the biblical Obadiah's warning, to which the fictional Obadiah eventually heeds, has to do with the pride of the eagle: "Though thou be exalted as an eagle, and though thou set thy nest among the stars: thence will I bring thee down, saith the Lord" (Obadiah 1:4, Rheims-Douay). His middle name is "Elihue," another common Old Testament name with six references, which means God is He; the closing scene in the story is a symbolic transformation of Parker to God, giving "Elihue" its literal meaning.

Sarah Ruth is the daughter of a "Straight Gospel preacher but he was away, spreading it in Florida" (662). His influence on her life is apparent in her worldview: churches are "idolatrous," and she prefers Parker in total darkness or "dressed and with his sleeves rolled down" (663). She preaches Parker's doom at "the judgment seat of God" (664), and she extends her ascetic sense of decorum to food preparation: "Sarah Ruth just threw food in the pot and let it boil" (664). She shares a name with the biblical Sarah, wife of Abraham, who, surprisingly late in life, gave birth to Isaac; with her attitude about Parker, Sarah Ruth's pregnancy is also surprising. The biblical Ruth, after her husband dies, follows her mother-in-law Naomi into a land different from her own, declaring "thy people shall be my people, and thy God my God" (Ruth 1:16, Rheims-Douay). O'Connor's character is an ironic inversion of the biblical Ruth; she does not subscribe to Parker's view of religion. But both are driven souls: Sarah Ruth wants to deny the flesh, and Parker wants to feel the pain of the flesh.

Part of the attraction of acquiring the tattoos was the pain to the flesh, "just enough to make it . . . worth doing" (658). Parker's frustration in the marriage reflects his dissatisfaction with his life. He wants something more; he interprets this vague yearning in terms of another tattoo. The effect of the sun in his eyes as he bales hay on the afternoon of his wreck predicts the tattoo he will seek: "The sun, the size of a golf ball, began to switch regularly from in front to behind him, but he appeared to see it both places as if he had eyes in the back of his head" (665). As the tractor propels into the only tree in the field, it bursts into flame, but not before separating Parker from his shoes, which also catch on fire. Parker himself screams out in capital letters, "GOD ABOVE!" (665), as a curse and as a direct address. The scene and the details of the cast-off shoes reflect the biblical story of Moses speaking to God in the burning bush: "And [God] said: Come not nigh hither, put off the shoes from thy feet: for the place whereon thou standest is holy ground" (Exodus 3:5, Rheims-Douay). Parker's vague malaise disappears; he knows "that there [has] been a great change in his life, a leap forward into a worse unknown, and that there [is] nothing he could do about it" (666).

What Parker knows is that he must get God, literally, on his back. When the tattoo artist wants help on defining the specific area of the God subject matter, Parker's response is ambiguous: "Just God. . . . Christ. I don't care. Just so it's God" (666). "Christ" in his reply works in two directions—as a curse and as a synonym for God. When Parker, again through some mystery, is directed to the Byzantine Christ, he notes the "all-demanding eyes" (667). Parker's sacrifice is complete: he pays the artist's price, he gives the two days' time, he sleeps fitfully in the Haven of Light Mission with a "phosphorescent cross glowing at the end of the room" (669), taunting him from a history he is about to unconsciously enter, and he suffers the taunts of his peers, who remind the conscious Parker that he has "got religion" (671). A fight erupts, started by the "whirlwind" that is Parker, and ends when his buddies throw him out of the pool hall, "as if the long barnlike room were the ship from which Jonah had been cast into the sea" (672). Parker has become a "stranger to himself" (672).

Parker's realization that he needs Sarah Ruth, that her "icepick eyes" are "soft and dilatory" compared to the "all-demanding eyes" of Jesus on his back (669–70), sends him home. Returning to his literal home, he meets rejection, for Sarah Ruth does not recognize the Byzantine Jesus as God. To her, God is a spirit that "no man shall see" (674). Her retort is a heated reference to his idolatrous behavior: "Enflaming yourself with idols under every green tree!" (674), which O'Connor takes from Jeremiah 2:20, who quotes God as saying: "For on every high hill, and under every green tree thou didst prostitute thyself" (Rheims-Douay). Taking the weapon she prizes above all, the broom, she begins to thrash Parker, as she had on their first meeting when she heard the blasphemous tirade of "Jesus Christ in hell! Jesus God Almighty damm!" and he was face-to-face with a "tall raw-boned girl with a broom" (656).

He had married that girl and now she was his pregnant wife, lighting into his shoulders and then "nearly knock[ing] him senseless," causing "large welts [to form] on the face of the tattooed Christ" (674). When she takes the last look, at story's end, Parker has become symbolically a crucified Christ on Calvary. He leans against the lone "tall pecan tree on a high embankment" (655) "crying like a baby" (675). His hands, no doubt, cover his eyes as he faces into the tree and cries, giving his body against the straight trunk a crosslike appearance; outwardly, the barebacked Parker's flat Byzantine face of Christ would be puffy with welts, to give the appearance that Christ, too, cries in the lonely night. Figuratively, Parker understands his moment with the Omega Point, and the religious burden he will from this moment have to suffer. But he is not alone in the scene. Sarah Ruth moves into the realm of symbolic substance, for she stares square into the face of her own culpability, her own part in denying Christ, and misses its whole significance. In O'Connor's world, there is no middle ground; Sarah Ruth represents those who have yet to begin movement toward the Omega Point.

"Judgment Day"

The final story in the collection is a reworking of O'Connor's first story in her M.A. thesis, "The Geranium." In a letter to her editor five weeks before her death, she explains its history: "I have had [it] around since 1946 and never been satisfied with, but I hope I have it now except for details maybe."[44] A comparison of the earlier story with the rewrite marks the growth of O'Connor's talent.[45] Unlike any story O'Connor wrote, "Judgment Day" is set in the North, specifically New York City, which Tanner bemoans in the story as "no kind of place" (676). He has gone North to live with his daughter because he had refused to run "a still for a nigger" (685). Tanner's discovery in the city is that the South is home and being a "nigger's white nigger" (685) is preferable to staring out the window at a brick wall all day and missing Coleman. A literal play on "coal man," Tanner elevates his lifelong relationship with Coleman above his familial ties with his daughter.

O'Connor lived and wrote in a segregated South. In the early 1960s, new laws were beginning to make old ways illegal, but people's habits die hard. By casting a black man as Tanner's best friend, O'Connor ties the theme of accountability at Judgment Day to a topical recognition of race relations. Tanner is Coleman's double, "a negative image of himself" (683). In youth, it was Coleman's bear to Tanner's monkey, but when they grew old, they also reversed these images. When Coleman first puts on the whittled glasses Tanner has made and looks through air surrounded by white man's crafted frames, he instinctively knows how to see the world in a way that conforms to the white man's expectations. Through those glasses, Coleman sees a man, a white man, and Tanner makes his point: "Well, you treat him like he was white" (684). Coleman thus becomes the "monkey" on his back (684). For Tanner, as is true of the dominant white class, is perfectly satisfied with being the controller of Coleman, but he is not about to have the situation reversed: "Let [a black man] make a monkey out of you and all you can do is kill him or disappear" (684). When Tanner is an old man, the "brown porpoise-shaped" Doctor Foley (680) strolls into the yard and offers Tanner the opportunity to tend his still. Tanner will not stand for the insult: "The governmint ain't got around yet to forcing the white folks to work for the colored" (684). Doctor Foley's response and prediction fall on deaf ears: "The day coming . . . when the white folks IS going to be working for the colored and you might's well to git ahead of the crowd" (685). Once in the North, Tanner regrets his quick rebuke.

Through the years of his friendship with Coleman, Tanner believes he can extrapolate from that relationship an understanding of all black people. When the new tenants occupy the "hutch" next door (687), Tanner knows that this man must be a "South Alabama nigger" (688), who wants to be addressed as "Preacher" because "it had been his experience that if a negro tended to be sullen, this title usually cleared up his expression" (689). The man is not real to Tanner, who has already reduced all Northerners to little more than rabbits and pigeons in their respective hutches. Tanner is not open to reason even when he hears the new neighbor is not from South Alabama but from New York City and is not a preacher but an actor. To understand, Tanner needs harsher treatment from the actor; he is "slammed" against the wall and called a "wool-hat red-neck son-of-a-bitch peckerwood old bastard" (690).

When he recovers from this incident, he fantasizes about going home, playing a trick on his old friend, jumping from the coffin and shouting "Judgment Day! Judgment Day!" (692). Returning to the South, dead or alive, becomes his sole obsession. His new fear is that his daughter, who had promised to bury him in the South, has no intention of keeping her word. If he is going there, he has to take the responsibility himself. On a symbolic level, the story suggests that when Judgment Day comes and the sheep are separated from the goats, Tanner clearly wants to be on the sheep side. It is this hope that has kept him from "killing a nigger" (684). When he discovers his daughter is going to betray him by burying him right there in New York City, he gives her the

Judgment Day lecture: "The Judgment is coming. . . . The sheep'll be separated from the goats. Them that kept their promises from them that didn't" (686). O'Connor refers to Matthew 25:32: "And all nations shall be gathered together before him, and he shall separate them one from another, as the shepherd separateth the sheep from the goats" (Rheims-Douay). Tanner fears the everlasting fire and brimstone that is promised the goats; his daughter and the new neighbor see this as "hardshell Baptist hooey" (678) and as "crap. There ain't no Jesus and there ain't no God" (690).

Once the daughter has left for the store, Tanner begins his long walk to the South, but the stairwell becomes a trap of unlighted steps where Tanner pitches forward, landing "upsidedown in the middle of the flight" (694). He is caught halfway in a purgatorylike existence. He flees from this Northern hell, where even his own kin flaunt their power over God's omnipotence, to the Southern heaven that awaits him, now that he has learned the lesson that transcends regional limitations. His last words are to the neighbor, still in his old belief that "Preacher" is a correct address: "Hep me up, Preacher. I'm on my way home" (694). Tanner dies in the stocklike spokes of the stairwell banister where the neighbor, who denies Judgment Day, puts him. Tanner has done everything in his power to return home to the South he understands so well, where his language and attitude contradict his behavior toward his lifelong friend, Coleman. By himself, however, he is unable to accomplish this goal, for his daughter buries him in New York City. Noticing the peril to her health, she ships the body home to Corinth, a Georgia city that shares a name with the biblical place that houses a church of God; her "good looks" return (695), and her movement toward an Omega Point can begin. It was to the Corinthian people that Paul delivered his profound words on love. O'Connor suggests, at the end, that Tanner has seen through a glass darkly but will now see face to face (Corinthians 13:12). Tanner's Omega Point can come only when he returns to Corinth.

Notes

1. Flannery O'Connor, *The Habit of Being,* ed. Sally Fitzgerald (New York: Farrar, Straus and Giroux, 1979) 498.

2. O'Connor, *Habit* 498.

3. O'Connor, *Habit* 449.

4. O'Connor, *Habit* 575.

5. O'Connor, *Habit* 580.

6. Her reviews have been compiled by Leo J. Zuber in *The Presence of Grace and Other Book Reviews by Flannery O'Connor,* ed. Carter W. Martin, Athens: U of Georgia P, 1983.

7. Flannery O'Connor, "Outstanding Books, 1931–1961," *American Scholar* 30 (Fall 1961): 618.

8. O'Connor, *Habit* 388.

9. O'Connor, *Presence* 161.

10. O'Connor, *Habit* 571.

11. Pierre Teilhard de Chardin, *The Phenomenon of Man* (New York: Harper & Row, 1959) 258.

12. Teilhard, *Phenomenon* 271.

13. O'Connor, *Habit* 368.

14. Quoted in the foreward by Max H. Begouen, *Building the Earth,* by Pierre Teilhard de Chardin (New York: Avon, 1965): 11.

15. "Nothing but the Truth," *New Yorker* 11 Sept. 1965: 221.

16. Robert Drake, "Hair-Curling Gospel," *Christian Century* 19 May 1965: 656.

17. Granville Hicks, "A Cold, Hard Look at Humankind," *Saturday Review* 29 May 1965: 23–24.

18. Richard Poirier, "If You Know Who You Are You Can Go Anywhere," *New York Times Book Review* 30 May 1965: 6, 22.

19. Webster Schott, "Flannery O'Connor: Faith's Stepchild," *Nation* 13 Sept. 1965: 142.

20. "Grace through Nature," *Newsweek* 31 May 1965: 86.

21. Irving Howe, "Flannery O'Connor's Stories," *New York Review of Books* 30 Sept. 1965: 16–17.

22. Flannery O'Connor, *Flannery O'Connor: Collected Works,* ed. Sally Fitzgerald (New York: Library of America, 1988) 490. All parenthetical citations from the stories in *Everything That Rises Must Converge* are from this edition.

23. Rosemary M. Magee, ed., *Conversations with Flannery O'Connor* (Jackson: UP of Mississippi, 1987) 110.

24. See John C. Shields, "Flannery O'Connor's 'Greenleaf' and the Myth of Europa and the Bull" *Studies in Short Fiction* 18 (1981): 421–31.

25. See Kristen Meek, "Flannery O'Connor's 'Greenleaf' and the Holy Hunt of the Unicorn" *Flannery O'Connor Bulletin* 19 (1990): 30–37.

26. O'Connor, *Habit* 175.

27. O'Connor, *Habit* 175.

28. O'Connor, *Presence* 130.

29. O'Connor, *Habit* 186.

30. O'Connor, *Habit* 190.

31. Elsdon C. Smith, *Dictionary of American Family Names* (New York: Harper and Brothers, 1956) 78.

32. O'Connor, *Habit* 354.

33. Frederick Asals, "The Double in Flannery O'Connor's Stories," *Flannery O'Connor Bulletin* 9 (1980): 68. See also Asals, *Flannery O'Connor: The Imagination of Extremity,* Athens: U of Georgia P, 1982. Asals also explores a Jungian interpretation.

34. Marshall Bruce Gentry, "The Hand of the Writer in 'The Comforts of Home,'" *Flannery O'Connor Bulletin* 20 (1991): 62.

35. John Hawkes, "Flannery O'Connor's Devil," *Sewanee Review* 70 (Summer 1962): 399–400.

36. Robert Fitzgerald, introduction, *Everything That Rises Must Converge,* by Flannery O'Connor (New York: Farrar, Straus and Giroux, 1965): 28.

37. O'Connor, *Habit* 491.

38. The Holy Bible. Rheims-Douay Version (Rockford, IL: Tan Books and Publishers, 1989): 893.

39. O'Connor, *Habit* 546, 552.

40. O'Connor, *Habit* 577.

41. O'Connor, *Habit* 427.

42. O'Connor, *Presence* 107–8.

43. See Karl-Heinz Westarp, "Teilhard de Chardin's Impact on Flannery O'Connor: A Reading of 'Parker's Back,'" *Flannery O'Connor Bulletin* 12 (1983): 93–113.

44. O'Connor, *Habit* 588.

45. In the Library of America edition, this story is slightly different from the first edition of the published collection. Final changes O'Connor made on her typescript were not incorporated into the 1965 edition. For an overview of the story's various drafts, see Karl-Heinz Westarp, "'Judgement Day': The Published Text versus Flannery O'Connor's Final Version," *Flannery O'Connor Bulletin* 11 (1982): 108–22.

CHAPTER SIX

Mystery and Manners

Mystery and Manners is a collection of O'Connor's occasional writings, selected and edited by Sally and Robert Fitzgerald. According to the book's foreword, they deleted repetitions from over fifty typescripts to present "interesting arguments in their best available form," rearranging and transposing where necessary, but making every effort to be "scrupulous to retain Flannery O'Connor's thought and phrasing."[1] The volume, which includes fourteen essays in six sections, was published by Farrar, Straus and Giroux in 1969, five years after O'Connor's death. Still in print a quarter century later, the collection has lasted through twenty printings. The first and the last selections are a reprinted article, "The King of the Birds," and an introduction to *A Memoir of Mary Ann.* The middle four sections contain essays that O'Connor first wrote as talks for the lecture circuit to university students in both literature and writing classes, Catholic organizations, regional literary symposia, and the club ladies. The first group of three essays addresses writing concerns in a regional, specifically Southern, milieu. The second group of three essays confronts the nature and activity of fiction. The third coupling of two essays faces questions of how literature should be taught. The fourth cluster of four essays demonstrates how the Catholic novelist is imbued with pertinent responsibilities for the Catholic church.

Contemporary reviews of *Mystery and Manners* blend the writer's life with the messages of the essays. For O'Connor is past tense now, and her while-she-lived questionable prosaic efforts are replaced with reviewer sympathy and dogmatic assurance: O'Connor's work was "brilliant," and these essays can "shed light on her profound but sometimes difficult work."[2] In a lengthy review in the *New York Review of Books,* Richard Gilman rhapsodizes about his friendship with O'Connor, interpreting the book through his personal knowledge of the writer. Gilman panders to his readers; knowing that O'Connor was an "intense, unapologetic, and unshakable Catholic" who "expected so little beyond internal satisfactions," he subjugates the power of the ideas in the essays to the pathetic and strong woman he is trying to immortalize. Calling her life "lonely, besieged, and unnoticed," he shifts the emphasis from her words to her self.[3] The *New York Times Book Review,* after expressing gratitude for the essays, which provide "sensible and significant reflections on the business of writing," goes to the book's pith: this book explains the "synergetic influence" of both mystery and manners in O'Connor's writing, that she was unwilling to "separate spirit from matter," grounding, as O'Connor says, "the supernatural . . . in the concrete."[4]

Other reviews are somewhat careless in their comments. *Harper's Magazine* wrongfully cites "The King of the Birds" as "originally published in *Esquire.*"[5] "The King of the Birds" appeared in *Holiday* under a different title. The *New Yorker* miscounts the number of essays, but notes that Henry James is "the writer most frequently quoted." The reviewer has high praise for the collection, suggesting that the writings are "truer and sounder and wiser about the nature of fiction and their responsibilities of reader and writer than anything published since James's 'The Art of the Novel.'"[6]

UNDERSTANDING FLANNERY O'CONNOR

"The King of the Birds"

When the article was previously published as "Living with a Peacock" in the September 1961 issue of *Holiday,* it appeared with a full-page color reproduction of "Limpy" with his four-foot erect tail of shimmering suns, one of O'Connor's forty-some peacocks. The article chronicles O'Connor's fascination with fowl in general—from her childhood days with a pet Cochin Bantam chicken that walked backward, through her growing passion for pheasants, quail, turkeys, geese, mallard ducks, Japanese and Polish bantams, and a cross between them. O'Connor claims she "felt a lack" (4), until instinct led her to the peacock.

O'Connor does not attempt to justify her interest in the peacock. To questions often asked of her about the obsession— why does she raise peacocks and what are they good for—she has no "short or reasonable answer" (4), and the latter query "gets no answer . . . because it deserves none" (10). Her attraction to them is one of reverence, even awe—respect for the peacock's attitude, with or without his flourished tail. While the cock itself is saved only by its "bearing . . . from being a laughingstock" (9), the spread tail elicits a range of emotions, none of them "laughter," instead, usually "silence" (9). O'Connor is fully aware of the humility she feels in the peacock's presence, and as a crafter of language, the fact that the peacock can stop language and demonstrate the "inadequacy of human speech" (10) is not lost on her. Noting the responses of visitors to her home, O'Connor found that many people were "congenitally unable to appreciate the sight of the peacock" (10), being reduced to utterances that diminished their reaction to the moment—"Never saw such long ugly legs" (12), "Get a load of that bastard!" (10). In spite of their

trouble to others, she delights in their thriving, in their multiply-
ing, for she recognizes "that, in the end, the last word will be
theirs" (21).

Peacocks appear in one of her stories, "The Displaced
Person," and function as both themselves and symbols of the
transfiguration of Christ. In this story, Father Flynn's reverence
for the peacock is contrasted with Mrs. McIntyre's annoyance
with their presence. She is one of the "congenitally" disabled.
Moreover, characters in other stories walk as peacocks do; for
example, Manley Pointer in "Good Country People" and Julian
in "Everything That Rises Must Converge." Manley Pointer
becomes a momentary Christ symbol in his story as he appears to
walk on water, but Julian's attitude is one of martyrdom, false
bravado, an ironic turn on the peacock's bearing.

O'Connor includes in her essay the indifferent reaction of
the peahen to the peacock, the peahen's laying of her five or six
eggs, and the twenty-eight-day wait for the hatching of the
peachicks, but this is empirical data and much less interesting
than the mystery of the peacock's dazzling tail. The sound of the
peacock's cry is, for O'Connor, "like a cheer for an invisible
parade" (15). This is something that cannot be explained or
taught to others, for the melancholy will interpret the peacock's
cry as melancholy. In other words, people will see and hear as
they are capable or so inclined. When a visitor comes to buy a
calf, his "churren" ask him what "thet thang" is. The old man has
O'Connor's appreciation, for he recognizes that the peacock is
"the king of the birds!" (13). The children's response to their
father is similar to young Nelson's regard for Mr. Head in "The
Artificial Nigger," for upon hearing his answer, "their expres-
sions [appear] annoyed, as if they disliked catching the old man

in the truth" (13). O'Connor has a kinship with those people she perceives value the peacock; together, silently, they partake in the mystery that is beyond understanding.

"The Fiction Writer and His Country"

Appearing first in a 1957 collection called *The Living Novel, A Symposium,* edited by Granville Hicks, this essay responds to questions posed in a *Life* editorial. Arguing for a literature that reflects the unparalleled prosperity of America and not one that sounds "as if it were written by an unemployed homosexual living in a packing-box shanty on the city dump while awaiting admission to the county poorhouse," the editorial asks "who speaks for America today?"[7] O'Connor notes that no one had answered who spoke "from the standpoint of Christian concerns" (26). To this writer, America as "country" becomes less important than the depiction of "country" as "everything from the actual countryside . . . , on to and through the peculiar characteristics of his region . . . and on, through, and under all of these to his true country . . . what is eternal and absolute" (27).

The editorial attacks the South in particular because it is "isolated" and "should produce the most anguished writing."[8] O'Connor feels that this would be a surprise to most Southern writers, who recognize that the anguish comes because the South "is not alienated enough, that every day we are getting more and more like the rest of the country" (28–29). Being threatened is one of the South's advantages, manifest in its manners, and to a writer, manners "are of such great consequence . . . that any kind will do. Bad manners are better than no manners at all" (29). She makes a connection between her use of these manners and her conscience; the fading manners have to be used "in the light of an ultimate concern" (29).

O'Connor makes a reference to the "Manichean spirit of the times" (33). Manicheism is a heresy that has its origins in the third century from a Persian dreamer variously named Mani, Manes, or Manicheus, whose teachings included a dual principle of creation—a good from God, manifested in a human's spirit, and an evil from Satan, situated in the body. The two are in constant struggle with each other.[9] O'Connor was fiercely anti-Manichean, believing in the impossibility of separating mystery from manners, judgment from vision, and good from evil. O'Connor's vision was Christian orthodoxy, a position that she knows could not "be taken halfway or one that is particularly easy in these times to make transparent in fiction" (32). Because the writer with Christian concerns is likely to be the least tolerant of that which is unacceptable, that which is "halfway," O'Connor suggests it is this writer's task to point out to the audience that which is unacceptable, which may not appear as such to the audience. The writer then proceeds to use distortion to make the point: "To the hard of hearing you shout, and for the almost-blind you draw large and startling figures" (34).

The *Life* editorial calls for novels that show the "joy of life," and O'Connor suggests that this could best be accomplished by the advertising agencies. The artist's job is different, for the talented know that to respond to their "country," they must know themselves in their world and must see one through the other, the outside from the inside. If they know this much, they also know what they lack, their limitations, so humility is the result of self-knowledge, "and this is not a virtue conspicuous in any national character" (35). Who speaks for America must speak for Truth, not joy. O'Connor elicits St. Cyril of Jerusalem, a fourth-century bishop noted for his valuable lectures on Catholic instructions. In one such lecture, Cyril warns the wary traveler that the "dragon sits by the side of the road," and all must pass him to get to the "Father of Souls." It is the "mysterious passage past [the dragon] . . . that stories of any depth will always be concerned to tell" (35). To turn toward the storyteller, the Truth, should be America's task. Transmittal of joy is not the novelist's business.

"Some Aspects of the Grotesque in Southern Fiction"

O'Connor begins this essay with what may appear to be a contradiction. Moving backward and forward in time, as she does throughout the essay, she suggests there was once a time when writers could speak collectively, citing the Vanderbilt group of the 1920s in *I'll Take My Stand,* but that the time has come for each writer to speak for the self. However, she then speaks for all writers when she says that "every writer . . . hopes to show that . . . he is a realist" (37). O'Connor notes that readers point out to her "that life in Georgia is not at all the way [she] picture[s] it" (38). Her characters have been called "grotesque" by the Northern reader, and her effort in this essay is to interpret her use of the grotesque, a tool that for her is an extension of realism. This kind of realism drives deep and is determined by the writer's concern that characters have "an inner coherence, if not always a coherence to their social framework. Their fictional qualities lean away from typical social patterns, toward mystery and the unexpected" (40). None of O'Connor's characters conforms to "typical social patterns," and the more interesting ones operate in response to a mysterious source that ultimately conveys the character's "inner coherence."

She uses the grotesque to connect one image with two points: "One is a point in the concrete, and the other is a point not visible to the naked eye" (42). Hazel Motes's eyes can serve as such an image; they are concretely in his head and every other character in *Wise Blood* has something to say about them, but when Haze blinds himself, his eyes take on a mysterious meaning. O'Connor acknowledges that this fiction "is going to be wild, that it is almost of necessity going to be violent and comic" (43). Haze Motes meets this description soundly. He is an example of a freak. Southern writers know about freaks because, as O'Connor says, they are "still able to recognize one" (44). Characters, as well as people, are measured against a concept of a whole human, and "in the South the conception of man is still . . . theological," not "Christ-centered," but "certainly Christ-haunted" (44).

Further, Southern writers have other Southern writers with whom to contend. Nobody wants to do "badly what has already been done" (45). O'Connor acknowledges Faulkner's presence among them, calling attention to his syntactical power: "Nobody wants his mule and wagon stalled on the same track the Dixie Limited is roaring down" (45). Each Southern writer, then, must look more deeply into the same terrain, and this is how they become "realist[s] of distances" (46).

The serious writer, ultimately, is going to be called on to deal with the "tired reader" who wants "her heart lifted up" (48), and grotesque characters do not "satisfy the tired reader" (50). When Dante wrote, he could divide his territory "pretty evenly between hell, purgatory, and paradise" because he lived in a time when "that balance was achieved in the faith of his age" (49). O'Connor sees the challenge of the novelist to write novels that have not yet been written, where vision alone serves as guide in an age "which doubts both fact and value, which is swept this way and that by momentary convictions" (49). The writer must "distort without destroying" and avoid writing novels "about men in gray-flannel suits" (50). The latter is a reference to Sloan Wilson's *The Man in the Gray Flannel Suit,* a 1955 best seller with a happy ending, a book that would be suitable for the "tired reader." O'Connor wants never to appeal to the "tired reader."

"The Regional Writer"

O'Connor delivered this talk to the Georgia Writers' Association when she received a scroll for *The Violent Bear It Away.* Particularly honored by this award, O'Connor notes that any award is "valuable in direct ratio to how near they come from home" (52). Remembering that when she was in college twenty years earlier, in the mid to late 1940s, Hawthorne, Melville, James, Crane, and Hemingway "were balanced on the Southern side by Br'er Rabbit" (56). In equal company this emblematic animal from the Uncle Remus tales of Joel Chandler Harris could hold his own, "but here too much was being expected of him" (56). Noting the progress of Southern arts in the intervening twenty years, she comments on the proliferating number of Southern arts festivals where "someone who is a part of what he writes about . . . is recognized as such" (56).

Her concern is for what may be in the process of being lost in the South. Having read a collection of student stories on one of her visits to a college campus, she remarks that all the stories "hadn't been influenced by the outside world at all, only by the television" (56). She ponders the irony of a writer discovering he or she can live in the South and a Southern audience becoming aware of its literature "just in time to discover that being Southern is relatively meaningless" (57). In the midst of these concerns about a grim future, she acknowledges the "positive signifi-cance" of being a Georgia writer, and not in the local color sense (57). An identity is not found on the surface, but it lies deep within a community. The artist will be the one who comes most close to appreciating its mystery.

Discussing ways in which regional literature grows beyond provincialism, she makes a case for the best American fiction being regional—"it has passed to and stayed longest wherever there has been a shared past, a sense of alikeness, and the possibility of reading a small history in a universal light" (58). She feels that the South has the advantage here because in losing the Civil War, the people of the South entered the "modern world with an inburnt knowledge of human limitations and with a sense of mystery" (59). This historical defeat gave the South an opportunity for another Fall, an allusion to the biblical story of Adam and Eve leaving the Garden of Eden. Innocence was replaced by an acute awareness of and a dependence on an older story. O'Connor notes that in H. L. Mencken's 1920 scathing indictment of the South, "The Sahara of the Bozart," he "called the South the Bible Belt, in scorn and thus in incredible inno-cence" (59). Southern people carry with them visions of various biblical faces; this knowledge felt and known in the community is what separates Georgia from Hollywood or New York. When the writer can no longer find this old biblical knowledge there, a literature that transcends provincialism will cease to exist. The writer's task is to find the "peculiar crossroads where time and place and eternity somehow meet" (59). For O'Connor, the crossroads existed concretely in middle Georgia and mysteri-ously in a deeper biblical history that probed an invisible world.

UNDERSTANDING FLANNERY O'CONNOR

"The Nature and Aim of Fiction"

This essay is a composite of talks O'Connor gave on the college circuit. At the beginning, she is addressing a writing class on the subject of "How the Writer Writes." Taking immediate offense at the title, she makes clear "there is no such thing as THE writer" (63). She believes that few people really care about writing well, but many are interested in publishing, selling their work, and being a writer. O'Connor speaks for the serious writer, who has developed the "habit of art," as Jacques Maritain called it. O'Connor's interpretation of Maritain is that a writer becomes serious when he or she develops a "certain quality or virtue of the mind" (64–65) and writes "something that is valuable in itself and that works in itself" (65). Maritain was a twentieth-century French Roman Catholic philosopher, who believed that one could know reality through diverse legitimate ways, which included philosophy, science, poetry, and mysticism. Maritain was important to O'Connor as an interpreter of St. Thomas Aquinas and for his firm belief that to exist is to act. Having the gift of art, O'Connor was compelled to act on that gift, to create something good within itself, for the "person who aims after art in his work aims after truth, in an imaginative sense, no more and no less" (65).

She indicates two things that should be common starting places in the development of any story, whether that story is a short story or a novel: that the story is grounded in the concrete and that the activity of the story unfolds around the reader—that it is presented, not reported because "when you write fiction you are speaking *with* character and action, not *about* character and action" (76). A symbol grows out of the concrete details, such that the symbol has an "essential place in the literal level of the story,

[and] operate[s] in depth as well as on the surface, increasing the story in every direction" (71). She cites Haze Motes's rat-colored Essex as an example of a symbol, for it is a "pulpit and his coffin," "means of escape," and "death-in-life" symbol (72). In order for a symbol to work on "different levels of reality," a writer needs to develop "anagogical" vision, which she defines as having to do with "the Divine life and our participation in it" (72). By extension, the anagogical level of any story is that level in which the reader becomes aware that the surface antics and the bizarre twists of the lunatic fringe are much more deeply intertwined with a mystery that is of eternal consequence. In order to arrive at the anagogical level, the writer must make every selection for a reason; every word, detail, and incident must be arranged in a "certain time-sequence for a reason" (75). Her own comments reflect St. Thomas of Aquinas's definition of art: "reason in making" (82). A thirteenth-century Dominican, Thomas is considered by many to be the greatest of the Catholic theologians and philosophers.

On speaking about the role of teachers, O'Connor notes that their work should be negative. A teacher should do nothing if there is no gift present in the student, except to squelch that student's penchant to write, for "there's many a best-seller that could have been prevented by a good teacher" (84–85). If the student has a gift, then the teacher should keep that student from heading in the wrong direction. A person with a gift should stare at everything, for there "is nothing that doesn't require his attention" (84). The writer needs to "contemplate experience, not to be merged in it" (84). Competence is not enough to write a story, thinks O'Connor; there is no substitute for vision. Teachers do their best work when they stifle those with no gift.

UNDERSTANDING FLANNERY O'CONNOR

"Writing Short Stories"

O'Connor prepared the core of this essay for delivery at a Southern Writers' Conference. She had been sent seven short stories, and her task was to read the stories and make comments that would be helpful to the writers. The point she makes in this essay is one she repeats often: people know what a story is until they try to write one. For O'Connor, formula, technique, and theory cannot replace the story or guide the story. A writer must write the story first and then speculate on those components that come together to accomplish the writing of it. A story must start with a person who shares in the "general human condition" and in some "specific human situation" (90). Problems and abstract issues must be secondary to people and concrete situations. For a reader to feel the person in a situation, the fiction must operate through the senses. O'Connor knows that a writer cannot learn this in "the head," but must develop this ability "in the habits" (92). In a reference to Jacques Maritain's insistence on the "habit of art," O'Connor makes clear that a writer has to develop a way of seeing that embodies all the senses. This vision is guided by a writer's judgment and therefore judgment determines selection of details.

Making reference to two of her own stories, she illustrates her emphasis on vision directed by judgment. First, in "The Life You Save May Be Your Own," she has Tom T. Shiftlet, the one-armed tramp, marry his employer's idiot daughter in order to obtain a car. He abandons the idiot in a roadside diner. O'Connor's selection of specific details all assist in her story's meaning, so this "is a complete story. There is nothing more relating to the mystery of that man's personality that could be shown through that particular dramatization" (94). However, when the story was adapted for television, the adapter had the tramp "have a change of heart and go back and pick up the idiot daughter and the two of them ride away, grinning madly" (94–95). O'Connor was aware that this ending satisfied many people because it answered a question readers asked: What happened to the idiot daughter? But this ending destroyed O'Connor's story. She understood "there will always be people who will refuse to read the story you have written" (95). The second story to elucidate her point about judgment in vision is "Good Country People." One-legged Joy/ Hulga Hopewell is the heart of the action, and her wooden leg becomes paramount as the story develops. O'Connor explains how the leg moves from its surface reality to an important symbol, so that when it is stolen by Manley Pointer, the Bible salesman, the theft is far more than a "low joke" (98). Because O'Connor starts with people in concrete situations, their created personalities dictate their actions. When Joy/Hulga's leg is stolen, the reader is shocked, and O'Connor's belief is that "it produced a shock for the writer" as well (100).

O'Connor's concern about the seven stories she had been sent to read included these basic deficiencies: no memorable images nor metaphors, no local idioms, and no penetration inside the characters. In the South, there is no reason for characters to sound like television. The characters had no memorable person-alities because they had no distinct use of Southern speech patterns. Fiction must employ a sense of mystery that comes through a character's manners, which emanate from a concrete situation. Make the characters real, she advises her audience, so that both reader and writer can "discover something" (106).

UNDERSTANDING FLANNERY O'CONNOR

"On Her Own Work"

Within this patchwork of commentaries, the most important is an introduction O'Connor used at Hollins College in October 1963 to prepare the students for listening to her read "A Good Man Is Hard to Find." Before she approaches the grist of her remarks, she expresses her concern about the state of literary dissection: "Every time a story of mine appears in a Freshman anthology, I have a vision of it, with its little organs laid open, like a frog in a bottle" (108). She feels something is wrong when a story is reduced to "a problem to be solved" (108). The proper use of literary analysis is to find more ways to enjoy a story.

By way of introducing "A Good Man Is Hard to Find," O'Connor develops two specific points—her use of both violence and the devil. This story is one that "should elicit from [the reader] a degree of pity and terror, even though its way of being serious is a comic one" (108). In thinking about how a story works, O'Connor claims she is after a gesture that is "both totally right and totally unexpected . . . both in character and beyond character . . . to suggest both the world and eternity" (111). The gesture, when it works, moves the story to the anagogical level, where mystery resides. The gesture in "A Good Man Is Hard to Find" is the moment when the grandmother reaches out to touch the Misfit, calling him one of her own children. O'Connor accomplishes this moment in the midst of violence. The grandmother faces the "most significant position life offers the Christian. She is facing death" (110). Only at this point are people capable of being their best selves, when they will reveal all they "will have to take into eternity" (114). The grandmother's son and his family have just been murdered by the Misfit and his henchmen, and she faces the ultimate sting of violence, her own imminent death. This is the brand of violence that can return "characters to reality and prepar[e] them to accept their moment of grace" (112). The gesture, which anticipates the coming moment of grace, is not without the presence of the devil, who behaves as an "unwilling instrument of grace" (118). This is not to say that the Misfit is the devil itself, but the character does exist in the "territory held largely by the devil" (118). The Misfit, who instantly puts three bullets through the grandmother upon hearing her words of revelation that he is her own child, will not be free from those words. O'Connor suggests the grandmother's words, "like the mustard-seed, will grow to be a great crow-filled tree in the Misfit's heart" (113). Viewed with an emphasis on the "action of grace . . . not for the dead bodies" (113), the violence is placed in perspective: "Violence is a force which can be used for good or evil" (113). The moment just before death is optimum for revealing "what we are essentially" (113).

"The Teaching of Literature"

O'Connor presented the core of this essay to a group of secondary school English teachers. She came to this audience with clear assumptions about the roles of writer, teacher, and reader. The writer must continue to "render what he sees and not what he thinks he ought to see" (131). The teacher must serve as the "middleman" (122) and try to "change the face of the best-seller list" (128). The reader serves as the authority because, after all, the novelist "writes about life, and so anyone living considers himself an authority on it" (122).

Speaking from the vantage point of one who is doing the primary work of literature, writing the text, O'Connor addresses those whose mission is to deliver the literature to a nation of would-be readers. O'Connor's suggestion is that the study of novels "must be a technical study" (124). O'Connor believes that the writer and the teacher have a mutual concern—"a love of language and what can be done with it in the interests of dramatic truth" (124), but that the student/reader is an inescapable part of the triangle. She feels that teachers have been avoiding their responsibility in teaching literature by teaching literary history (who wrote what when and what was happening in the world at the time), teaching the author and his or her psychology (why was Hawthorne melancholy, why did James prefer England to America), teaching sociology (how a text represents a social problem), or "integrat[ing] it out of existence" (127) by teaching literature *with* any other subject in the school curriculum. O'Connor speaks for new criticism, a critical perspective that takes its name from John Crowe Ransom's 1941 *The New Criticism*. New criticism stresses the importance of turning attention to the text as an object in itself, without contextual interference. Literature has an intrinsic worth and the demonstration and defense of this worth is the teacher's duty.

O'Connor explores her interpretation of Henry James's use of mystery and manners: "The mystery he was talking about is the mystery of our position on earth, and the manners are those conventions which, in the hands of the artist, reveal that central mystery" (124). O'Connor encourages the teacher to teach the form of the novel, which is inseparable from its meaning. Through an understanding of form, the student should then be able to contemplate "the mystery embodied in it" (129). In defense of the battle-weary novelist, who feels the attack from a public seeking happy books that reflect America's prosperity, she claims that her books are about the poor because the poor are the common denominator for making the point that the "basic experience of everyone is the experience of human limitation"

(131). The fiction writer is delighted that the poor will be always present because they best can demonstrate how the "mystery of existence is always showing through the texture of their ordinary lives" (133).

"Total Effect and the Eighth Grade"

This essay first appeared 21 March 1963, in the *Georgia Bulletin,* a Catholic paper associated with the Diocese of Atlanta. It was then titled "Fiction Is a Subject with a History; It Should Be Taught That Way." O'Connor is responding to parents' concerns about the modern fiction their children are assigned in school, making reference to two contemporary legal suits involving John Steinbeck's *East of Eden* and John Hersey's *A Bell for Adano.* The title, reinstated from her typescript, is a reference to terminology used in the courts—a book is not judged by its isolated parts but by its "total effect" (136). O'Connor suggests that students in high school are not equipped to determine the "total effect" of modern fiction because teachers in the eighth and ninth grade have not served their students well; teachers have been "haphazard" in the selection of assigned books from a "safe" state reading list (136). O'Connor is perplexed by an educational system that "has asked the child what he would tolerate learning" (137) in the study of literature, but does not consult the child about algebra or "if he finds it satisfactory that some French verbs are irregular" (137). In past generations, students learned Homer and Virgil, but "our children are too stupid now to enter the past imaginatively" (137).

In a time that predates canonical questioning, O'Connor provides all-male suggestions; students need to know the best of James Fenimore Cooper, Nathaniel Hawthorne, Herman Melville, the early Henry James, and Stephen Crane. These works should be preceded with the "better English novelists of the eighteenth and nineteenth centuries" (138). O'Connor suggests there is much to learn about how a "sea-change" effects a literary form (139). With this knowledge, students are more apt to be prepared to meet the demands of modern fiction, which appears simpler but is not. As an example of the complexity of modern fiction, O'Connor cites the morality problem. A historical background will help students understand that adultery in the Bible or in *Anna Karenina* is a sin; whereas in modern fiction, adultery is, "at most, an inconvenience" (140). Because students live in a "fractured culture" where adults in responsible positions cannot agree on moral matters or that "moral matters should come before literary ones when there is a conflict between them" (140), it is essential that students have a strong foundation. Students should not be consulted in the matter; their tastes are being formed.

"The Church and the Fiction Writer"

This essay first appeared in the 30 March 1957 issue of *America,* a small Catholic weekly magazine with an editorial policy that places Catholic interests at its forefront. O'Connor connects the writer who is Catholic with the concerns of the Catholic church. Always aware of audience, O'Connor counters the perceived popular opinion that the Catholic "suffers from a parochial aesthetic and a cultural insularity" (144) by suggesting that his or her problem is deciding what the Catholic church demands of its believers. For the modern world, a term here that excludes the devout Catholic, is divided about the depths of mystery—"part of it trying to eliminate mystery while another part tries to rediscover it in disciplines less personally demanding than religion" (145). Some Catholic writers may be using fiction to prove the truth of their faith, but O'Connor reminds the reader that all the writer has is "what-is"; "fiction can transcend its limitations only by staying within them" (146). She uses Henry James's reference to "felt life" to reiterate her position on the Catholic writer who "will feel life from the standpoint of the central Christian mystery" (146). Every time O'Connor uses this expression she is referring to the death of Jesus Christ on the cross and His resurrection, and the Catholic person's understanding of that event in his or her individual and ongoing life. The Catholic writer who believes that God has found humans "worth dying for" will have a vision that is enlarged, not narrowed, by the Catholic religion (146).

O'Connor submits that the average Catholic reader is likely to want to separate nature and grace, flesh and spirit, and when this separation occurs, the conception of the supernatural is reduced to "pious cliché" (147). Nature is recognized in literature as either sentimental or obscene. O'Connor points out the similarity of these portrayals. Both are distortions, for "sentimentality" is an excess, an overemphasis on innocence, and "obscenity" is an excess, an overemphasis on lust, disconnecting "sex with its hard purpose" (148). By "hard purpose," O'Connor means the biblical call for procreation. The Catholic reader needs to resist the pull to separate; fiction works when it reinforces a "sense of the supernatural by grounding it in concrete, observable reality" (146).

Acknowledging the possible gap between the response of the reader and the intention of the writer, O'Connor knows that the reader may stare into the face of sin while the writer sees salvation. An example from her writing is Haze Motes's blinding in *Wise Blood*. For the writer, when Haze blinded himself, he achieved salvation, but the Manichean reader could easily see this act as the moment of Haze's damnation. O'Connor, who uses François Mauriac as her support, chooses not to be responsible for the reader. Winner of the 1952 Nobel Prize for Literature, Mauriac was a French Catholic writer who cast in each of his novels a religious soul struggling with the problems of sin, grace, and salvation. He concluded that the reader could be dismissed by this advice: "Purify the source" (149). In a letter, O'Connor explains the reference.[10] A young man had written Mauriac that his reading of one of Mauriac's novels had caused him to think of committing suicide. At first dismayed, Mauriac concluded in his 1929 *God and Mammon* that he was not responsible for the immaturity of his reader's mind; his responsibility was to "purify the source"—his own mind.

For O'Connor, belief in a "fixed dogma" adds dimension. Working from "what-is" in reality with characters adequately motivated in a credible imitation of a way of life, the writer still needs more to have a story. The mystery must come through the manners, "grace through nature," and once everything is presented, looming beyond and beneath must be "that sense of Mystery which cannot be accounted for by any human formula" (153).

"Novelist and Believer"

At a symposium at Sweetbriar College in March 1963, O'Connor expresses her dissatisfaction with the organizer's definition of the symposium's topic—that "we conceive religion broadly as an expression of man's ultimate concern rather than identify it with institutional Judaism or Christianity" (154). O'Connor feels that to enlarge religion's definition may be to vaporize it. So important is the Judeo-Christian tradition that O'Connor claims its role in shaping the West's secularism and its modern atheism. The ties are there, "which may often be invisible, but which are there nevertheless" (155). Because O'Connor is a novelist who speaks for the Church and for Christ "without apology" (155), she sees her task as finding an appropriate symbol for the feeling embodied in the work. Her theology will have a bearing on her choices. How the symbol is lodged "tells the intelligent reader whether this feeling is adequate or inadequate, . . . moral or immoral, . . . good or evil" (156). O'Connor's maimed people are examples of where she has chosen to lodge these symbols, for while Joy/Hulga's wooden leg, Tom T. Shiftlet's one arm, and Rufus Johnson's club foot are all first the things themselves, they all carry symbolic weight, which tells the reader something more of the character's feeling.

O'Connor cites St. Augustine, the fourth-century confessor, who wrote about how "things of the world pour forth from God in a double way: intellectually into the minds of the angels and physically into the world of things" (157). With Joseph Conrad, O'Connor wants to "render the highest possible justice to the visible universe" (157). By penetrating the concrete world, she believes she can move toward a depth in which the "sacred is reflected" (158). This comment reiterates her anti-Manichean position, that spirit and matter cannot be separated. Because O'Connor is a writer who speaks with those writers who believe in the "God of Abraham, Isaac, and Jacob" (161), her inclination is to agree with the Blaise Pascal quotation: "If I had not known you, I would not have found you" (160). A seventeenth-century mathematician, Pascal was also a religious philosopher whose *Pensées,* a numbered listing of proverbial thoughts, was influential for many writers of strong faith.

Establishing the position from which she writes, O'Connor delves into her key problem of dealing with the position from which she is read, which is "going to be difficult in direct proportion as your beliefs depart from [your readers' beliefs]" (162). O'Connor uses *The Violent Bear It Away* as an example of the challenge. In this novel, the central action is baptism, and her dilemma is how "to make the reader feel, in his bones if nowhere else, that something is going on here that counts" (162). She accomplishes the task by both distorting and exaggerating the baptism, in order to "reveal," not "destroy" (162) its importance to readers for whom baptism is not personally significant. She also refers to readers' misunderstanding of Haze Motes, "whose presiding passion was to rid himself of a conviction that Jesus had redeemed him" (164), but could not do so.

O'Connor suggests that the modern age lacks a religious sense, and when the age appears to shift with the moment, effective allegory will not work. The serious novelist writes about people in a world where something is missing, and for that writer the greatest drama is the "salvation or loss of the soul." When the audience does not believe in the soul, "there is very little drama" (167). This dilemma, however, also creates a source of great humor, for "the maximum amount of seriousness admits the maximum amount of comedy" (167), which begins to explain why O'Connor's short stories where people die can be simultaneously horrible and funny. O'Connor concludes that there can be no "great religious fiction until we have again that happy combination of believing artist and believing society" (168). Until then, the novelist and believer must reflect "our broken condition and, through it, the face of the devil we are possessed by" (168).

"Catholic Novelists and Their Readers"

Parts of this essay were delivered at the College of St. Teresa in Winona, Minnesota, and published as "The Role of the Catholic Novelist" in *Greyfriar, Siena Studies in Literature* in 1964. O'Connor begins with an analogy matching the novelist and the Catholic church with the legend of the wolf of Gubbio and St. Francis. When St. Francis converted the wolf, it remained a wolf, but it became a better wolf. When a novelist sees by the light of the Church, the novelist becomes likewise better. O'Connor sees a novelist's talent as God-given; the receiver is charged with doing a particular thing within the talent, not outside of it. O'Connor shares St. Thomas Aquinas's belief about art: "It is wholly concerned with the good of that which is made" (171). In the broad scope, this definition encompasses what is specifically meant by a "Catholic novel," a novel "in which the truth as Christians know it has been used as a light to see the world by" (173). In a Catholic novel or in any art that exists for the sake of the good that is in the art, the artist need not be concerned with the reader's taste, happiness, or morals.

As examples of Catholic writers who fit this definition, O'Connor cites J. F. Powers as having a "terrible accuracy" for seeing the "vulgar, ignorant, greedy, and fearfully drab." Powers writes about these character traits not "to embarrass the Church," but because "he can't write about any other kind" (173). In other words, these are the people that Powers sees in the world; he is being faithful to his talent. She gives writer Paul Horgan the distinction of being true to what he sees, and yet he does not "offend the ordinary Catholic" (186). On the other hand, Cardinal Francis Spellman's best-selling 1951 *The Foundling* is a work that does not advance "the standards of Catholic letters" (175). O'Connor notes that the proceeds from the book go to help the orphans, "and afterwards you can always use the book as a doorstop" (175). Most contemporary reviewers agreed with O'Connor's assessment, calling the book "amateur," "mediocre," and satisfactory material for a sermon topic. Baron von Hugel, a nineteenth-century Roman Catholic philosopher and author who wrote about the importance of the mystical experience, suggested that the "lowliest" causes the deepest response (176). O'Connor's own choice of characters was often from among "the lowliest."

The novelist's concern is "with mystery as it is incarnated in human life" (176). Fixed dogma, according to O'Connor, helps the writer to look at the universe with more certainty, to be "true to time and eternity both, to what he sees and what he believes" (177), to become a "realist of distances," one who distorts "appearances in order to show a hidden truth" (179). If a writer tries to disconnect faith from vision, then this will result in "violence to the whole personality" (181). A goal for the Catholic novelist is to make the Church so much a part of the personality that the writer "can forget about her" (181). O'Connor uses biblical allusions to explain the Catholic writer's difficulty in reaching this goal, for God does not talk to the writer "mouth to mouth" as He did with Moses, but rather God speaks to the writer as He did with Aaron and Mary, "through dreams and visions"

(181). Aaron and Mary, the sister and brother of Moses, found fault with Moses for taking an Ethiopian wife, so God retaliated: "He said to them: Hear my words: if there be among you a prophet of the Lord, I will appear to him in a vision, or I will speak to him in a dream" (Numbers 12:6), and not as God had spoken to His "most faithful" Moses, which was "mouth to mouth" (Numbers 12:7–8). If the Church could be so integrated into the whole of the personality, then the writer, too, could have verbal communication with God. More likely, though, the Catholic writer is like a "doubtful Jacob" who "wonders if he will come out of the struggle at all" (183), a reference to Jacob's struggle with the angel (Genesis 32).

When fiction works, the reader is left "like Job, with a renewed sense of mystery" (184). Job's story in the Bible is an exploration of the mysterious question—why do bad things happen to good people? Tested by Satan, Job's faith remains strong in the midst of all manner of plagues and ill winds. At the end, he is restored beyond his former state of prosperity. O'Connor cites St. Gregory I, a contemporary of St. Augustine, a pope and prolific writer: "every time the sacred text describes a fact, it reveals a mystery" (184). When O'Connor suggests the Christian storyteller "is like the blind man whom Christ touched, who looked then and saw men as if they were trees, but walking" (184), she makes an unstated reference to her own "A View of the Woods" where trees thicken "into mysterious dark files that were marching across the water and away into the distance."[11] At this point in the story, the mystery deepens.

The Catholic novelist's duty is to art, or, truth—that which is seen in the world by a writer whose vision is connected to faith. Art is never "democratic . . . ; it is only for those who are willing to undergo the effort needed to understand it" (189). The Catholic writer has the challenge of being true in art so as not to be suspect "in matters of religion" (190). O'Connor speaks for total integration—faith and vision, art and truth, the concrete world that opens to mystery. The Catholic novelist writes with the whole personality.

"The Catholic Novelist in the Protestant South"

This lecture was delivered at Georgetown University in 1963 and published in its *Viewpoint* in the spring of 1966. O'Connor establishes how the Catholic novel has failed itself and its audience by gravitating toward the abstract. The Catholic novelist who is Southern and pays attention to the region's ways of doing will heed the ear, for "when one Southern character speaks, regardless of his station in life, an echo of all Southern life is heard" (199). Because the American Catholic church is "not central to this society" (201), there is no one place that reflects its "particular religious life" (200). However, the Catholic writer who lives in the South has an advantage because the South is the Bible Belt, and the fact that "Sam Jones' grandma read the Bible thirty-seven times on her knees" (201) is an influence that cannot be shaken "in even several generations" (202). O'Connor refers to H. L. Mencken's satiric essay "The Sahara of the Bozart," in which the South becomes a "desert of the fine arts," as he mourns the passing of a genuine culture. The essay appeared in Mencken's 1920 *Prejudices,* second series. Mencken's reference to the South as a "Bible Belt" was meant to belittle, but O'Connor is thankful for its reality. Stories of some mythic and shared dimension must exist by which other stories can be measured. In the South, these stories were the Scriptures.

MYSTERY AND MANNERS

Catholics have paid too much attention to the abstract and "consequently impoverished their imagination and their capacity for prophetic insight" (203). On the other hand, "in the South the Bible is known by the ignorant" as well as the educated, which provides for a greater intensity of the life experience, for "every action to be heightened and seen under the aspect of eternity" (203). Northerners see this "religious enthusiasm" as "one of the South's more grotesque features" (204), but O'Connor encourages the Catholic to find that "kinship with backwoods prophets and shouting fundamentalists" (207). O'Connor is attracted to those aspects of Southern life where religious feeling is the most intense, calling the area ripe for the "invisible Church" (208).

O'Connor believes the Catholic writer can emphasize the South's religious legacy, and the South can assist the novelist's ear for real dialogue in a concrete setting. The South's greatest gifts to a Catholic writer include its "thriving literary tradition" in its felt knowledge of the Bible, its efforts to maintain its identity "to know manners under stress," and because it is a Bible Belt, "belief can be made believable" (208). What a writer, character, and reader share is what makes fiction possible. Because of O'Connor's vision and the South's preoccupation, the result is literarily theological.

"Introduction to *A Memoir of Mary Ann*"

In the spring of 1960, O'Connor received an invitation from Sister Evangelist, the Sister Superior of Our Lady of Perpetual Help Free Cancer Home in Atlanta, to write the story of Mary Ann, a cancer patient who had lived with the nuns for twelve years with a tumor on the side of her face that had resulted in the removal of one eye. O'Connor believed she had been asked to write Mary Ann's story because the nuns mistakenly thought that a talent to write meant "a talent to write anything at all" (215). O'Connor had no intention of complying. However, when she looked at the picture of Mary Ann, the face haunted her, and she told the nuns they should write the story, but she would be glad to look over the manuscript upon its completion. She expected not to hear from them again. The completed text arrived in August, and it made the "professional writer groan" (222). However, besides the small stylistic irritations of their language, the nuns had succeeded in conveying the "mystery of Mary Ann" (223).

When O'Connor saw the picture of Mary Ann's face, she was reminded of Nathaniel Hawthorne's story "The Birthmark," where Aylmer decides to remove the birthmark from his otherwise perfect wife's face and, in doing so, kills her. The story suggests that Aylmer is a "menace" (227), one who cannot accept human imperfection. O'Connor believes that this menace has multiplied. Dostoevski and Camus are such examples of writers who feel that suffering children "discredit the goodness of God" (227). She cites *The Brothers Karamazov*'s intellectual, atheistic son Ivan, who "cannot believe, as long as one child is in torment" (227). She also cites "Camus' hero [who] cannot accept the divinity of Christ, because of the massacre of the innocents" (227). This is a reference to the narrator Bernard Rieux of Camus's *The Plague* (1947). O'Connor notes that in earlier ages, people were able to look with an "unsentimental eye of acceptance" (227) into the face of goodness, to dwell inside the mystery.

Though most people would believe that the face of evil is grotesque, Mary Ann's story helped O'Connor see that goodness has its own grotesque nature and that "the good is something under construction" (226). The nuns' story of Mary Ann addresses the question of why she had to die; O'Connor believes that most people might wonder why she was ever born. O'Connor found the nuns' version "affected by traditional hagiography and even a little by Parson Weems" (224–25). In other words, the nuns had read too much of saints' lives and paid too much attention to fabrication of tales that showed a person to be better than he or she actually might have been.

Nathaniel Hawthorne's notebooks recount a story in which he once picked up a disfigured child in a Liverpool workhouse, believing that not to have done so would have been unforgivable. Hawthorne's daughter, Rose, believed the account was her father's "greatest words" (219). This same daughter founded the Dominican Congregation of the Servants of Relief for Incurable Cancer, the Order of Sisters that years later would care for Mary Ann. O'Connor champions the wonder of both the Mary Anns of the world and those who spend their lives caring for "human imperfection and grotesquerie" (228). O'Connor has no interest in easy logical answers; only total acceptance of faith is admissible.

Notes

1. Sally and Robert Fitzgerald, eds., *Mystery and Manners,* by Flannery O'Connor (New York: Farrar, Straus and Giroux, 1969) ix. All parenthetical citations from the essays are from this edition.

2. Jean Kellogg, "We Have Had Our Fall," *Christian Century* 9 July 1969: 927.

3. Richard Gilman, "On Flannery O'Connor," *New York Review of Books* 21 August 1969: 24–25.

4. D. Keith Mano, "Mystery and Manners," *New York Times Book Review* 25 May 1969: 6.

5. Review of *Mystery and Manners, Harper's Magazine* 238 (June 1969): 94.

6. Review of *Mystery and Manners, New Yorker* 19 July 1969: 84.

7. "Wanted: An American Novel," *Life* 12 Sept. 1955: 48.

8. "Wanted," 48.

9. *The Catholic Encyclopedia Dictionary* (New York: Gilmary Society, 1941) 589.

10. Flannery O'Connor, *The Habit of Being,* ed. Sally Fitzgerald (New York: Farrar, Straus and Giroux, 1979) 143.

11. Flannery O'Connor, *Flannery O'Connor: Collected Works,* ed. Sally Fitzgerald (New York: Library of America, 1988) 546.

CHAPTER SEVEN

The Habit of Being

A collection of O'Connor's letters, edited by Sally Fitzgerald, was published by Farrar, Straus and Giroux in 1979. The 600-page volume contains 789 letters O'Connor wrote to forty-six correspondents from June 1948 until July 1964. Most of the letters—662—were written to fifteen people. Letters to relatives are not included, and most especially absent is the daily exchange between mother and daughter that Fitzgerald says was a part of O'Connor's diurnal ritual when she lived with the Fitzgeralds in rural Connecticut for almost two years.[1] Jacques Maritain provided a concept of the "habit of art" from which O'Connor learned the necessity of adding to her God-given talent an "attitude or quality of mind" (xvii). Fitzgerald extends Maritain's idea to a "habit of being," which she defines as "an excellence not only of action but of interior disposition and activity that increasingly reflected the object, the being which specified it, and was itself reflected in what she did and said" (xvii). The letters testify to such a person of lucid and deep-seated integrity.

When the letters appeared, ten years after the celebrated collected essays, *Mystery and Manners,* O'Connor scholarship accelerated. Magazine reviews of the letters were considerably longer than the responses to O'Connor's fiction. Even though the letters chronicle extensively O'Connor's ideas about faith and the progress of her writing, most reviews emphasize her life, often creating a sentimental portrait of some "maiden lady with a fatal illness"[2] who "spent most of her adult life with her mother on a dairy farm just outside Milledgeville, Ga., up the road a piece from Macon and a middling way from Atlanta."[3] Every review includes references to her fatal illness in precisely the manner she so adamantly resisted while she was living.

Richard Gilman's assessment of her stature is one of high praise, suggesting it is not "eccentric to regard her as at least the equal of any American writer of short stories." As a letter writer, he places her in the company of "Byron, Keats, Lawrence, Wilde, and Joyce," all producers of "correspondence that gleams with consciousness."[4] Robert Towers of the *New York Review of Books,* like Gilman, has difficulty stopping the review, wanting to keep giving one more example of the life depicted in the letters, and also shares his belief in O'Connor's reputation—"despite the small body of her work and the narrowness of its range, [she] seems as permanently seated among the American immortals as Emily Dickinson or Hawthorne." Towers places her in a bygone age, with a fierce belief in the Catholic faith, so much that her own suffering from lupus seemed unnoteworthy. Towers's assessment is that O'Connor measured her own pain by that of "the Crucifixion and a belief in Hell."[5]

Paul Gray of *Time* says, "the most memorable character that O'Connor ever got down on paper was her own." In the midst of sadness for a life "cut off much too soon," Gray claims that "the emotion that Flannery O'Connor conveyed most often was joy." However, he misrepresents the reality of the collection when he catalogs the list of correspondents: "Old friends like Lowell" (eight letters), "literary figures like Katherine Anne Porter" (one letter) "and Walker Percy" (one letter), "college chums" (one chum, nine letters), "priests" (one priest, twenty-seven letters), "questioning students" (one student, three letters), "aspiring authors, fans, cranks."[6] The collection contains no cranks, unless two unnamed English professors with insipid questions fall into this category. Many of her fans were also aspiring authors who became friends of long standing. In fact, the person to whom O'Connor wrote 193 of the collection's letters, identified only as "A," began as a fan and became a friend as well as an aspiring author. Another fan, a college instructor and writer, Cecil Dawkins, became one of the top four correspondents.

The Letters to "A"

The letters to "A" are O'Connor's most articulate expression of her faith, which was never defined by personal whim, but by what her faith called on her to do. She never moved to mold that faith to suit her ways; rather, she accepted what was her perception of a given. Here, also, in these 193 letters are O'Connor's most personal revelations of her life in Milledgeville.

In July 1955, O'Connor responded to the first letter she received from "A" with enthusiasm, asking her to write again, for O'Connor wanted to know "who this is who understands my stories" (90). Though it was to be almost three months before O'Connor suggested that they both stop addressing each other as "Miss" and the following summer of 1956 before they meet face-to-face, O'Connor's letters from the beginning are detailed, presumptive, and surprisingly personal. From the start, there is an exchange about authors and their books, which moves directly to a literal exchange of the books themselves, for "A" agrees to check them out of the Atlanta Public Library for O'Connor if she cannot find them in Milledgeville. Writing to "A" helped O'Connor "clarify" what she thought (103). The reader learns those writers most important to O'Connor's development; however, what matters more about this correspondence is what and how O'Connor writes about her personal life: learning to use crutches, being touched by a Christmas gift of a poinsettia with an unsigned card, agreeing to be "A's" sponsor when she enters the Church, mailing "A" a copy of her own self-portrait. O'Connor often thanked "A" for the correspondence: "These letters from you are something in my life" (153); "you sometimes appear to know better what I am trying to say than I do; and also it is you now who is in a position to help me. And do" (169).

As the years wear on, the affection O'Connor has for "A" permits her to speak freely, and "A" becomes the recipient of diverse information: stories about company that come to Andalusia who sound like characters from her fiction; her affinity for W. C. Fields; her ability to turn down the White House before she could refuse to write a piece called "Woman's Day" for her mother's "colored friend Annie" (515); her response to President Kennedy's death on the day after the assassination—"I am sad about the President. But I like the new one" (549). According to Fitzgerald's notes, it is to "A" that she makes the first mention of a "possibly serious development in [her] fragile health" (554) and of her "possible surgery" (565). In one of the last letters O'Connor writes to "A," she says that "A's" "great natural grace is finding the good in people" (587); it is clear from the range and depth of the correspondence that O'Connor knew she had a friend who also saw the good in her.

Letters to Maryat Lee

Most of O'Connor's enduring adult friendships were initiated first by someone who appreciated her writing; only later did the two meet face-to-face. Maryat Lee filled a unique position in O'Connor's life. They met each other on the last day of Lee's 1956 Christmas visit with her brother, the president of O'Connor's alma mater, the local Georgia State College for Women. At the end of this visit, Lee received a letter from a friend suggesting that she try to meet O'Connor; coincidentally, on that same day, O'Connor called and invited her over. Neither one knew the work of the other; both were responding more to good manners than to a desire to meet one another. From the beginning, both acknowledged a kinship between them. Lee recalls: "Even before we were introduced I met her eyes in a brief searching look of instant recognition, although I was not at all clear *what* was recognized."[7]

The Habit of Being includes seventy-nine letters to Lee, spanning the last eight years of O'Connor's life, from early January 1957 until six days before her death. The last letter O'Connor wrote was to Lee. Fitzgerald describes the letters as "slambang" (193), an apt word for the lexical sparring that was an ongoing part of their often cryptic exchanges.

The dominant theme of the letters is clearly race, with an occasional nod to religion. The tone of the correspondence is set in the first letter. O'Connor admits that the need for delicacy in matters of race "is often so funny that you forget it is also terrible." She also admits her steadfast religious position on orthodoxy, a "ceiling" she had come through "with a deepened sense of mystery and always several degrees more orthodox" (195). The liberal Lee was inclined to break the rules of time-honored white Southern manners in regard to race relations, whereas O'Connor felt a loyalty to Southern propriety. She refuses to meet James Baldwin in Georgia, but claims it would be nice to meet him in New York. However, when Baldwin's name arises five years later in their correspondence, he has become a type to her: "About the Negroes, the kind I don't like is the philosophizing prophesying pontificating kind, the James Baldwin kind" (580). On one hand, this comment smacks of racism; on the other, it is emblematic of O'Connor's often brutal honesty. The sentence is mitigated by her further comment: "My question is usually, would this person be endurable if white?" (580). O'Connor is more likely to tolerate a person for a person's sake and not for some correct political agenda.

With Maryat Lee, O'Connor lowered her personal guard. She has found the person she can be silly enough with to ask for a saber-toothed tiger, to admit a "secret desire to rival Charles Dickens upon the stage" (265), to denigrate the fiction of Ayn Rand—"as low as you can get re fiction" (398), and to express absolute and sincere delight at receiving a "Waring Blendor" (435) on her birthday. While "A" is far more likely to receive a thoughtful and detailed response, Lee is O'Connor's alter ego, perceiving intuitively the bargain in acquiring a tackle box to hold O'Connor's paints for two books of green stamps and understanding the deal in a pair of $65 swans "because the female is blind in one eye" (448). For O'Connor, Lee is a quick first draft; she is the perfect recipient of slapdash, a side of O'Connor to which Lee alone is privy.

Letters to Cecil Dawkins

In May of 1957, Cecil Dawkins, with what must have been a degree of uncertainty, wrote her first letter to O'Connor. O'Connor opens and closes her response by thanking her for writing and "mailing the letter," and she invites Dawkins to "stop and see [her]" if she is ever nearby (221). *The Habit of Being* contains sixty-three letters to Dawkins from O'Connor over the remaining seven years of her life. In some ways, Dawkins is the middle ground between "A" and Lee. Born and raised in Alabama, teaching at Stephens College in Columbia, Missouri, at the time she first wrote O'Connor, she was herself a writer. O'Connor encouraged her by writing detailed commentary on Dawkins's stories, recommending her for a Guggenheim, and supporting her admission to Yaddo. As the friendship developed, O'Connor gave Dawkins permission to turn "The Displaced Person" into a play. O'Connor did not live to see the play presented at the American Place Theatre in New York in 1965.

Letters to Sally and/or Robert Fitzgerald

Sally Fitzgerald is the editor of *The Habit of Being* and sixty-five letters from O'Connor to her and her late husband Robert are included in the collection. O'Connor tells the Fitzgeralds she has without permission decided to dedicate her first collection of short stories, *A Good Man Is Hard to Find,* to them: "You all are my adopted kin and if I dedicated it to any of my blood kin they would think they had to go into hiding" (74). The letters possess an affectionate tone that never wavers, even after their regularity decreases. O'Connor had friends to whom she confided more, but none with whom she so joyfully ran the gamut of subjects. The Fitzgeralds, in being "adopted kin," had special status in O'Connor's life.

Letters to Janet McKane

Janet McKane was a Northerner who entered O'Connor's life by way of a letter in the winter of 1963. *The Habit of Being* contains thirty-two letters to McKane in the last nineteen months of her life. O'Connor and McKane never met in person. McKane was a devout Catholic who kept O'Connor in her prayers, for which O'Connor never failed to thank her.

UNDERSTANDING FLANNERY O'CONNOR

In the last month of O'Connor's life, she sends McKane a copy of the prayer to St. Raphael; this is a prayer O'Connor admits to saying "every day for many years" (590). St. Raphael's task was to lead "you to the people you are supposed to meet" (590). In mentioning the prayer to McKane, O'Connor suggests that she believes that McKane is one of those people she was "supposed to meet." Her prayer was answered. Sally Fitzgerald reports that after O'Connor died, in memory of her McKane invited Robert Giroux to a Byzantine rite requiem Mass in a Second Avenue church in New York. The two of them "were the only ones who attended" (572).

The Remaining Letters

The rest of the fifty-three correspondents in *The Habit of Being* consist of a priest; English professors, both named and unnamed; friends and teachers from her college days in Georgia, from her graduate days in Iowa, and from her writing days in the North at Yaddo, New York; journal editors; nuns; poets and writers; students; and assorted fans.

Among the fans, Louise Abbot, who lived close by in Louisville, Georgia, cast aside her notion to pose as a "lady-journalist" (205), and in O'Connor's first letter to Abbot she invites her for a visit. Although the collection contains only nine letters to Abbot, she frequently visited O'Connor. In one of the letters to Abbot, O'Connor gives what many critics consider her most profound theological advice: "What people don't realize is how much religion costs. They think faith is a big electric blanket, when of course it is the cross. It is much harder to believe than not to believe.... A God you understood would be less than yourself" (354). Disclaiming her status as a spiritual advisor, O'Connor wanted Abbot to know that questions of faith plagued her as well. In her very last written words to Abbot, she taps on their mutual spiritual devotion: "Prayers requested. I am sick of being sick" (581). It is the closest O'Connor ever comes to showing outward weariness from the toll of lupus on her daily energy.

Reading the letters straight through provides a chronological overview of O'Connor's life and is, until the publication of Sally Fitzgerald's authorized biography of O'Connor, the most we can know of O'Connor's life. However, grouping the letters by correspondent renders a deeper view, for as O'Connor grows in her affection for these various people, she reveals more complex and personal insights that are intensified when read together. The letters solidify the Church as the taproot from which O'Connor uncompromisingly and unapologetically developed her "habit of being."

Notes

1. Flannery O'Connor, *The Habit of Being* ed. Sally Fitzgerald (New York: Farrar, Straus and Giroux, 1979) xii. All parenthetical citations from the letters are from this edition.

2. "Short Reviews: *The Habit of Being,*" *Atlantic* 243 (June 1979): 96.

3. Paul Gray, "Letters of Flannery O'Connor," *Time* 5 Mar. 1979: 86.

4. Richard Gilman, "A Life of Letters," *New York Times Book Review* 18 Mar. 1979: 1.

5. Robert Towers, "Flannery O'Connor's Gifts," *New York Review of Books* 3 May 1979: 3.

6. Gray, 86.

7. Maryat Lee, "Flannery, 1957," *Flannery O'Connor Bulletin* 5 (1976): 40.

CHAPTER EIGHT

Other Stories

Nineteen stories were published in O'Connor's two collections. When Robert Giroux prepared *The Complete Stories* in 1971, the volume contained thirty-one stories.[1] The twelve stories not in her collections appeared in book form for the first time. The first six stories had comprised her M.A. thesis for the State University of Iowa in June 1947. Of the remaining six, three eventually became chapters in her first novel, *Wise Blood:* "The Peeler," originally appearing in *Partisan Review* (December 1949); "The Heart of the Park," debuting in *Partisan Review* (February 1949); and "Enoch and the Gorilla," first in *New World Writing* (April 1952). "You Can't Be Any Poorer Than Dead," which became the first chapter of *The Violent Bear It Away,* was first published in *New World Writing* (October 1955). These four stories will not be addressed in this chapter.

"The Partridge Festival," a story submitted to the second collection and then retrieved by O'Connor, made its earlier appearance in the *Critic* (March 1961). Finally, O'Connor's novel-in-progress at the time of her death was tentatively titled *Why Do the Heathen Rage?,* which drew local publicity when the fragment surfaced in *Esquire* (July 1963). In a letter to "A" she responds: "I am much amused by the local reaction to my appearing in *Esquire.* You would think that at last I was really going places."[2] *Flannery O'Connor: Collected Works,* edited by Sally Fitzgerald for the Library of America series in 1988, contains a revised version of one of the thesis stories, which

OTHER STORIES

Giroux's 1971 collection does not include, called "An Afternoon in the Woods."[3]

When the early thesis stories appeared in *The Complete Stories* (1971), Thomas Gullason, writing for the *Saturday Review,* called them "one-dimensional tales." He noted, however, that "they only periodically display the striking imagery and sharply etched details of her more mature work." Though the themes that would concern her throughout her writing life were already present, she was moving in "piecemeal fashion . . . in the direction of her major fiction."[4] Walter Clemons, reviewing for *Newsweek,* notes that "her force and droll acerbity are already visible" in the thesis stories, adding "singly, none of the uncollected pieces is indispensable," for each early story contributes to an understanding of O'Connor's "development of her profound moral vision."[5] *Time*'s reviewer acknowledges the value of the early work in an encompassing statement: "Every one is good enough so that if it were the only example of her work to survive, it would be evident that the writer possessed high talent and a remarkable unclouded, unabstract, demanding intelligence."[6]

"The Geranium"

O'Connor's first story in her thesis was published by *Accent* in the summer of 1946. Old Dudley, whose name reflects the "dud" that he is, has left the South for New York City to live out his days with his dutiful daughter, who had caught him in a moment he now regrets, wishing she had "let him stay where he was back home and not be so taken up with her damn duty" (701). The movie that Old Dudley had seen on his only trip to Atlanta, "Big Town Rhythm," had been the impetus to see New York. The movie O'Connor cites is as fictional as the Coa County Old Dudley hails from. Until "The Geranium" is rewritten as "Judgment Day" at the end of her career, it is the only story set outside the South. O'Connor describes the apartment, six floors up, and Old Dudley's view from his window across to "another window framed by blackened red brick" (701), and the subways where people "boiled out of trains and up steps and over into the streets" (705) before she ever visits the city herself. O'Connor has Old Dudley think that "big towns were important places" (702), and "Big Town Rhythm" had convinced him there would be room for him there. However, when Old Dudley arrives, sees the apartment building, the halls "that reminded you of tape measures strung out with a door every inch" (704), he has had enough, and realizes he "must have been sick when he said he [would go with her]" (702). His days consist of staring out the window at a geranium on the ledge across from his own. The geranium serves as a symbol of memory—his own recollections of how much he misses the black couple back home in the basement of his boardinghouse: Rabie, with whom he spent time fishing and hunting, and Lutisha, who "could root anything" (701).

Sally Fitzgerald has pointed out the significance of T. S. Eliot's poetry on O'Connor's early work. Eliot links a geranium with memory in "Rhapsody on a Windy Night": "Midnight shakes the memory / As a madman shakes a dead geranium."[7] Fitzgerald links the idea of O'Connor's Dudley with the old man of "Gerontion." In this poem, an "old man in a dry month," possessing "a dull head among windy spaces," "in a draughty house / Under a windy knob" takes signs for wonder. Eliot's old man has had "tears . . . shaken from the wrath-bearing tree,"[8] like Old Dudley himself, whose "pain in his throat was all over his face now, leaking out his eyes" (711). He is being watched by a

OTHER STORIES

man in the window where the geranium usually rested who asks, "What you cryin' for? . . . I ain't never seen a man cry like that" (711). Eliot's old man is linked with Christian gestures, a theme O'Connor does not plumb in this story.

Rather, O'Connor comments on race relations as perceived by a longtime Southerner gone North. Old Dudley can live in the same Southern boardinghouse with a black couple, praise their gardening abilities, fish every Wednesday with Rabie in the familiar river he could see from his boardinghouse window, 'possum-hunt with Rabie at night, eat Lutisha's food, but he cannot imagine the possibility of living side by side with a member of their race in New York City. When he sees "a nigger . . . [wearing] a grey, pin-stripe suit and a tan tie" (706) go into the apartment next door, he figures the people living there have a servant. When his daughter suggests the black man is "looking at [the apartment] for himself" (706), Old Dudley thinks she "could be right funny when she wanted to" (706). He is eager to find out the servant's day off so that they can go fishing; this same person's status as neighbor, however, is unacceptable to him. As fond as he is of Rabie and Lutisha, the old man cannot fathom this reality: "You ain't been raised to live tight with niggers that think they're just as good as you, and you think I'd go messin' around with one er that kind!" (707).

Rabie calls Old Dudley "boss," shares any problems for which Dudley alone is responsible, stops whatever he is doing to be with Dudley, does Dudley's running for him, but this new neighbor calls him "old timer," laughs at him, and speaks to him in "a voice that sounded like a nigger's laugh and a white man's sneer" (710). When he offers to help Dudley up the stairs, his language suggests a superior gun knowledge: "I went deer hunting once. I believe we used a Dodson 38 to get those deer.

What do you use?" to which Dudley replies, "a gun" (710). In a later story, it would have a richer meaning that a Dodson 38 does not exist, that a "38" would be illegal to use because it is too small to kill a deer. When the neighbor suggests that New York is "a swell place—once you get used to it" (711) and pats him on the back as he ushers Dudley through his daughter's front door, Dudley is out of control with his throat about to pop: "He was trapped in this place where niggers could call you 'old timer'" (711).

In time, the story closes where it opens, with Dudley sitting at the window waiting for the people across the way to set out the geranium. But the tenant tells Dudley it has fallen off the ledge and lies shattered below, where Dudley sees it "at the bottom of the alley with its roots in the air" (713). In the last lines of the story, the geranium as symbol of memory of good times with Rabie and Lutisha becomes symbol of Old Dudley himself, whose Southern roots have been pulled from him and, like the geranium, he hangs "in the air," resisting the ways of a culture foreign to him in name, but, ironically, dear to him in reality. Rabie and Lutisha, though black, are friends closer than family, but such a claim in language, the Southern Dudley would never utter.

"The Barber"

"The Barber" was included in *New Signatures,* 1947, an anthology of student writing, according to Sally Fitzgerald.[9] However, when the story appeared in the October 1970 *Atlantic,* Robert Fitzgerald claims in a note that "'The Barber' has never been published."[10] O'Connor portrays a stereotypical small town Southern barbershop, in fictional Dilton, where it is "trying on liberals" (714), in which various types are represented—the liberal-thinking college teacher, the conservative-redneck, nonthinking barber, and his black cleanup boy, George, a young "Yessir" man, who knows to say only what he knows he must say to keep his job. Although titled "The Barber," the story's protagonist is Rayber, a teacher at the local college, who tries to defend in the barbershop his sensible political support for candidate Darmon over the more popular racist "demagog" Hawkson; however, it is the barber who wins the day. Rayber is an early model for the Rayber character-type O'Connor struggles to make authentic in *The Violent Bear It Away.*

The story explains why Rayber has had to find a new barbershop after the "Democratic White Primary." Because O'Connor chooses to use this expression, she places the story within a historical context. From the Civil War through the Civil Rights Movement, the "Solid South" moniker designated clear support for the Democratic Party. Because primaries are more important than general elections in single-party states, Southern whites established private elections to exclude black voters. It took Supreme Court legislation, beginning with *Smith vs. Allwright* in 1944, to rule that preventing blacks from the primary elections was unconstitutional. By midcentury, white primaries were not supposed to exist.[11] When the barber asks Rayber who will receive his vote, his choice for Darmon nets him a "nigger-lover" jeer. Not thinking fast enough, Rayber regrets not having told the barber he was "neither a negro- nor a white-lover" (714). To the barber, on the other hand, "there ain't but two sides now, white and black" (714).

Through a repetition, O'Connor uses the racist barber to apply Mother Goose characters to ways of behaving. The heroine of the well-known rhyme—Old Mother Hubbard / Went to the

UNDERSTANDING FLANNERY O'CONNOR

cupboard / To get her poor dog a bone. / When she got there, / The cupboard was bare, / And so the poor dog had none—is used eight times in the story to refer to pathetic men, incapable of stocking their own cupboards, showing up only to discover how bare they are. According to the barber, these are men who are so wrong-headed that they do not understand the need for white supremacy. O'Connor assumes the South's position is not a secret; the barber laments: "Why, lemme tell you this—ain't nothin' gonna be good again until we get rid of them Mother Hubbards and get us a man can put these niggers in their places. Shuh" (715). The barber thinks Rayber is a Mother Hubbard, the people who listen with skepticism to Hawkson are Mother Hubbards, those who call Hawkson a "demagog" are Mother Hubbards, and Hawkson has no choice but to lay those Mother Hubbards low every time he makes a speech in the fictional towns of Mullin's Oak, Bedford, Chickerville, Spartasville, and Mulford. Only Tilford, a part of Atlanta, is real. The barber reports Hawkson's use of Mother Goose's "Little Boy Blue" as well. The sleeper in the rhyme—Little Boy Blue / Come blow your horn. / The sheep's in the meadow / And the cow's in the corn. / Where is the little boy who looks after the sheep? / He is under the haystack fast asleep—is Hawkson's image of Darmon: "Why, he was Little Boy Blue, blowin' his horn. Yeah. Babies in the meadow and niggers in the corn" (716). The barber then extends the Darmon image to include those who support Darmon, ultimately becoming the same as Mother Hubbards. In summing up Hawkson's speech at Spartasville, the barber regales: "There wasn't a Mother Hubbard left standin', and all the Boy Blues got their horns broke" (716). O'Connor suggests that adult men who speak in a child's Mother Goose character have a stunted development. Ironically, though, the barber, who knows clearly the role of white man keeping black man in his place, also knows the deep pleasure of the black man's role in his own life: "There ain't nothing like taking a nigger and a hound dog and a gun and going after quail. . . . You missed a lot out of life if you ain't had that" (722).

Rayber prepares a speech to defend himself against barbers that both his wife and his colleague Jacobs respond to with a high degree of passiveness. His barbershop audience response is even worse; they laugh at him. Even George is put on the spot by the barber, asking him after Rayber's speech who he will vote for: "I don't know is they gonna let me vote. . . . Do, I gonna vote for Mr. Hawkson" (724). George will have no vote in a Democratic White Primary, but his response is the one that is instilled in him from the Southern code of manners. Rayber, impotent in the face of ignorance, hits the barber and with his face half-lathered with shaving cream, and with the barber's bib "dangling to his knees" (724), he flees this shop. This is the scene that explains the first lines of O'Connor's tale—why they are "trying on liberals in Dilton" and why Rayber has to change barbershops. There is no clear-cut victory for either Rayber or the barber in this story, no win for either intelligence or ignorance. The South's racial relationships are too complex, but, in this early story, O'Connor suggests that discrepancy exists between language spoken and behavior displayed.

"Wildcat"

O'Connor submitted "Wildcat" to the *Southwest Review,* who rejected it in the summer of 1946. It appeared for the first time in print in the spring 1970 *North American Review.* Of all her thesis stories, critics consider this one the weakest, but few have given it much attention. This is the first story in which O'Connor explores a physical disability, blindness, to suggest a keener insight. The experimentation here is important, however, for, in addition, O'Connor casts a full slate of black characters. Eight years later, she remarks in a letter to a friend that she "can only see [colored people] from the outside."[12] The mature O'Connor does not dare to go inside their heads, and in "Wildcat" the venture inside Old Gabriel's head is tentative. Divided in three parts, the first and last are set on the same day, where an old blind man smells a wildcat nearby and asks those who plan to hunt it in the woods to stay at the cabin; he knows the wildcat will come there, seeking and smelling folks' blood. A group of young people, by whom O'Connor suggests just how powerful is Old Gabriel's ability to smell, approach the cabin to be greeted by "Who that? . . . I smells fo' niggers" (725). When the visitors ask Gabriel to identify them by name, he is able to do so for the first three, stumped only by the fourth. The conflict, such as exists between the generations, concerns old Gabriel's committed belief that this wildcat wants human blood and the youths' equal assurance that the big cat is satisfied by the blood of cows. The second part makes clear why old Gabriel's warning should be heeded.

The middle part is a flashback to the blind boy Gabriel, who remembers being left with a cabin full of women, who call him inside because they fear the approach of the wildcat. As a young boy, Gabriel knew that he would be attacked after Reba was, who also had the power to smell the wildcat. But young Gabriel is excited by the match: "He'd lock his arms 'round [the wildcat's] body an' feel up for its neck an' jerk its head back an' go down wit it on the floor until its claws dropped away from his shoulders.

OTHER STORIES

Beat, beat, beat its head, beat, beat beat" (727). Reba knows that cat is coming; she has powers that transcend the others' abilities, and her groans become an old spiritual that predicts the day's events: "Lord, Lord, / Gonna see yo' pilgrim today" (727). When worry shifts to Nancy and Old Hezuh in a nearby cabin, Reba warns that the cat is close by, nobody should leave. Her words are no sooner released when they hear the shriek, made flesh by Nancy at their door, screaming: "Got him, sprung in through the winder, got him in the throat. Hezuh, . . . ol' Hezuh" (728).

In the last part, old Gabriel smells the cat, clambers on a shelf over the chimney, which sags, cracks, and throws him to the floor. Smell becomes sound as the wildcat approaches outside. When Gabriel knows the wildcat has got a cow, he knows he can fall asleep for this night. The stubborn youth, however, are convinced they will have the wildcat the following night, having built a trap in the woods, which they plan to watch: "We goin' up in a tree over the trap every night an' wait 'til we gits it" (731). When Gabriel resists their plan, knowing it will be his throat that night, they can only rely on their belief in empirical data: "How many wildcats you killed, Granpaw?" (731). Gabriel's knowledge is more profound than if he had killed a wildcat himself, as if killing one is the only way to know something.

O'Connor chose the biblical name Gabriel for her protagonist, the angel who interprets Daniel's vision of the ram and the he-goat (Daniel 8). Because Gabriel can smell so much better than any other character, and because smell is the sense most instantaneously connected with memory, Gabriel "knows what [he] knows, boy" (731). Further, he knows that the Lord is waiting on him, and he "didn't want to be on no floor with a wildcat stuck in his face." No one hears Gabriel, interpreter of visions, blind seer, who must face in darkness his coming death, as sure as he feels the "animal cries [that] wailed and mingled with the beats pounding in his throat" (731).

"The Crop"

"The Crop" is O'Connor's only venture in telling a story about the process of writing and reading fiction. The framing story concerns a family of four adult children, living together with prescribed roles—Willie, forty-four, who crumbs the table, Lucia and Bertha, who do the dishes, and Garner, fifty, who removes himself to the parlor to work the crossword puzzle. The sisters look after Garner, but Lucia minds everybody's business and directs the affairs of this superbly organized household. She also "Bissells" the floor, a brand-name carpet sweeper used as a verb to mean "vacuum." To escape from the monotony of "regular habits" (732), Miss Willerton delights in crumbing the table, the process of removing from the tablecloth all manner of stray crumbs that have fallen during the meal, with a silver crumber and its matching crumb-catcher. While she occupies her outward self with this proper task, she uses the time to think of subjects for stories she plans to write.

The "Willie" who would be spontaneous, frivolous, and lusty is trapped inside "Miss Willerton" who cannot help but be restrained by conventional behavior. She dismisses the subject of bakers when her mind moves to "French bakers . . . great tall fellows—blond and . . ." (733). She resists even thinking about what these men must look like, how she might describe them. Next, she moves to teachers as a possibility, but her own experience at the Willowpool Female Seminary reminded her that "[the school's name] sounded biological" (733). She is satisfied finally with sharecroppers because "they would give her that air of social concern which was so valuable to have in the circles she was hoping to travel!" (733). The first sentence that O'Connor gives Miss Willerton to write comes easy: "Lot Motun called his dog" (734). O'Connor's first sentence of "The Crop" is grammatically similar and as direct: "Miss Willerton always crumbed the table" (732).

Once Miss Willerton begins the story, her mind moves to commentary she has made about the activity of writing at a gathering of the United Daughters of the Colonies. O'Connor spoofs the Daughters of the American Revolution and the United Daughters of the Confederacy, moving the historical connection to predate these groups. The kinds of comments Miss Willerton makes to the women also predate what O'Connor will one day say about writing to the "club ladies" that will be a part of her future. Moving away from thoughts about writing to the story itself, Miss Willerton's focus once again shifts to her influences: "But a sharecropper, she knew, might reasonably be expected to roll over in the mud" (724). O'Connor makes a subtle reference to Erskine Caldwell's *Tobacco Road,* which begins with Ellie May and Lov rolling around in the dirt while the rest of the Jeeter Lester family looks on. To reenforce why Miss Willerton might be under such constraints, O'Connor has Lucia find this book and burn it, knowing that "it couldn't be [Willie's]" (735). Once one family member has entered Miss Willerton's mind, she then reflects on what each family member would think of her "passionate scenes" (735).

This intrusion from reality out of the way, Miss Willerton once again returns to the story, planning how Lot Motun and his woman will look. As she ruminates how the story will work itself out, O'Connor moves the narrative into a story-within-a-story.

UNDERSTANDING FLANNERY O'CONNOR

She has Miss Willerton kill the woman and become a character in the story she is writing. Miss Willerton becomes Willie, wife of Lot Motun. She fixes him grits, he helps with household chores, they walk the property, talk of the crop and the coming rain, and then "there'd be a baby next year instead of a cow" (737). What Miss Willerton cannot let herself think in the world she inhabits, she gives full submission to in the world she invents. Details are not included; no actual sex scenes exist. A baby is born, but Willie can only mourn the loss of the crop, which they did not harvest before the rains came. Lot has to tell her she has had the baby: "We got a daughter. . . . two Willies instead of one" (738). Willie ignores the child and only knows to ask, "And what can I do to help you more?" (738). Miss Willerton cannot write more for Willie to say than she knows, and she has had no experience with sex, with the birthing process, with harvesting a crop, with children.

The reverie is over for Willie, though, for her question is answered by her sister, Lucia; she can go to the grocery store. The story-within-a-story ends as Miss Willerton casts Lot aside and pushes herself "back from the typewriter" (738). The grocery store becomes a scene of actual life, where she notices a couple who look exactly like Lot Motun and the woman Willie killed. Their reality sobers Miss Willerton, who, home again with the eggs and tomatoes, returns to her typewriter, finds only the first three sentences she had written, and knowing how the plot played out in her mind and on the street in front of the grocery story where she had just seen the couple, determines her work "sounds awful" (740). Another topic, the Irish, comes to mind. As long as she knows nothing about them, she can always begin. O'Connor ends the story with a physical description of the Irish—"red-haired, with broad shoulders and great, drooping mustaches"

OTHER STORIES

(740). For Miss Willerton, once the description above the shoulders is complete, her squeamishness about things physical, sexual, and biological will prevent her from moving forward. She will have to turn to another subject; Miss Willerton is incapable of giving Willie her freedom.

"The Turkey"

"The Turkey" first appeared as "The Capture" in the November 1948 *Mademoiselle* magazine. The surface action of the story concerns eleven-year-old Ruller McFarney's afternoon in the woods playing with his imaginary friends and chasing a turkey. On a deeper level, the story explores Ruller's first personal experience with God and his own movement from innocent, unusual child to tough-cussing bad boy to bewildered, isolated, and frightened youth. The afternoon has been more than Ruller bargained for, and beyond his capability to understand. "The Turkey" is the first of O'Connor's stories to deal overtly with a religious theme, where presentation leads to resolution, but not for the character.

As the story opens, Ruller is playing a Western version of cops and robbers, good guys against bad guys, when he catches sight of a turkey, described before named: "a touch of bronze and a rustle and then . . . the eye, set in red folds that covered the head and hung down along the neck" (741). Wishing he had a real gun, Ruller quickly discovers the turkey is lame and plots to take it home if he has "to chase it out of the county" (742). Repeatedly, Ruller reflects on his parents would-be delight and wonder at his success: "Look at Ruller with that wild turkey!" (742), "Good Lord look at Ruller!" (744), "Lord look at Ruller!" (747). Catching this turkey will distinguish him from his older brother

UNDERSTANDING FLANNERY O'CONNOR

Hane, who had gone bad at fifteen, taking up pool and smoking and staying out late. Ruller's plans disintegrate, however, as quickly as he makes them. The turkey disappears, and the story moves to a theological level: "It was like somebody had played a dirty trick on him" (744).

Running into a tree, scratching his arms, tearing his shirt had all been for nothing. It is enough to make him cuss. The words, first thought, slip cautiously out of his mouth. When nothing happens, the words grow more bold: "Oh hell" prompts "God!" which escalates to "God dammit" which extends to "God dammit to hell, good Lord from Jerusalem" which enters the realm of silly with "Good Father, good God, sweep the chickens out the yard" (745). Laughing out of control, he cannot remove his mother's response to his cussing from his mind. When the laughter suddenly stops, however, he is aware of a new thought, and his mind moves to his grandmother's words of warning to Hane: "The only way to conquer the devil was to fight him" (746). He has no choice but to oppose his grandmother's warning, to cuss at her in his mind, suggest "some booze" so that they can "get stinky" (746). The minister, too, he flaunts in his mind. His warning about "walking in the tracks of Satan" was ridiculous because the biblical threat of "weeping and gnashing of teeth" (747), which O'Connor takes from any number of places in Matthew or Luke (Matthew 8:12, 13:42, 50, 22:13, 24:51, 25:30; Luke 13:28), is not pertinent to men: "Men didn't weep" (747).

The "somebody" that Ruller had blamed for the dirty trick becomes "God." As soon as God as responsible party becomes full in Ruller's mind, he catches sight once more of the turkey, described again before named: "A pile of ruffled bronze with a red head lying limp along the ground" (747). Thoughts of himself as family hero once again come to mind, and God becomes worth

OTHER STORIES

considering in some other way than a curse word: "Maybe God wanted him to be a preacher" (748). Ruller and God then talk with each other, and God becomes the hail-fellow-well-met. Ruller has in these ensuing moments grown to perfect understanding of God, and if "God wanted him to do something, he'd turn something up" (749). God then provides opportunities along the way home through town for family friends to praise Ruller's accomplishment, and God answers Ruller's prayer for the beggar to appear so he can give her a dime. This token gesture, all the money Ruller has, is Ruller's way of thanking God for the turkey. Ruller, however, has asked only for a beggar—"Lord, please send me a beggar! . . . one right now" (751). Ruller mistakes Hetty Gilman for the beggar God has sent and promptly delivers to her his only dime. The country boys, who had been tailing Ruller all along, and to whom Ruller brazenly shows the turkey, also walk away with that turkey.

Ruller, stunned, watches the turkey disappear, the night grow dark, and fear fill his heart, which runs "as fast as his legs . . . certain that Something Awful was tearing behind him with its arms rigid and its fingers ready to clutch" (752). O'Connor suggests that God is something full of awe, not to be understood, not to be reduced, not to be anybody's diminutive pal. God is a mystery that cannot be figured out by a young boy in his afternoon play. Who "the turkey" is at story's end shifts to Ruller himself.

"The Train"

The last story of O'Connor's thesis is an early draft of the first chapter of what will be her first novel, *Wise Blood*. Published in the April 1948 *Sewanee Review,* "The Train" appears with only her name and no explanation of the author nor the nature of the fiction. Early readers considered the piece of fiction, then, a short story. A man named Hazel Wickers is on a train heading for Taulkinham, but he is obsessed with his lost home, the subject on which every facet of the story is riveted. First, Haze focuses on the porter, a man who is so like old Cash from his own home in Eastrod, Tennessee, that Haze cannot keep his eyes off him. Haze wants to talk with the porter, but he makes several false starts before he is able to mention Eastrod. When the porter says he is from Chicago, Haze has trouble processing this information, repeating his home several times to himself: "He was from Chicago" (756). Haze resists believing him, so much does he want the man to be from his own hometown, which no longer exists. Haze yearns for conversation about home. When he looks for the porter to assist him into the upper berth, Haze holds onto this hope: "They might have a little conversation before he got in the berth" (758). The porter, however, appears to be interested only in doing his job. The last words the misguided Haze says to the porter include a reference to Cash: "Cash is dead. He got the cholera from a pig" (759), to which the porter repeats that he is from Chicago. None of this matters to Haze. He strongly needs to believe that the porter is from Eastrod, that he is related to Old Cash, either his runaway son or a cousin.

Mrs. Wallace Ben Hosen, formerly Miss Hitchcock, boards the train in Evansville, and "Haze was glad to have someone there talking" (754). The conversation they have is more strange than the ones Haze has with the porter. When Mrs. Hosen asks if Haze is going home, he responds by telling her he "get[s] off at Taulkinham" (755), which she assumes is his home, moving directly to place someone she knows there. When Haze corrects her, she asks where he lives, but his answers are vague: "It was there. . . . I don't rightly know, I was there but . . ." (755). Even a break to speak with the porter and a return to hear Mrs. Hosen's ceaseless prattle does not deter him from thoughts of home. She speaks of her sister's husband who turned to liquor in Waterloo, and Haze interrupts: "I went back there last time. . . . I wouldn't be getting off at Taulkinham if it was there; it went apart like, you know, it . . ." (756). Mrs. Hosen has lost Haze; his answers do not make sense in her world. When the two meet in the train aisle after she has prepared for her berth by becoming "heavily pink" (758), and he tries to get around her, she can only demand of him: "What IS the matter with you?" (759). The answer to her question is only partially demonstrated in this story.

When Haze retires to his upper berth, he is free once again to remember the place that is no more, his visit to Eastrod, the decaying home, his mother, who "could rest easier knowing [the shifferrobe] was guarded some" (761). But Haze's berth is reminiscent of his mother's casket. He had seen the "shadow that came down over her face" (761) and his own situation in this berth, with no window and darkness closing in on him, forced him to spring up and throw his head over the side and hang there "wet and cold" (761), gazing at the rug below. When the tracks curve, though, Haze falls "back sick into the rushing stillness of the train" (762). O'Connor develops an odd character here, one still interested in other people, but more consumed with a desire to figure out how to replace the home he has lost. This early Haze represents a marked departure from other thesis characters. He is interior man, her first character that is to be consumed by the vertical relationship of man to God that will take O'Connor another five years to prepare for publication in novel form.

"An Afternoon in the Woods"

When O'Connor was selecting her stories for the first collection, *A Good Man Is Hard to Find,* she wrote to her editor, Robert Giroux, that she was including "the story that was in *Mademoiselle*—with the title changed to 'An Afternoon in the Woods' and the whole thing much rewritten."[13] Within the month, she suggested that he cut "An Afternoon in the Woods" because of space limitations. Two months later, she reported the completion of a brand new story, "Good Country People," which would take the place of "An Afternoon in the Woods" in the published collection. Until Sally Fitzgerald's 1988 *Flannery O'Connor: Collected Works* appeared, "An Afternoon in the Woods" remained unpublished.

O'Connor is successful in this rewrite of "The Turkey" in bringing the religious theme of the story toward a more precise focus. The action is calculated, and the boy, at story's end, appears more sobered than frightened. The new name for the protagonist, Manley, anticipates a younger version of the character who becomes Manley Pointer in "Good Country People." Manley, "a fat white-haired boy of ten with pale blue eyes that watered constantly behind a thick pair of silver-rimmed spectacles" (763), has fled the child's party he was supposed to attend, and in his white suit has retreated to the woods. Once in the woods, Manley destroys the child's present: "He took a good-sized rock and crushed the bottle and buried it with the paper and ribbon in a ditch" (763). His response to the disposal of a heart-shaped bottle of perfume selected by his mother and grandmother is one of "exquisite pleasure" (763). The violent act heightens his senses and makes the woods around him come to life. In this mood, he sees "a dark wine-colored eye watching him with a fierce tranquility" (764). O'Connor evokes the biblical story of

Isaac, about to be sacrificed by his own father (Genesis 22): "[Manley] squatted there, trembling as if he were waiting for an ax to strike the back of his neck" (764). Manley's approach toward the turkey duplicates the ending of the story: "His arms were rigid and his fingers ready to clutch" (764). Manley anticipates the surprise from family if he can bring the turkey home: "Manley! where in the world did YOU get that turkey!" (764); "Where did YOU get that wild turkey?" (765). He has learned from older brother Roy Jr. that the turkey will divert his mother's attention from his ripped white coat, dirty white pants, and broken glasses. The turkey eludes him, "like God had played a dirty trick on him" (766).

Manley responds to the trick by cussing, and one word becomes, ultimately, a string of words spoken alternately softly and loudly. "Oh hell" moves to "God" which grows to "God dammit" which combines to "God dammit to hell" which become short directives in "Good Father, Good God, back the truck in-to the yard" and diversions on a theme in "Our Father Who art in heaven, shoot em six and roll em seven" (766). When Manley's laughter abruptly ceases, he tallies up the cost of his broken glasses and dirty clothes and anticipates the trouble at home. Manley thinks salvation rests in "doing something that was so bad that being killed dead for it wouldn't be as bad as what you had done" (767). The feeling of evil comes on him, and he knows what he is about to say is like nothing he has ever said before: "Goddam God" (768). After the blasphemy is uttered, he spots the dead turkey "that must weigh twenty pounds" (768), decides to take it home, determines "it must weigh thirty or forty pounds" (769), and realizes that what has just "happened was a clear call to the ministry" (769). And no sooner is Manley aware of this call than a voice appears on the scene. The voice is a reminder that

God's way is not an easy way. The voice is the devil, arguing the other side: "There would be more in it for you if you went bad" (769).

When Manley is ready to talk with God, he does so in the guise of his imaginative play role. He tells the boys the turkey is from God, acknowledges God directly for the gift, and then God takes his turn: "Only the best for a valuable man. . . . Glad to have you on my side, Mason" (769). On the way home through town, people Manley does not know come to see his turkey. Manley notices also the tenant children who walk behind him and hopes they will come closer to look at his turkey, for Manley "felt an urgency to do something for God" (770). He prays for a beggar, out loud, to come "before [he] get[s] home" (770). He remembers the preacher's words, from Matthew 7:7, "knock and it would be opened to you, ask and you would receive!" (771). He opens his eyes and Hetty Gilman turns the corner, the perfect recipient for his dime, he thinks. The beggar woman is sinister—dressed in black, a face "the color of a dead chicken's skin," a mouth that "cracked," and a "voracious leer"—and with a "razor-like scrape" she secures the dime from Manley's hand (771). Manley's wrong-headed interpretation is "that a miracle had been performed for his sake" (771).

When he turns to offer the tenant boys a look at his turkey, they have other designs: "Lemme see it here" (772), says the tallest boy, and he slings the turkey over his back and walks away. Manley has no verbal response to the departing boys. As he turns toward home, only the coming darkness causes him to run. While running, however, he is "certain that Something Awful was tearing behind him with its arms rigid and its fingers ready to clutch" (772), exactly the position he had been in back in the woods with his first encounter with the turkey. The afternoon has exposed him to his first perception of God, but as he runs toward home, he is only aware of a mystery in the universe that is beyond his comprehension to decipher in one afternoon in the woods.

"The Partridge Festival"

"The Partridge Festival" appeared in the March 1961 the *Critic*. O'Connor considered the story for possible inclusion in *Everything That Rises Must Converge* but decided "[she] didn't want it in the collection."[14] O'Connor used the events of a local murder for the story, which she altered so significantly that the historical event is sufficiently obscured. The event she began with is the same murder that Pete Dexter researched for his 1988 award-winning *Paris Trout*. Marion Stembridge, a grocer and loan shark, was charged with the murder of a young black girl in 1949. He was found guilty and sentenced to one to three years in prison. He never actually served time. Then in 1953, he went on a rampage and killed two lawyers, Marion Ennis and Pete Bivins. Next, he turned the gun on himself. A man named Singleton rode up and down the street, honking his horn, trying to alert everyone.[15] A line and a character from an early O'Connor draft is much closer to the title character of Dexter's book. Kenneth Scouten refers to the earlier Singleton as "a usurer of questionable character: 'he owned a dry goods store on the back street where colored people traded . . . [and] he lent money at a high rate of interest' (a, 1–2)."[16] Dexter focuses on the 1949 episode in his book, whereas O'Connor bases her final draft on the killing rampage that Stembridge launched in 1953.

Calhoun is an aspiring writer, who, for "three summer months of the year . . . lived with his parents and sold air-conditioners, boats, and refrigerators," so that he could bring his "rebel-artist-mystic" (776) self to life the other nine months. O'Connor paces for the reader Calhoun's success at selling, and later the similarities with his great-grandfather, "the most forward-looking merchant Partridge ever had" (774), become apparent: "Selling was the only thing he had proved himself good at; yet it was impossible for him to believe that every man was not created equally an artist if he could but suffer and achieve it" (789). However, his writing desires are thwarted by a vision that does not square with reality. Calhoun visits his two maiden aunts in the small town of Partridge, which is celebrating its annual azalea festival, not for the festival, but because he is attracted by the bizarre murder of six innocent people that has taken place in conjunction with the festival. Singleton, the murderer, had refused to purchase a ticket for the activities of the festival and had been "imprisoned in a pair of stocks . . . with a goat that had been tried and convicted previously for the same offense" (774). Ten days later, Singleton returned for his revenge. Apparently, the mock jail, meant in the spirit of community fun, was no laughing matter to Singleton, who mowed down six people with a "silent automatic pistol" (774). Calhoun is convinced that the town of Partridge is at fault and that Singleton is the real victim, caught in the clutches of crass commercialism.

A familiar motif in O'Connor stories includes the simpleminded, dottering, yet kind and well-intentioned female, who actually knows a great deal more than is first supposed, pitted against the young, upstart intellectual who will eventually see fully the error of his ways. The aunts and Calhoun fill these roles perfectly. His aunts know that Singleton is insane. Calhoun feels that Singleton is his double. Calhoun's plan is to expose the town in his novel, while the aunts hope Calhoun will be "another

Margaret Mitchell" (776), a reference to the author of *Gone with the Wind*. When Calhoun stares them down with a fiercely retorted John 8:32: "Know the truth . . . and the truth shall make you free," the aunts are pleased he is "quoting Scripture" (776). O'Connor also brings in a subtle reference to Herman Melville's "Benito Cereno" when she suggests that Calhoun needs "to mitigate his own guilt, for his doubleness, his shadow, was cast before him more darkly than usual in the light of Singleton's purity" (776).

Scouten has noted some parallels between O'Connor's azalea festival with its cold-blooded murder drama and the Greek dramatic festival, the archetypal fertility ritual of Dionysia, which demands a sacrifice. The people Calhoun meets on his walk through town—the young boy, the old man, the girl "whose tongue was curled in the mouth of a Coca Cola bottle" (780), the barber—become the chorus, that body, speaking as one, who affirm the reality of the drama.[17] Calhoun pushes his position on each person he meets, but he scores no points until his return to dinner at his aunts' home. They have included Mary Elizabeth, an unattractive intellectual with a matching disposition. Mary Elizabeth is Calhoun's true double; she is a writer interested in a nonfiction piece on Singleton, whom she views as a mythic Christ figure.

O'Connor inserts a brief debate between novelist and nonfiction prose writer. Calhoun values the importance of seeing Singleton, for the "novelist is never afraid to look at the real object" (787). Mary Elizabeth, on the other hand, is satisfied with what Calhoun calls her "narrow abstractions" (787). Calhoun is more talk than action, and Mary Elizabeth must goad him into making the offer for both of them to visit Singleton together. On the ride out to Quincy State Hospital, patterned on Central, the Georgia state facility for the mentally disabled, Mary Elizabeth quotes from Dante's *Divine Comedy* as they drive through the entrance: "Abandon hope all ye who enter here" (791). Besides the candy and cigarettes, Mary Elizabeth takes three books to Singleton: Friedrich Nietzsche's *Thus Spake Zarathustra,* a book about the possibilities of a Superman in our society; José Ortega y Gasset's *The Revolt of the Masses,* which anticipates mass-man negating the system that has spawned him; and "a thin decorated volume of Housman" (793). A. E. Housman's poems stress the transitory nature of existence. Mary Elizabeth obtains their passes, which identify them as relatives of Singleton, and, thus, of each other. When Singleton appears from his room, after he has been "got ready" (793), Calhoun is rendered mute, while Mary Elizabeth manages in a "barely audible voice, 'We came to say we understand'" (794). Singleton, as the chorus has intoned all along, is insane. He shrills and shrieks, exposing himself to Mary Elizabeth, which causes both of his alleged kin to race for the car and drive five miles before stopping from exhaustion.

The intellectual and her double have been brought low by the reality of Singleton's insanity. Her face mirrors the "nakedness of the sky," while the artist in Calhoun has been claimed by the image of himself in Mary Elizabeth's glasses; he is nothing more than his great-grandfather, "a master salesman" (796), who began the festival in Partridge and from whom his heir is doomed to inherit it. Calhoun is not the artist he thinks he is; Mary Elizabeth's abstractions have become startlingly concrete. The horror is more than either of these limited people could have imagined.

OTHER STORIES

"Why Do the Heathen Rage?"

This fragment of what might have been O'Connor's third novel was published in the July 1963 *Esquire*. The Flannery O'Connor archives at Georgia College have a total of 378 manuscript pages of this work, but all the pages do not tally an almost finished novel; rather, only a half-dozen episodes exist, with seventeen versions of a porch scene.[18] The title comes from a paid ad that was "a fixture on the pages of Atlanta newspapers." The author of the column, Robert Scott, was an eccentric with a deep interest in Bible missionary work.[19]

In the four-page published fragment, O'Connor is well on her way to depicting Walter Tilman as a monk. He is the son, not understood by his mother, who is dealing with his father, who has just returned from the hospital, where he stayed two weeks because of his stroke. Walter's unnamed mother thinks that her husband's stroke will "wake Walter up" (797). His sister, Mary Maud, is another schoolteacher type, with a take-charge personality. The unnamed mother, Mary Maud, and Walter share similar personality types with other O'Connor characters.

Upon his return home, the old man gives Roosevelt, the yardman turned nurse, "the only gesture of affection he had given any of them" (798). This response causes Roosevelt to cry: "Then, all at once, tears glazed [his eyes] and glistened on his black cheeks like sweat" (797). But attention in this fragment is directed at the relationship between Walter and his mother. She wants him to assume responsibility for managing the place, but he knows she would serve that role better than he could. In a Southern lady's whine, his mother replies: "Walter, you're a man. I'm only a woman" (799). Walter's interest is reading, not

UNDERSTANDING FLANNERY O'CONNOR

bossing others around, but his mother does not understand him. Her assessment of him is limited by the reality of her day-to-day existence: "The man she saw courted good and evil impartially and saw so many sides of every question that he could not move, he could not work, he could not even make niggers work" (799). It was his reading that stumped her, for Walter read "books that had nothing to do with anything that mattered now" (800). When she perceives that the books are stories of the early days of the church, a letter from St. Jerome to Heliodorus, his world appears in a mysterious light to her. The published fragment ends with her revelation "that the General with the sword in his mouth, marching to do violence, was Jesus" (800). It is a theme O'Connor and her readers know well.

Notes

1. See Flannery O'Connor, *The Complete Stories* (New York: Farrar, Straus and Giroux) 1971.

2. Flannery O'Connor, *The Habit of Being,* ed. Sally Fitzgerald (New York: Farrar, Straus and Giroux, 1979) 526.

3. Flannery O'Connor, *Flannery O'Connor: Collected Works,* ed. Sally Fitzgerald (New York: Library of America, 1988). All parenthetical citations from these other stories are from this edition.

4. Thomas Gullason, A Review of *"Flannery O'Connor: The Complete Stories," Saturday Review* 13 Nov. 1971: 57, 63.

5. Walter Clemons, "Acts of Grace," *Newsweek* 8 Nov. 1971: 116.

6. "At Gunpoint," *Time* 29 Nov. 1971: 88.

7. Sally Fitzgerald, "The Owl and the Nightingale," *Flannery O'Connor Bulletin* 13 (1984): 56.

8. T. S. Eliot, *Collected Poems, 1909–1962* (New York: Harcourt, Brace and World, 1963) 29–30.

OTHER STORIES

9. Sally Fitzgerald in O'Connor, *Flannery* 1242.

10. Robert Fitzgerald, note, "The Barber," by Flannery O'Connor *Atlantic* 226 (Oct. 1970): 111.

11. Harold Chase, et al., *Dictionary of American History,* V (New York: Charles Scribner's Sons, 1976) 407.

12. O'Connor, *Habit* 159.

13. O'Connor, *Habit* 72.

14. O'Connor, *Habit* 580.

15. Sharon Thomason, "Milledgeville Remembers Real Paris Trout," *Atlanta Journal and Constitution* 8 May 1991, C10.

16. Kenneth Scouten, "'The Partridge Festival': Manuscript Revisions," *Flannery O'Connor Bulletin* 15 (1986): 36.

17. Kenneth Scouten, "The Mythological Dimensions of Five of Flannery O'Connor's Works," *Flannery O'Connor Bulletin* 2 (1973): 59–72.

18. See Stuart L. Burns, "How Wide Did 'The Heathen' Range?" *Flannery O'Connor Bulletin* 4 (1975): 25–41; Marian Burns, "The Chronology of Flannery O'Connor's 'Why Do the Heathen Rage?'" *Flannery O'Connor Bulletin* 11 (1982): 58–75; Marian Burns, "O'Connor's Unfinished Novel" *Flannery O'Connor Bulletin* 11 (1982): 76–93.

19. "Q & A on the News," *Atlanta Journal and Constitution* 8 Apr. 1991, A2.

BIBLIOGRAPHY

Books by Flannery O'Connor

Wise Blood. New York: Harcourt Brace, 1952. London: Neville Spearman, 1955. Novel.

A Good Man Is Hard to Find. New York: Harcourt Brace, 1955. Retitled as *The Artificial Nigger and Other Tales.* London: Neville Spearman, 1957. Short Stories. Contents: "A Good Man Is Hard to Find," "The River," "The Life You Save May Be Your Own," "A Stroke of Good Fortune," "A Temple of the Holy Ghost," "The Artificial Nigger," "A Circle in the Fire," "A Late Encounter with the Enemy," "Good Country People," and "The Displaced Person."

The Violent Bear It Away. New York: Farrar, Straus and Cudahy, 1960. London: Longmans, Green, 1960. Novel.

Everything That Rises Must Converge. New York: Farrar, Straus and Giroux, 1965. London: Faber and Faber, 1966. Short Stories. Contents: "Everything That Rises Must Converge," "Greenleaf," "A View of the Woods," "The Enduring Chill," "The Comforts of Home," "The Lame Shall Enter First," "Revelation," "Parker's Back," and "Judgment Day."

Mystery and Manners. Ed. Sally and Robert Fitzgerald. New York: Farrar, Straus and Giroux, 1969. London: Faber and Faber, 1972. Occasional Prose.

The Complete Stories. New York: Farrar, Straus and Giroux, 1971. Short Stories. Contents: "The Geranium," "The Barber," "Wildcat," "The Crop," "The Turkey," "The Train," "The Peeler," "The Heart of the Park," "A Stroke of Good Fortune," "Enoch and the Gorilla," "A Good Man Is Hard to Find," "A Late Encounter with the Enemy," "The Life You

BIBLIOGRAPHY

Save May Be Your Own," "The River," "A Circle in the Fire," "The Displaced Person," "A Temple of the Holy Ghost," "The Artificial Nigger," "Good Country People," "You Can't Be Any Poorer Than Dead," "Greenleaf," "A View of the Woods," "The Enduring Chill," "The Comforts of Home," "Everything That Rises Must Converge," "The Partridge Festival," "The Lame Shall Enter First," "Why Do the Heathen Rage?," "Revelation," "Parker's Back," and "Judgment Day."

The Habit of Being. Ed. Sally Fitzgerald. New York: Farrar, Straus and Giroux, 1979. Collected Letters.

The Presence of Grace and Other Book Reviews by Flannery O'Connor. Comp. Leo J. Zuber. Ed. Carter W. Martin. Athens: U of Georgia P, 1983.

Flannery O'Connor: Collected Works. Ed. Sally Fitzgerald. New York: Library of America, 1988.

Secondary Sources

Books about Flannery O'Connor

Asals, Frederick. *Flannery O'Connor: The Imagination of Extremity.* Athens: U of Georgia P, 1982. The most extensive commentary on O'Connor's use of the "double" figure motif; a focus on the tensions and polarities of her imagination.

Bacon, Jon Lance. *Flannery O'Connor and Cold War Culture.* Cambridge: Cambridge UP, 1993. Argues that O'Connor attacks consumerism within the American way of life.

Baumgaertner, Jill P. *Flannery O'Connor: A Proper Scaring.* Wheaton, IL: Harold Shaw, 1988. A Christian reading of O'Connor's work.

BIBLIOGRAPHY

Brinkmeyer, Robert H., Jr. *The Art and Vision of Flannery O'Connor.* Baton Rouge: Louisiana State UP, 1989. Explores levels of dialogue between narrator and character.

Browning, Preston M., Jr. *Flannery O'Connor.* Carbondale: Southern Illinois UP, 1974. An overview of the two novels and the two collections of short stories that stresses the moment of connecting opposites, the tension created when violence and the holy come together.

Coles, Robert. *Flannery O'Connor's South.* Baton Rouge: Louisiana State UP, 1980. A reading of O'Connor as a realistic writer.

Desmond, John F. *Risen Sons: Flannery O'Connor's Vision of History.* Athens: U of Georgia P, 1987. An examination of how O'Connor's historical sense functions within her creative efforts.

Di Renzo, Anthony. *American Gargoyles: Flannery O'Connor and the Medieval Grotesque.* Carbondale: Southern Illinois UP, 1993. Connects O'Connor's comic genius to medieval art and satire.

Driggers, Stephen G., and Robert J. Dunn, with Sarah Gordon. *The Manuscripts of Flannery O'Connor at Georgia College.* Athens: U of Georgia P, 1989. A catalogue explaining the 297 files of O'Connor's manuscripts housed in the O'Connor Collection in Milledgeville.

Driskell, Leon V., and Joan T. Brittain. *The Eternal Crossroads: The Art of Flannery O'Connor.* Lexington: UP of Kentucky, 1971. Exploration of influences of Mauriac and Teilhard. Contains early, yet fairly thorough bibliography.

Eggenschwiler, David. *The Christian Humanism of Flannery O'Connor.* Detroit: Wayne State UP, 1972. Explores O'Connor as a Christian humanist.

BIBLIOGRAPHY

Farmer, David. *Flannery O'Connor: A Descriptive Bibliography.* New York: Garland, 1981. Comprehensive listing of O'Connor's work in print.

Feeley, Kathleen. *Flannery O'Connor: Voice of the Peacock.* New Brunswick, NJ: Rutgers UP, 1972. Perceptive readings of O'Connor's work; commentary based in O'Connor's reading of theology and history.

Fickett, Harold and Douglas R. Gilbert. *Flannery O'Connor: Images of Grace.* Grand Rapids: Eerdmans, 1986. Theological perspective on O'Connor's work with photographs from the O'Connor Collection and around rural Georgia.

Friedman, Melvin J., and Lewis A. Lawson, eds. *The Added Dimension: The Art and Mind of Flannery O'Connor.* New York: Fordham UP, [1966], 1977. Important early essays, demonstrating variety of critical approaches to O'Connor.

Friedman, Melvin J., and Beverly Lyon Clark, eds. *Critical Essays on Flannery O'Connor.* Boston: G. K. Hall, 1985. Contains selected early reviews and essays offering broad range of approaches to O'Connor's fiction; introductory essay provides overview of history of O'Connor scholarship.

Gentry, Marshall Bruce. *Flannery O'Connor's Religion of the Grotesque.* Jackson: UP of Mississippi, 1986. Examines the struggle for authority between narrator and character.

Getz, Lorine M. *Flannery O'Connor: Her Life, Library and Book Reviews.* New York: Edwin Mellen, 1980. Uncertain reliability. Partially corrected by Linda Schlafer, "Monitum: Beware the Getz." *Flannery O'Connor Bulletin* 11 (1982): 43–57.

———. *Nature and Grace in Flannery O'Connor's Fiction.* New York: Edwin Mellen, 1982. Theological implications of O'Connor's representation of grace.

BIBLIOGRAPHY

Giannone, Richard. *Flannery O'Connor and the Mystery of Love.* Urbana: U of Illinois P, 1989. Exploration of guilt and love in each work; biblical texts used in literary form.

Grimshaw, James A., Jr. *The Flannery O'Connor Companion.* Westport, CT: Greenwood, 1981. Includes an alphabetical description of O'Connor characters, brief annotations on fiction and nonfiction.

Hawkins, Peter S. *The Language of Grace: Flannery O'Connor, Walker Percy, and Iris Murdoch.* Cambridge, MA: Cowley, 1983. Addresses language, audience, and belief.

Hendin, Josephine. *The World of Flannery O'Connor.* Bloomington: Indiana UP, 1970. A biographical reading of O'Connor's fiction.

―――. *The Otherness Within: Gnostic Readings in Marcel Proust, Flannery O'Connor, and François Villon.* Baton Rouge: Louisiana State UP, 1983. A study of Proust's "negative space" illustrated by O'Connor's metaphor of physical violence.

Hyman, Stanley Edgar. *Flannery O'Connor.* Minneapolis, U of Minnesota P, 1966. Early overview of O'Connor's life and career.

Kessler, Edward. *Flannery O'Connor and the Language of the Apocalypse.* Princeton: Princeton UP, 1986. Emphasizes O'Connor's use of metaphor.

Kinney, Arthur F. *Flannery O'Connor's Library: Resources of Being.* Athens: U of Georgia P, 1985. Catalogue by subject matter of O'Connor's personal library holdings.

McFarland, Dorothy Tuck. *Flannery O'Connor.* New York: Frederick Ungar, 1976. Emphasizes O'Connor's demonic thrust.

BIBLIOGRAPHY

McKenzie, Barbara. *Flannery O'Connor's Georgia.* Athens: U of Georgia P, 1980. A collection of photographs of middle Georgia that illustrate O'Connor's fiction.

Magee, Rosemary M., ed. *Conversations with Flannery O'Connor.* Jackson: UP of Mississippi, 1987. Previously published interviews and panel discussions.

Martin, Cartin W. *The True Country: Themes in the Fiction of Flannery O'Connor.* Kingsport, TN: Vanderbilt UP, 1969. Among the earliest book-length studies. Exploration of O'Connor's religious themes.

May, John R. *The Pruning Word: The Parables of Flannery O'Connor.* Notre Dame: U of Notre Dame P, 1976. A biblical interpretation of O'Connor's fiction.

Montgomery, Marion. *Why Flannery O'Connor Stayed Home.* LaSalle, IL: Sherwood Sugden, 1981. Focuses on depth of characterization grounded in Western intellectual thought.

Muller, Gilbert H. *Nightmares and Visions: Flannery O'Connor and the Catholic Grotesque.* Athens: U of Georgia P, 1972. Historically connects O'Connor's use of the grotesque to Roman art.

Orvell, Miles. *Flannery O'Connor: An Introduction.* Jackson: U of Mississippi P, 1991. A reissuing of *Invisible Parade.*

———. *Invisible Parade: The Fiction of Flannery O'Connor.* Philadelphia: Temple UP, 1972. Early attempt to place O'Connor's fiction in American literature.

Paulson, Suzanne Morrow. *Flannery O'Connor: A Study of the Short Fiction.* Boston: Twayne, 1988. A representative assortment of essays from theological to modern secular perspective.

BIBLIOGRAPHY

Ragen, Brian Abel. *A Wreck on the Road to Damascus: Innocence, Guilt, and Conversion in Flannery O'Connor.* Chicago Loyola UP, 1989. Focuses on use of car as symbol in three works.

Shloss, Carol. *Flannery O'Connor's Dark Comedies: The Limits of Inference.* Baton Rouge: Louisiana State UP, 1980. Examination of O'Connor's rhetoric of violence.

Stephens, C. Ralph, ed. *The Correspondence of Flannery O'Connor and the Brainard Cheneys.* Jackson: UP of Mississippi, 1986. Chronicles the friendship from both sides.

Stephens, Martha. *The Question of Flannery O'Connor.* Baton Rouge: Louisiana State UP, 1973. Early attempt to examine O'Connor outside of a theological perspective.

Walters, Dorothy. *Flannery O'Connor.* New York: Twayne, 1973. A formalist methodology with attention to the grotesque.

Westarp, Karl-Heinz, and Jan Nordby Gretlund, eds. *Realist of Distances: Flannery O'Connor Revisited.* Aarhus, Denmark: Aarhus UP, 1987. A collection of twenty papers, representing seven countries, delivered at a symposium in Sandbjerg, Denmark, in August 1984.

Westling, Louise. *Sacred Groves and Ravaged Gardens: The Fiction of Eudora Welty, Carson McCullers, and Flannery O'Connor.* Athens: U of Georgia P, 1985. Feminist perspective; close look at O'Connor's mothers and daughters.

Wood, Ralph C. *The Comedy of Redemption: Christian Faith and Comic Vision in Four American Novelists.* Notre Dame: U of Notre Dame P, 1988. Contains two chapters on O'Connor as Christian satirist and comedian.

BIBLIOGRAPHY

Flannery O'Connor Journals

Critique: Studies in Modern Fiction 2 (Fall 1958). Eds. Joan Griscom, et al. An issue dedicated to the work of Flannery O'Connor and J. F. Powers. Three articles on O'Connor by Caroline Gordon, Louis D. Rubin, Jr., and Sister M. Bernetta Quinn, O.S.F.; includes a list of publications and reviews.

Esprit 8 (Winter 1964). Ed. John H. Scanlin. Upon O'Connor's death, the University of Scranton in Scranton, Pennsylvania, dedicated this issue to O'Connor's life and work. Includes tributes from over fifty writers, poets, editors, and critics. Also photographs and drawings of O'Connor and scenes from the fiction.

The Flannery O'Connor Bulletin. Ed. Sarah Gordon. Milledgeville: Georgia College. A journal dedicated to O'Connor's life and work. Continuous yearly publication since 1972. Includes articles, reminiscences, poems, reviews, notes, art, cartoons, and photographs.

Selected Contemporary Reviews

WISE BLOOD

"Briefly Noted." *New Yorker* 14 June 1952: 118.

Goyen, William. "Unending Vengeance." *New York Times Book Review* 18 May 1952: 4.

LaFarge, Oliver. "Manic Gloom." *Saturday Review* 24 May 1952: 22.

Simons, John W. "A Case of Possession." *Commonweal* 27 June 1952: 297–98.

"Southern Dissonance." *Time* 9 June 1952: 108, 110.

BIBLIOGRAPHY

Stallings, Sylvia. "Young Writer with a Bizarre Tale to Tell." *New York Herald Tribune Book Review* 18 May 1952: 3.

"To Win by Default." *New Republic* 7 July 1952: 19.

The United States Quarterly Book Review 8 (Sept. 1952): 256.

A GOOD MAN IS HARD TO FIND

"Briefly Noted." *New Yorker* 18 June 1955: 105.

Gordon, Caroline. "With a Glitter of Evil." *New York Times Book Review* 12 June 1955: 5.

Greene, James. "The Comic and the Sad." *Commonweal* 22 July 1955: 404.

"New Books." *Catholic World* 182 (Oct. 1955): 66–67.

Prescott, Orville. "Books of the Times," *New York Times* 10 June 1955: 23.

Stallings, Sylvia. "Flannery O'Connor: A New, Shining Talent among Our Storytellers." *New York Herald Tribune Book Review* 5 June 1955: 1.

"Such Nice People." *Time* 6 June 1955: 114.

Wyllie, John Cook. "The Unscented South." *Saturday Review* 4 June 1955: 15.

THE VIOLENT BEAR IT AWAY

"Added Attractions." *Christian Century* 1 June 1960: 672.

"Briefly Noted." *New Yorker* 19 Mar. 1960: 179.

Davidson, Donald. "A Prophet Went Forth." *New York Times Book Review* 28 Feb. 1960: 4.

"God-Intoxicated Hillbillies." *Time* 29 Feb. 1960: 118–19.

Greene, James. "The Redemptive Tradition of Southern Rural Life." *Commonweal* 15 Apr. 1960: 67–68.

Hicks, Granville. "Southern Gothic with a Vengeance." *Saturday Review* 27 Feb. 1960: 18.

BIBLIOGRAPHY

Nyren, Dorothy. "Review of *The Violent Bear It Away*." *Library Journal* 1 Jan. 1960: 146.

"Set Fair for Happiness?" *Times Literary Supplement* 14 Oct. 1960: 666.

Warnke, Frank J. "A Vision Deep and Narrow." *New Republic* 14 Mar. 1960: 18–19.

EVERYTHING THAT RISES MUST CONVERGE

Drake, Robert. "Hair-Curling Gospel." *Christian Century* 19 May 1965: 656.

"Grace through Nature." *Newsweek* 31 May 1965: 85–86.

Hicks, Granville. "A Cold, Hard Look at Humankind." *Saturday Review* 29 May 1965: 23–24.

Howe, Irving. "Flannery O'Connor's Stories." *New York Review of Books* 30 Sept. 1965: 16–17.

Kiely, Robert. "The Art of Collision." *Christian Science Monitor* 17 June 1965: 7.

"Nothing but the Truth." *New Yorker* 11 Sept. 1965: 220–21.

Poirier, Richard. "If You Know Who You Are You Can Go Anywhere." *New York Times Book Review* 30 May 1965: 6, 22.

Schott, Webster. "Flannery O'Connor: Faith's Stepchild." *Nation* 13 Sept. 1965: 142–44, 146.

MYSTERY AND MANNERS

"Books in Brief." *Harper's Magazine* 238 (June 1969): 94.

"Briefly Noted." *New Yorker* 19 July 1969: 84.

Gilman, Richard. "On Flannery O'Connor." *New York Review of Books* 21 August 1969: 24–25.

Kellogg, Jean. "We Have Had Our Fall." *Christian Century* 9 July 1969: 927.

BIBLIOGRAPHY

Mano, D. Keith. "*Mystery and Manners.*" *New York Times Book Review* 25 May 1969: 6–7, 20.

COMPLETE STORIES

"At Gunpoint." *Time* 29 Nov. 1971: 88, E3.

Clemons, Walter. "Acts of Grace." *Newsweek* 8 Nov. 1971: 115–17.

Gullason, Thomas. "*Flannery O'Connor: The Complete Stories.*" *Saturday Review* 13 Nov. 1971: 57, 63–64.

HABIT OF BEING

Clemons, Walter. "Letters from the Farm." *Newsweek* 19 Mar. 1979: 87–88.

Gilman, Richard. "A Life of Letters." *New York Times Book Review* 18 Mar. 1979: 1, 32–33.

Gordon, Mary. "The Habit of Genius." *Saturday Review* 14 Apr. 1979: 42–44, 46.

Gray, Paul. "Letters of Flannery O'Connor." *Time* 5 Mar. 1979: 86–87.

Shaw, Robert B. "Jane Austen in Milledgeville." *The Nation* 28 Apr. 1979: 472–74.

"Short Reviews." *Atlantic* 243 (June 1979): 96.

Towers, Robert. "Flannery O'Connor's Gifts." *New York Review of Books* 3 May 1979: 3–6.

Selected Articles on Flannery O'Connor

Allen, William Rodney. "The Cage of Matter: The World as Zoo in Flannery O'Connor's *Wise Blood.*" *American Literature* 58 (May 1986): 256–70. By fusing images of animals and confinement, the modern world becomes a "zoo for the human animal."

BIBLIOGRAPHY

Archer, Jane Elizabeth. "'This Is My Place': The Short Films Made from Flannery O'Connor's Short Fiction." *Studies in American Humor* 1 (June 1982): 52–65. Discussion of problems and choices filmmakers have in converting five short stories into hour-length films.

Asals, Frederick. "The Double in Flannery O'Connor's Stories." *Flannery O'Connor Bulletin* 9 (1980): 49–86. Examines the role of the protagonist's double and the resulting revelations.

Bishop, Elizabeth, and Elizabeth Hardwick. "Flannery O'Connor, 1925–1964." *New York Review of Books* 8 Oct. 1964: 21, 23. Two separate obituaries: one from someone who knew O'Connor's work and not her, and one from someone who knew O'Connor but was less familiar with her work.

Bonney, William. "The Moral Structure of Flannery O'Connor's *A Good Man Is Hard to Find.*" *Studies in Short Fiction* 27 (Summer 1990): 347–56. Each of the stories in the collection has a character who is hopeful the world of "materialism can be transcended."

Bryant, Hallman B. "Reading the Map in 'A Good Man Is Hard to Find.'" *Studies in Short Fiction* 18 (Summer 1981): 301–7. Bryant follows Bailey and his family along the route that he drives toward Florida, suggesting why O'Connor makes the references to places, both real and fictional, that she does.

Burns, Marian. "The Chronology of Flannery O'Connor's 'Why Do the Heathen Rage?'" *Flannery O'Connor Bulletin* 11 (1982): 58–75. A dismantling of Stuart Burns's argument. Dates the unfinished novel later and suggests the stories came first.

———. "O'Connor's Unfinished Novel." *Flannery O'Connor Bulletin* 11 (1982): 76–93. Suggests an impasse in development because of problems in dealing with Walter Tilman, a protagonist who is neither grotesque nor violent.

BIBLIOGRAPHY

Burns, Stuart L. "How Wide Did 'The Heathen' Range?" *Flannery O'Connor Bulletin* 4 (1975): 25–41. A study of the 378 manuscript pages of the third novel. Dates the novel early and suggests the short stories came from it.

Clasby, Nancy T. "'The Life You Save May Be Your Own': Flannery O'Connor as a Visionary Artist." *Studies in Short Fiction* 28 (Fall 1991): 509–20. A Jungian reading.

Coulthard, A. R. "Flannery O'Connor's Deadly Conversions." *Flannery O'Connor Bulletin* 13 (1984): 87–94. A look at three stories where redemption and death occur simultaneously.

———. "From Sermon to Parable: Four Conversion Stories by Flannery O'Connor." *American Literature* 55 (Mar. 1983): 55–71. Coulthard argues that O'Connor's characters often receive grace and death simultaneously; in four stories, however, the protagonist lives long enough to accept grace.

Ensor, Allison R. "Flannery O'Connor and Music." *Flannery O'Connor Bulletin* 14 (1985): 1–13. A catalog of O'Connor's use and misuse of music.

Fennick, Ruth. "First Harvest: Flannery O'Connor's 'The Crop.'" *English Journal* 74 (Feb. 1985): 45–50. Fennick argues that O'Connor's early story is appropriate for high school anthologies.

Fitzgerald, Sally. "The Owl and the Nightingale." *Flannery O'Connor Bulletin* 13 (1984): 44–58. Explores O'Connor's debt to and use of T. S. Eliot in her early fiction.

Foster, Shirley. "Flannery O'Connor's Short Stories: The Assault on the Reader." *Journal of American Studies* 20 (Aug. 1986): 259–72. Foster suggests O'Connor's "deflationary technique" includes the audience as well as her main characters.

BIBLIOGRAPHY

Gentry, Marshall Bruce. "The Hand of the Writer in 'The Comforts of Home.'" *Flannery O'Connor Bulletin* 20 (1991): 61–72. A thorough assessment of Thomas and Sarah/Star as siblings, showing how O'Connor unifies the genders.

Gordon, Sarah. "Flannery O'Connor, the Left-Wing Mystic, and the German Jew." *Flannery O'Connor Bulletin* 16 (1987): 43–51. Gordon explores O'Connor's interest in Simone Weil, an "outsider" who struggled with her faith, and Edith Stein, an "insider," once she converted and joined the Carmelites.

Griffith, Benjamin. "After the Canonization: Flannery O'Connor Revisited." *Sewanee Review* 97 (Fall 1989): 575–80. Combination review of O'Connor's *Collected Works* and reflections on Griffith and O'Connor's friendship.

Hawkes, John. "Flannery O'Connor's Devil." *Sewanee Review* 70 (Summer 1962): 395–407. The first commentary to take issue with O'Connor's own explanation of the devil.

Highsmith, Dixie Lee. "Flannery O'Connor's Polite Conversation." *Flannery O'Connor Bulletin* 11 (1982): 94–107. An examination of clichés, popular sayings, and slogans.

Katz, Claire. "Flannery O'Connor's Rage of Vision." *American Literature* 46 (Mar. 1974): 54–67. An exploration of O'Connor's use of violence in the narrative voice.

Kinney, Arthur F. "Flannery O'Connor and the Art of the Holy." *Virginia Quarterly Review* 64 (Spring 1988): 215–30. Overview of the "incarnational writer" who proclaims a message through her fiction that her readers are "potentially temples of the Holy Ghost."

Kowalewski, Michael. "On Flannery O'Connor." *Raritan* 10 (Winter 1991): 85–104. Kowalewski argues that O'Connor's subjects have often dimmed the attention that he directs on O'Connor's use of language.

Lee, Maryat. "Flannery, 1957." *Flannery O'Connor Bulletin* 5 (1976): 39–60. Lee reflects on her first meeting with O'Connor and the growth of the friendship.

Meek, Kristen. "Flannery O'Connor's 'Greenleaf' and the Holy Hunt of the Unicorn." *Flannery O'Connor Bulletin* 19 (1990): 30–37. Makes a biblical connection with the events of the story.

Mellard, James M. "Flannery O'Connor's Others: Freud, Lacan, and the Unconscious." *American Literature* 61 (Dec. 1989): 625–43. Mellard suggests that O'Connor feared Freud because the congruence of the unconscious and grace was a threat to her theology; however, a reinterpretation of Freud's work focusing on the nature of language offers a restoration of O'Connor to theology.

Nisly, Paul W. "The Prison of the Self: Isolation in Flannery O'Connor's Fiction." *Studies in Short Fiction* 17 (Winter 1980): 49–54. Nisly examines O'Connor's characters who willfully seek isolation in order to find their own truths.

Park, Clara Claiborne. "Crippled Laughter: Toward Understanding Flannery O'Connor." *American Scholar* 51 (Spring 1982): 249–57. An exploration of why readers fail to see the humor in O'Connor's stories.

Parks, John G. "Losing and Finding: Meditations of a Christian Reader." *Christianity and Literature* 38 (Summer 1989): 19–23. Reflective essay that suggests the crises of O'Connor's characters parallel the predicament of the Christian reader.

Rath, Sura. "Comic Polarities in Flannery O'Connor's *Wise Blood.*" *Studies in Short Fiction* 21 (Summer 1984): 251–58.

An examination of the characters as comic archetypes—self-deprecator, impostor, and buffoon.

Roos, John. "The Political in Flannery O'Connor: A Reading of 'A View of the Woods.'" *Studies in Short Fiction* 29 (Spring 1992): 161–79. An exploration of O'Connor's use of Locke and Aquinas.

Rubin, Louis D., Jr. "Flannery O'Connor's Company of Southerners: Or 'The Artificial Nigger' Read as Fiction Rather Than Theology." *Flannery O'Connor Bulletin* 6 (1977): 47–71. Rubin examines the importance of the Southern milieu in O'Connor's work, suggesting that O'Connor follows the tradition of Southern humor begun by Joel Chandler Harris and Augustus Longstreet.

Satterfield, Ben. "*Wise Blood,* Artistic Anemia, and the Hemorrhaging of O'Connor Criticism." *Studies in American Fiction* 17 (1989): 33–50. Against the current, Satterfield argues that no evidence exists to support Hazel Motes's redemption.

Scouten, Kenneth. "The Mythological Dimensions of Five of Flannery O'Connor's Works." *Flannery O'Connor Bulletin* 2 (1973): 59–72. By using Greek myths that show the impossibility of defying oracles, Scouten argues that O'Connor suggests God cannot be denied.

———. "'The Partridge Festival': Manuscript Revisions." *Flannery O'Connor Bulletin* 15 (1986): 35–41. A review of the eleven file folders of manuscript revisions on this story. Traces development of the Singleton character.

Shackelford, D. Dean. "The Black Outsider in O'Connor's Fiction." *Flannery O'Connor Bulletin* 18 (1989): 79–90. Refutes the argument that O'Connor is racist by examining how O'Connor uses the outsider in her fiction.

BIBLIOGRAPHY

Shields, John C. "Flannery O'Connor's 'Greenleaf' and the Myth of Europa and the Bull." *Studies in Short Fiction* 18 (1981): 421–31. A detailed study of how myth's portrayal of the union of sky and earth inform a reading of this story.

Sloan, Larue Love. "The Rhetoric of the Seer: Eye Imagery in Flannery O'Connor's 'Revelation.'" *Studies in Short Fiction* 25 (Spring 1988): 135–45. A close examination of looks, gazes, glances, and visions that lead to the "final blast of vision."

Spivey, Ted R. "Flannery O'Connor, the New Criticism, and Deconstruction." *Southern Review* 23 (Spring 1987): 271–80. Argues that O'Connor herself was an intertextual critic and that biographical and deconstructive criticism provide new ways of expanding O'Connor.

Tate, J. O. "O'Connor's Confederate General: A Late Encounter." *Flannery O'Connor Bulletin* 8 (1979): 45–53. Tate shows O'Connor's artistic appropriation of real people and historical events. Contains pictures reproduced from local newspaper accounts.

Walker, Alice. "Beyond the Peacock: The Reconstruction of Flannery O'Connor." *In Search of Our Mothers' Gardens.* New York: Harcourt Brace Jovanovich, 1983. 42–59. Walker's account of a visit to Andalusia with her mother ten years after O'Connor's death.

Weisenburger, Steven. "Style in *Wise Blood*." *Genre* 16 (Spring 1983): 75–97. In a stylistic analysis, Weisenburger focuses on similes that distort, images of containment, and a fugue structure.

Westarp, Karl-Heinz. "'Judgement Day': The Published Text versus Flannery O'Connor's Final Version." *Flannery*

BIBLIOGRAPHY

O'Connor Bulletin 11 (1982): 108–22. Westarp establishes that the story published in the collection is not the final draft. Fitzgerald corrected the situation in *Collected Works* in 1988.

————. "Teilhard de Chardin's Impact on Flannery O'Connor: A Reading of 'Parker's Back.'" *Flannery O'Connor Bulletin* 12 (1983): 93–113. Argues that in the order of the tattoos Parker chooses, he moves toward Christ, as the universe moves toward the Teilhardian Omega Point.

Westling, Louise. "Flannery O'Connor's Revelations to 'A.'" *Southern Humanities Review* 20 (1986): 15–22. A close examination of the ways "A" challenged O'Connor's resistance to accepting her womanhood.

Wyatt, Bryan N. "The Domestic Dynamics of Flannery O'Connor: *Everything That Rises Must Converge.*" *Twentieth Century Literature* 38 (Spring 1992): 66–88. In the posthumous collection of short stories, Wyatt examines females as protagonists, noting men as nonfunctional or substitute heads of households.

INDEX

The index does not include references to material in the notes.

INDEX

INDEX

INDEX

INDEX

INDEX